# THE LONGEST NIGHT

## A Personal History of Pan Am 103

**Helen Engelhardt**

*a memoir*

Blue Thread Communications

An Imprint of Jewish Currents Magazine

## Also by Helen Engelhardt

### Audio books

With Marjorie van Halteren:
*Coming Home To Us: A Trilogy of Love, Loss, & Healing*
2011, Midsummer Sound Company LLC

*The Longest Night*
*A Personal History of Pan Am 103*
excerpts from the memoir
2009, Midsummer Sound Company, LLC

With Leora Skolkin-Smith, author:
*Edges: O Israel O Palestine*
2007, Midsummer Sound Company LLC

Blue Thread Communications

ISBN 978-0-9851138-6-5

*For our son, Alan Lacey Richard,*
*the promise fulfilled*

*For my parents, Jacob and Beatrice Engelhardt,*
*and aunt, Rosalind Derman,*
*whose love sustains me*

*For Lacey and Claire Hawkins, who were spared this loss*

*For Tony's family, who embraced us*

# THE LONGEST NIGHT

Helen Engelhardt

# Contents

# Incident at Altitude 12/21/88

*For Tony/For Everyone*

*"All the controller saw was the aircraft breaking up. There were pieces all around the screen where there had been a single dot."* —1/2/89 *Newsweek*

AIR    The invisible ocean that has to be crossed. The Maid of the Seas cuts through the sky bearing its cargo, the burden of your dreams. You are on your way home to us.
(You are still trying to come home to us.)

FIRE    On the Prestwick radar screen, you are a green electronic blip. At 7:03 p.m. the blip bursts.

*"Like meteors falling from the sky. There were flames in the front and back garden and I could hear things falling on the roof.…We didn't know what hit us."* —Ann McPhail, Lockerbie

*There was fire everywhere. Ignited fuel was running along the street and balls of fire seemed to be everywhere."* —Irene Brown, Lockerbie

EARTH  Pasturelands dark green in the cold December night.
Sweet earth wounded
one by one by one by one they fell to earth
our husbands, our sons, our daughters, our wives, our sisters,
our brothers, our mothers, our fathers, our aunts, our uncles,
our nieces, our nephews, our cousins, our sweethearts,
our colleagues, our neighbors,
one by one
through the dark cold air they came back to earth
to Halldykes Farm you came at last to ground.

WATER  The ocean was supposed
to swallow the crime.
We have our tears
and time.

Helen Engelhardt Hawkins
Widow of Anthony Lacey Hawkins

# REFLECTIONS

**Winter 2012-13**

On December 21, 1988, a Boeing 747 aircraft named *Clipper Maid of the Seas* exploded at 7:03 p.m. over the market town of Lockerbie, in southern Scotland, killing all 259 on board and 11 people on the ground. Pan Am Flight 103 was Pan American's third daily scheduled transatlantic flight from Heathrow Airport, London to JFK Airport, New York. My husband was one of the passengers.

I began working on this memoir the night he died.

It began as an oral history, an intimate exploration of personal loss, as I recorded everything that was happening within me and within the circle of my family and friends. Then the Air Accidents Investigation Board of the U.K. and Scotland Yard officially announced to the world, on December 28th, that a bomb, not structural failure, had brought down Pan Am 103. Tony had not died in an horrific accident, but had been murdered. One month later, Cardinal O'Connor held a high mass for the families of the victims in St. Patrick's Cathedral, and I knew that my memoir had to include these people as well. By February, a group of family members formed the Victims of Pan Am Flight 103 to provide us with emotional support and represent our political and legal interests. I joined in March, and still remain actively involved today.

Almost all of the books published about Pan Am 103 focus on the disaster itself and the conspiracy responsible for it, or on the legal and political efforts that established Libya's guilt in courts of law. This is not one of those books. *The Longest Night* focuses on the impact Tony's death had on me and our six-year-old son Alan, during our first year of learning to live without him. In counterpoint with those twelve months of 1989 is the story of my marriage of sixteen years, compressed into our beginning and concluding months.

By telling the story of the person I knew best, I am personalizing the immeasurable loss of 270 souls. By telling the story of the formation, struggles and accomplishments of Victims of Pan Am Flight 103, I am honoring the people who would not let their loved ones die in vain.

# PRELUDE

**November 22ⁿᵈ, 1988**

*I'm desperately fighting to keep my head above water, calling out into the darkness. "Tony, where are you? Are you all right?"*

*He's more than thirty feet from me slipping below the surface into clear green water. I won't be able to reach him in time. TONY!!!!*

I lift myself out of my nightmare and back into my bed. My husband is sprawled at my side, snoring loudly, his head near my feet, where he had fallen asleep. I shake him awake.

"Wha', what is it, luv?"

He lifts himself awkwardly and moves up to lie down beside me, taking me in his arms.

"I've had a bad dream . . ."

But he was asleep again, snoring softly.

This is the morning of November 22ⁿᵈ, 1988, the twenty-fifth anniversary of John F. Kennedy's assassination. In twenty-nine days, my husband will also be dead.

# PART ONE

## CHAPTER ONE

### December 21st, 1988

"Hello, luv!"

"Tony! It's 5:30!"

"I'm sorry. I didn't mean to wake you. I miscalculated the time."

"I don't mind. I'm glad it's you."

"I'm taking the last plane out of London today. I should be arriving at Kennedy at 8:40. I'll take a cab, I guess."

"Alan and I could take car service and meet you — but it is kind of late."

"Not to worry. I'll take a cab. See you soon, luv."

"Miss you."

"Me too. Very much. Tonight!"

I placed the phone back in its cradle and hugged my pillow. We'd last spoken five days ago when Tony called asking permission to return a day later: "I'm feeling pressured to try to get everything done, to see everybody. I'd like to stay one more day. Would that be all right? It will give me some more time."

"I think we can manage one more day without you! Of course you can stay. Who knows when you'll get another chance to visit England again?"

Tony had flown to London ten days before in order to see an uncle with terminal cancer. While there, he had been trying to attend to as much personal and professional business as possible. His work situation was a chronic source of conflict between us. After a lifetime of working as a salesman of audio equipment, he wanted to devote his time and energies to designing and manufacturing his own furniture. It had become apparent to me that the income he could contribute on a freelance basis would never be sufficient as long as we continued to stagger under the immense obligations we had assumed. At my insistence, we had acquired a house in the Adirondacks that we couldn't afford. In his absence, I had decided to sell it as soon as possible and liberate ourselves from all outstanding debts. Then he could putter about in his basement workshop and we could afford to make some improvements in our old house in Brooklyn. We would live within our means and enjoy our life together again.

Tony had planned his visit to England to fit neatly into the week between our son Alan's sixth birthday party and our Christmas Day dinner. His nine-day absence had felt much longer. In a few hours he'd be home, and we'd have all the time we needed to talk and to enfold each other again. I'd been too shy and sleepy to promise him that I was going to give him all the time alone together he could possibly want or need; perhaps the warmth in my voice had told him that.

"Rise and shine, sweet boy, time to get up."

Alan lay flat on his back, like his father, surrounded by some of his favorite stuffed animals. His bed was against the window, tucked under the sloping roof. I sat on the edge of his blanket and tickled his cheek. He brushed my hand away and turned on his side towards the window. He was Tony in miniature, his small hands with their bowling-pin fingers, wider at the base than at the tip, and his square feet, a perfect recapitulation of his father's. I had tried to give him my long legs, but it looked like he would be Tony's height when he grew, a few inches shorter than me. And he had Tony's fair Irish/English skin and light blue eyes. I had given him my thick naturally wavy brown hair, though. I stroked it and caught his hand when he tried to stop me.

"Come on, sweetie. Don't you remember what day this is?"

Alan's eyes clicked open like a doll's and he turned to face me. "Tony's coming home today!"

Alan was our miracle baby, born when I was 43 years old and Tony 51 — a gift we had given ourselves in the tenth year of our marriage.

"Yes, he is! So let's get up and have a nice breakfast before you go to school so you can tell him what you did today!"

Ordinarily, Tony made him breakfast and lunch to take with him, and then drove him to school. During the week he was away, my next door neighbor took Alan along with her daughter, while I went off to work.

That evening, I altered my routine and did not turn the radio on and listen to *All Things Considered* while doing kitchen duty. That night I preferred to work in meditative silence. I had a lot of things to think about.

These nine days had given me more than an opportunity to see our situation anew, to thoughtfully arrive at a rational decision. These days of separation had also given me visions of disaster: cars crashing into trees, smashing head first into one another, planes bursting into flames, skidding off runways, exploding into pieces. These images had occurred randomly, flickering across the screen of my attention. I saw them as I walked down a street, sat at my desk, prepared dinner. I saw them again as I prepared this meal. They were unprecedented in my experience. Though Tony had traveled frequently during the early years in our marriage and again during the first two years after Alan's birth, I had never been excessively anxious in his absence; never before had I anticipated catastrophe.

I had interpreted these disturbing 'daymares' as metaphors for my financial anxieties. I had never mentioned them to Tony. What could he do, after all? He had to take an airplane in order to come home to us.

Alan and I ate dinner, discussing all we'd do when Tony returned in a couple of hours:

"Tony's going give us big hugs, and then he's going to make himself a cup of coffee and then . . ."

"First thing we're going to do is play splat!" ("Splat" was a game they had created together. It involved rolling tiny rubber wheels from advanced Lego sets across the floor and trying to stop and squash them with the palm of the hand. It was the last thing Tony had done with his son before he left to catch his cab to the airport.)

"Mom." Alan suddenly looked confused. "I don't remember what Tony looks like any more."

"Do you want to see a picture of him?"

"No, I'll remember when I see him tonight!"

Alan returned to the living room to play with his Legos and I resumed marking final exams. I wanted to be able to devote myself entirely to Tony as soon as he walked in the door.

At 9:00 p.m. the phone rang. "That was quick! Tony must have already finished with Customs." I leapt up from the couch where Alan and I were watching "A Child's Christmas in Wales." Picking up the phone in the hallway, I heard an English voice very far away. It was Tony's cousin.

"Helen, have you been listening to the news lately?"

"Oh, yes, I know all about the triple train crash outside of London last week. Tony called to tell me about it last Wednesday. He also told me that you're in charge of the official investigation, since you're now the Chief of the London Transport Police."

"Listen, Helen, we've had an airplane accident today."

Suddenly I was having difficulty standing, difficulty hearing. I carried the phone the few feet into the dining room and sat down in slow motion.

"We've had a rather serious crash in Scotland of a Pan Am flight, Flight 103. What plane was Tony on?"

"I don't know the flight number. He was flying Pan Am. When he called me this morning it was to tell me he'd be landing at 8:40 tonight. I thought he was calling me just now."

I could barely hold onto the phone. I braced my arm against the table, leaning into the receiver.

*I DID NOT DO THIS. I DID NOT MAKE THIS HAPPEN.*

I stared at the dark green tablecloth Tony had bought for our Christmas dinner a few years ago. It matched the dark green walls of the oak paneled dining room. I looked up at the photo of Tony's father beaming down on me. I had taken that picture on a sunny summer afternoon in a garden in Dorset, the year after Tony and I were married. *Lacey, Lacey, you were spared this. You will never know that Tony . . .*

"I've been trying to get through to the police in Scotland or to the Pan Am office. There was a T. Hawkins on the manifest. Wouldn't he have signed his name Anthony or Tony?"

"He usually signed his name 'A. Hawkins'. Why don't you think the 'T. Hawkins' on the manifest is Tony?"

"No one from the family saw him off to the airport, no one saw him get on the plane. We knew he intended to fly home on the 103, but we were hoping he had been delayed in traffic. We all know that Tony tended to leave things for the last minute."

"What are you trying to tell me? You're trying to tell me there aren't any survivors, aren't you?"

"Yes, that's right."

"And if there are any survivors, it would be better if Tony were dead, actually, the crash is that bad."

"That's right."

"In fact, the only hope we have is that Tony is not on that plane at all."

"Yes, that's why I've called you. We were hoping, the family was hoping."

"But he hasn't called me! Where is he? There are only three possibilities: Either he's been knocked unconscious in some sort of traffic accident, but then his papers would lead the police to contact me, so all his papers would have had to been stolen, that means he was mugged, or second, he's been kidnapped, or third, he's on that plane. Now which do you think is the likeliest possibility? The other situations aren't totally impossible, just utterly improbable. If he had missed the plane, he would have called me to reassure me that he's safe, not to worry. He has to be on that plane. HE HASN'T CALLED ME!"

There was this cool precise part of my mind clicking away, ticking off all of the logical possibilities, as though we were considering how many different ways someone could send a message, as though we were both detectives, as though we weren't discussing the end of the world, the victory of nightmare, the triumph of terror. There was the rest of me, my body trembling severely, uncontrollably, as though I had been plunged into icy water.

"Helen, are you alone?"

"Yes. No. Alan is here, and Jay the man who boards with us."

"Don't you have a friend who could pop 'round. You shouldn't be alone."

"I'm all right. I'll be all right. Thank you."

He had been the perfect messenger. His training as a policeman, his natural sympathies as Tony's cousin, his English reserve, had gently guided me, telling me only what I needed to know. In fact, all I knew was that Tony was dead. And so was everyone else on the plane. I called Pan Am and got through immediately.

"What was the scheduled arrival time for Flight 103 out of London today?"

"Eight-forty p.m."

"Do you have any other flights leaving London and arriving approximately that time?"

"No."

I walked back to the living room, grateful for the distraction of the television screen. Two fully dressed young men were marching with cavalier indifference into the sea. The waves obliterated them as Alan snuggled close, looking up at me with an anxious expression.

"Who was that on the phone? Why were you crying?"

"It was Tony. He just told me that he can't come home tonight because . . . because their plane developed engine trouble. It's being held overnight in London."

*Years ago, that is what happened to our plane. Engine troubles kept us in England overnight. It hasn't been confirmed yet 100 percent. I need more time. I need to try to understand what has happened to me, what has happened to us.*

Alan fell in slow motion sideways onto the couch, deflated. "I can't stand waiting anymore! I'm too tired. Let's go upstairs. I want to go to sleep."

He fell asleep instantly. I could hear the hum of the television set in Jay's room. I left Alan's side and walked the few feet to Jay's room, stood in the open doorway and watched the 11 o'clock news on the tiny black and white screen. Flames in the darkness. A town on fire. Sirens and hoses. The reporter with a microphone in the foreground trying to describe chaos.

"It was a bomb," I said with absolute certainty.

"They don't know that for sure, yet," Jay replied, surprised to see me standing there. "What's the matter?"

"Tony. Tony was on Pan Am 103."

"Oh my God!"

The reporter was talking about possible survivors. "What do they mean? How can there be any survivors?"

"They mean on the ground. In those houses. They don't know how many people have been killed from the impact of the plane on the town," Jay explained.

I nodded and walked into my bedroom and picked up the phone. I notified my chairman of the science department in the high school where I worked. I knew that he, too, knew about Pan Am 103, that by this time everyone knew.

"I can't come to work tomorrow, but I'll try to come in on Friday."

"Helen, you're not thinking clearly. Forget about us. First things first."

"But it's the last day before the school holidays."

"Don't worry about us. Do what you have to do. If there's anything I can do, please don't hesitate."

I made the second call. My parents had just arrived in their Florida home that very afternoon.

"Helen, is there anything wrong? It's after eleven."

"Mom have you been watching the news?"

"Yes, the television is still on. Some friends are here to help us get settled in."

"Are you sitting down?"

"Yes, I'm sitting down. What . . . ?"

"Tony. Tony was on Pan Am 103."

"Oh, Helen! Oh no! Not Tony! Jack! Jack! Tony was on that plane! We'll be with you as soon as we can arrange things. Oh dear, how dreadful. We'll talk tomorrow."

I called a friend who lived in the neighborhood. By now I had developed a routine. I delivered the news like a TV anchor.

It was after 11:30. I reached Jack, one of my oldest friends, a man I've known over thirty years.

"Shit! God damn it! Helen, I'm holding your hand."

"I know you are. Thank you. We'll talk again."

Jay came into the room. He sat down awkwardly on the "throne chair" that stood in the corner, a legacy from Tony's deceased mother. Neither of Tony's parents had lived long enough to live through this. The phone rang. Midnight.

"Is this Tony Hawkins' wife?"

"No. This is his widow."

It was a nervous young woman trying to be tactful. "I'm calling from Pan Am. We wanted to make certain before anyone called officially."

"Thank goodness I didn't learn from official sources."

"We're providing flights for people to attend funerals, close family. If you want to go to Lockerbie, we are providing free flights to Lockerbie."

"I can't think of a place in the universe I'd rather not be than Lockerbie."

"Is there anything else we can do?"

"Yes. You can guarantee me that this truly was an accident due to mechanical failure, not greed, not incompetence, not terrorism. Anything but terrorism."

"I can't say . . . I don't know."

"How old are you?'"

"Thirty-one."

"Have you ever done this before?"

"No. It's hard. I've been calling people for awhile. I have a long list."

Jay and I looked at each other. He stayed and talked with me until 4:00 a.m. I don't remember one word of our conversation, just the sense that we were bearing witness, keeping watch. I bundled myself under as many blankets as I could pile on top of me; distress always makes me shiver uncontrollably.

At 4:00 a.m., Heathrow Airport officially confirmed the death of Anthony Lacey Hawkins aboard Pan Am flight 103. They would fly me to Lockerbie without charge. Jay excused himself and went to bed to try to sleep.

I was wide awake. I hadn't stopped trembling from the moment I heard Tony's cousin say, "We've had an airplane accident today." I found my journal lying amidst the books and magazines piled along the bench under the windows. I began to write:

*"December 21st. The shortest day of the year. The longest night for the rest of my life. For the rest of Alan's life, though he doesn't know it yet."*

I glanced at the opposite page and read what I had written the night before:

*"December 20th . . . during these days of being alone with Alan without Tony . . . haven't really centered my attention on Tony. His absence has been neutral for Alan as well as myself. I know that it flows from certainty of continuity. Alan would be devastated if Tony never returned to him and the only way that would ever happen would be by a fatal accident or mortal disease. In this situation — a ghastly plane or car crash. The impact on me? I can't begin to imagine . . ."*

I turned off the light and began talking out loud to Tony: "Tony, where are you? Is this really happening?"

Realizing that I wasn't able to sleep, I turned the light back on, found a blank cassette tape, slipped it into the tape recorder on my night table, turned out the light, and resumed talking to him. I wanted to keep a record of my first raw thoughts. Tony used a tape recorder the way other people use a camera, to document their daily lives. It seemed fitting to me to use it to record the impact his death was having on me.

I trusted my body. It would sleep when it needed to and eat when it needed to. It had carried me through pregnancy, through birth; it would bear me through Tony's death.

"My darling Tony. I talk into your favorite machine, something you were an authority on. We were going to do such wonderful things with tape recording, weren't we? We've drifted so far away from our original dreams. We wanted to do radio plays, produce radio plays . . . Oh my darling. Nothing of you. Where is your shirt? Does it have your smell?"

I turned on the light, crawled across the bed, opened the doors of the old-fashioned armoire that Tony had used as his dresser, rummaged through his tee shirts, polo shirts, underwear, socks. Everything was too clean. I lifted the black plastic lid of the hamper. Empty. He used to peel off his socks, first one then the other, and fling them in the general direction of the hamper. They'd land on the floor, on the chair, on the closed lid. I'd hold my nose. Sometimes I was annoyed, sometimes exasperated, sometimes angry. Now I'd give anything to inhale any trace of him.

I found his navy blue fisherman's turtleneck, bought on holiday in Kennebunkport, and brought it back with me into the bed. It was rough, heavy. I crumpled it against my face. It smelled faintly of something that wasn't wool, wasn't the stale air of the dresser drawer. Tony's spoor. If I were a dog, I could sniff him out.

Was I hugging Tony's sweater spontaneously or because I was imitating a film I saw with him three years ago in which a new widow buries her nose in the sheets where she had recently made love? Because Tony had been by my side watching it with me, I had believed he would never die on me.

Last night I had imagined his death and tonight he had died. Why had I dreamt of his death? Why had I walked to the edge of the precipice and tried to peer down into the darkness?

"Oh my lovely love. Thinning hair, furrowed laugh wrinkles, double chin and all. I love you, Tony. I loved you. I have guilts, regrets, self recriminations but I know my love was real and enduring and I know that you knew that I loved you. Even that last awful argument in the basement. We were going to discover how much more we could still share together."

*Tony is leaning against a white pillar, his hands shoved deep into the pockets of his blue work coat. "Why do I have to defend myself? Don't tell me that we are both right. We haven't been spending enough time together. Why do I have to explain myself, justify myself?"*

*I think: We can't part like this! He's leaving in a few hours. He can't leave with anger between us. "How can I help you, Tony? What can I do to help make your departure as smooth as possible?"*

*"You can do the clothes and the food and like that. I'm still putting this rack together. It has to be shipped UPS tomorrow and I'm in a panic about it."*

"Alan," I said. "Alan will never be the same without you. This loss of his daddy, his daddy snatched away from him forever. His daddy who played Lego games with him and told him stories about his childhood and read to him and told him jokes and made him sandwiches and brought him to school every morning. His Tony. It will be a shadow over his life always. I have to help him get through these days, these weeks, these months. I don't know how I'm going to be able to guide him through this terrible time. I do know that if any part of you is left intact, coherent, you are grieving this untimely ripping away from your beloved child . . . You would have done everything in your power to return home to us. If only we were on our way to a hospital in Scotland to be with you while you mended from your grievous wounds, then to bring you home, even without an arm, even without a leg, even physically immobilized. If you could touch us, if you could do things with your hands and hug and kiss us, I think you would want to continue to be here with us. And Alan and I would want you here.

"Give me strength to guide Alan to school today so that he doesn't suspect anything worse than my disappointment that you haven't come home. I must protect him from knowing how and when this happened to his daddy. My darling . . . I wanted to tell you — I need you. I miss you. I'm going off into the unknown."

I stopped talking and stared into the darkness. And then, after awhile, when I found my voice again, I continued. "I pledge myself to the best of your memory and example to Alan's well being. All of my decisions of how I live my life — the choices I will make, the things I do — he will come first. I will, as soon as possible, begin to recollect our life together for Alan, for myself. I will not make you a god, a hero, a man no one else can possibly come next to. No. No, no, no, no. But the dear, precise, exact details of you and our best memories, what our problems were, your flaws as well as your strengths, so that a real sense of you exists. Your pictures and your voice, too. Some of your favorite possessions. I will have to decide what to do with our unfinished projects, tidy up what was left undone. I will do my best, my darling."

Never mind the future, what was I going to do in the next few days?

"Shall I go ahead with Christmas Day dinner without you? Who shall cook the turkey? Shall we have a tree? I don't know how to make a trifle! Wait! I have to organize a funeral. There might never be a body to bury. Everyone was probably blown to smithereens or burnt beyond recognition. Annette told me how grateful she was for the Jewish tradition of a speedy funeral and burial because only after she returned from the cemetery were she and her children able to mourn her husband.

"But you lost the faith you were born into and were so anti-religious that we didn't get married in a synagogue. I'll call the people who married us, the Ethical Culture Society, as soon as Alan is safely in school. But I want everything else to be in the Jewish tradition. I want to sit *shiva*. I know it will comfort me.

"Tony, you gave such wonderful hugs. I loved hugging you. When you lifted your right arm and shoulder very high, your left arm dropping down low so I could fit my arms to you and hold on tight and sometimes do a naughty little rub and kiss necks and you'd growl like a tiger and I'd pretend to swoon. . . .

"Friends. When shall I tell them? Today? What about Carol who is flying in a few hours? Before she flies? After she arrives?"

I myself was a ticking time bomb of shattering news. It was light enough now to see the clock radio, its red numbers glowing 7:00. I walked through Alan's bedroom to the bathroom. I heard his gentle breathing. Tony is still coming home to him. I showered and dressed and lay down beside him, stroked his thick brown hair, his soft face. He stirred. I breathed in his sweet fragrance. Tony used to stare down at the sleeping wonder of his son from the moment he was a newborn and exclaim, "God! He's so beautiful I can't stand it!"

I breathed deeply. Alan would not sniff me out. "Time to get up, sweet boy . . ."

## December 22nd

Alan refused to go to kindergarten. How long could I dissemble? "How about spending today with Leah?"

Leah lived down our block and was already on holiday. He nodded.

Leah's father answered the phone. "Would it be all right if Alan spent the day with Leah at your home? He doesn't feel like going to school this last day."

"Well, I'm not sure because we may be going shopping today."

I lowered my voice. "Actually, I need help. Tony was on Pan Am Flight 103. I have to organize a funeral, notify everyone."

"Oh, my God. Helen, send him over. He can stay as long as you need him to. If you want him to sleep over — that's fine. We'll help anyway we can."

"I haven't told Alan yet. It wasn't confirmed until after midnight. Please don't say anything while he is with you."

I didn't know when I would tell Alan.

"Alan, guess what? Leah's dad said it is a really great idea for you to play with Leah today! He's going to come and get you in a few minutes."

The doorbell rang while Alan was still putting on his shoes. He ran down the stairs and opened the door before I reached the first floor. Leah's father looked towards me and closed his eyes, nodding, before he focused on Alan. "Well, hello, young man. Are you ready?" Taking Alan's hand, and looking back towards me as they walked across the porch, he said, "Let us know when you want him back."

With Alan out of the house, I returned to bed and the telephone. The Ethical Culture Society of Brooklyn, the place where Tony and I had been married sixteen years earlier, was closed for the holiday weekend, so I called the Society's office in Manhattan and was told, "One of our Leaders will be in touch with you."

Michael Grupp called within the hour. I liked his deep resonant voice, his calm practical manner. I handed him my burden and he began solving problems. He agreed that a memorial service should be held as soon as possible, taking into consideration that my parents needed time to travel from Florida and Christmas was on Sunday. We agreed on Monday. Then he focused on my needs:

"Be yourself. Respond to what each person brings to you, but don't try to live up to their expectations of your behavior. You may feel like crying, you may not. You may feel angry, or calm. Just stay in touch with what you are actually feeling, or needing to do. Be open to what each person gives to you. Do not add to your stress by thinking that you have to play a prearranged role. There is no behavior that is inappropriate.

"When you tell Alan, try to have something warm that belonged to Tony — a sweater, a scarf, some article of clothing, to hold. It will help comfort him. I also want to meet and talk with you in your home. Perhaps tomorrow?"

"Tomorrow will be perfect."

I resumed calling my friends. I called and called. With each call, Tony died again. With each call, his death became more real for me. I felt as though someone else were making the calls, I was so cool, so matter of fact. Was this shock?

People began coming to my house. Fulfilling Mr. Grupp's prediction, each brought me something different, each needed something different from me. I felt that I was comforting everyone until my voice teacher, Shirley, gave me her pure intense grief, and I wept for the first time, in her arms. We joined the other women around the dining-room table, sipping tea and reminiscing. My friends offered me their fondest recollections of Tony, but I wouldn't let myself be comforted. I couldn't stop thinking of our last argument in the basement a few hours before he drove to the airport.

The phone rang. It was Leah's mother. "When are you planning to tell Alan?"

"Oh. Tomorrow is the Christmas party in school," I said. "Why shouldn't he have one last day with his friends and teacher? I've been considering not telling him the exact circumstances of Tony's death. He and Tony loved planes so much. They used to drive out to the airport just to look at them take off and land. He'll never be able to look at a plane again."

"You must not lie to him," she said. "Alan must be able to trust you implicitly. There is no way you can protect him from the facts. They are notorious. Tony did not die a private death. His name will appear in the papers, his face might appear on TV. Alan must learn the truth in the best way he can deal with it. You must not put him in a situation where he goes to school, to a party, when everyone else in his family is already grieving the death of his father. I know what I'm talking about talking about. My father died when I was about his age."

"You're right. I'll tell him tonight."

My brother Dan and his girlfriend arrived in the early evening. Dan hugged me and sobbed in my arms for perhaps the very first time in our lives. I rested my head on his shoulder. His nose was red and his eyes puffy. The last time I had seen him cry was the moment after hearing Tony announce to our family that he and I were planning to marry. But those were delicate tears that made his eyes glisten.

I called Leah's house and asked for Alan to come home. As soon as he saw the dining room filled with people, he went in to join the party. Dan, his favorite uncle, captured his attention. *When he looks around and asks me, "Where's Tony? Didn't you say he was coming home tonight?" that's when I'll tell him.* But Alan never asked. So I excused myself and went upstairs to be alone with my thoughts. I was at my desk in my study on the second floor, when a delegation of friends confronted me.

"You must tell him, Helen. The later it gets, the worse it will be for him," said Shirley.

"Alan will be confused and resentful if he learns later that his senses were not telling him the truth. While he was feeling happy and playing with his uncle and thinking that everything was normal, everyone was actually grieving for Tony," said Sue.

But before I could go to Alan, I took a call. It was Pan Am.

"We wanted you to know that 150 corpses have already been retrieved. We need some information from you in order to identify your husband. Would you give us the name of your dentist?"

"I can do more than that. I can describe his wedding ring, which is unique. I am the only other person who has a ring like it. It's a gold band, wide, with three rows of six tiny squares outlined like paving stones. In the top row, second from the right, a blue stone has been set. Tony designed it himself. All you have to do is find that ring and you've found his body."

"You should be hearing from own contact person within the next day or two. We're arranging that each family will be assigned to one of our people who will keep in touch with you, giving you any information you may require, answer any of your questions."

And now I had run out of excuses to delay telling Alan. Reluctantly, I went downstairs. I found him in the living room eating ice cream with Dan and his girlfriend Yvette. It was now after 9:00 p.m. I asked Sue to field any phone calls that might come through. No more interruptions.

I sat down on the couch beside Alan, with Tony's blue striped windbreaker over my arm, and two of Alan's favorite stuffed animals beside me. I was following Mr. Grupp's instructions. The jacket wasn't soft or warm, but

Chocolate the Bear and Rabbit were. And the jacket was Tony.

"Alan, I have something very important to tell you, but you have to finish your ice cream first."

"Why can't you tell me while I'm eating my ice-cream?"

"I just can't. You don't have to rush. I can wait."

Everyone became very quiet around the dining room table in the room behind us. Dan and Yvette shifted away from each other, each leaning against an arm of the loveseat opposite us. Dan's eyes began to fill with tears. I moved over to the middle of the couch to make room for Alan, who came to join me after he put his emptied bowl very neatly on the bench. He looked at me expectantly. I hadn't known how to do what I needed to do until I sat down.

"I have sad news. The plane Tony was on, had an accident. It crashed."

Alan asked in a very small voice, "He's hurt?"

"He's dead."

In slow motion, he bends forward and puts his head against my right breast as I enclose him with my right arm and one tear slides out of his left eye leaving a streak down his cheek. He murmurs, "I'm all alone with you, now?"

"We have all our friends and family, too."

I looked across the room to Dan and Yvette, who were weeping at each end of their couch. Alan looked again at my face and then put his head back down and spoke into my shoulder: "You could get married again."

For a second I could not understand what I had just heard. I had been prepared for Alan's rage, and for screaming and for throwing things and striking out at me — but not this.

"Why should I ever want to do that?"

"So I could have another daddy."

I considered what he was telling me: *You've just plunged me into the void. Fill the void. You've just destroyed my daddy. Buy me a new one.*

"Maybe. Someday. Not soon."

Alan jumped up. "One good thing, now I can move all my toys into Tony's office and you won't have to be angry any more for my not cleaning them up. And there won't be any yelling. Tony used to yell at me and I never knew why.

I was stunned and offended. "Now wait a minute! Tony loved you more than anyone else in the world! Even more than me, and he loved me very, very much. He didn't yell at you unless he was very tired or frustrated."

Alan noticed Chocolate and Rabbit for the first time and clutched them to his chest.

"One bad thing," he said. "We won't be able to finish playing our Lego game." He looked over at Dan and Yvette. "You don't have any animals to hug?"

"Why don't you bring down some more?" said Yvette, smiling and dabbing her eyes.

Alan handed over Chocolate and Rabbit to her and ran upstairs. He returned with the enormous Pooh Bear that Tony's mother had mailed to him shortly after his birth, and Winkleigh the Fox from Devon, a gift from Tony's stepmother. "Now everybody has something to hug!" he declared.

Each one of us sat there hugging a stuffed animal.

"You know something, Alan?" said Yvette. "It does make me feel a little better."

Alan looked at me. "Why couldn't Tony stop the plane from crashing? Why couldn't he help the pilots? He's a great driver. He knows a lot about planes."

"Oh sweetheart," I sighed, " If there were any way Tony could have stopped the accident, he would have. But it happened too quickly. The plane suddenly exploded and everybody was killed instantly. No one felt any pain." I didn't really know if this were true, but I needed to believe it and I needed Alan to believe it.

"Tony can't whistle any more. He can't laugh again when he reads Winnie-the-Pooh to me."

*I am in my bedroom when I hear Tony's deep-throated laughter. I find him sitting on the floor by Alan's bed, his glasses tipped up on his forehead, rubbing his knuckles into his eyes to stop the tears. "I had no idea this book was so great! I've just started, 'Rabbit's Busy Day.' Rabbit is like every boss I've ever worked for! Listen to this . . ."*

"Alan, I think you and I ought to go to bed now."

Everyone left except Sue and Shirley. I made up the couch for Sue to sleep on and gave Shirley the empty bedroom on the second floor.

"If we could find Tony's body, we could put his bones back together again," Alan said.

We were lying side by side on his narrow bed, the glow-in-the-dark plastic stars dimly shining on the sloping ceiling above us.

"His bones won't be able to come to Christmas Day. Christmas is supposed to be the best party and now it can't be. At least he came to my birthday." And then he was asleep. I had to transfer him from the top of the blanket to between the sheets, wash him around with a wet cloth and slip a pad under him, since he had crashed without a good-night pee.

I went to my bedroom and began to yawn for the first time in almost forty-eight hours. I had been awake from the time of Tony's last phone call 5:00 a.m. Wednesday morning. I slept deeply without dreaming.

## December 23rd

In the morning, Alan came into my room and crept into bed beside me.

"What does Tony look like now?" His voice was very low.

"We have pictures of him, sweetheart."

"Yes, but his whole body."

"It's not a body you can hug. It's not a good body to see now, Alan."

"Why can't we just put him in a museum?"

"Like a mummy? You don't want to do that to your daddy, do you? I don't think so. . . . It's very sad," I said at last. "It's very sad, Alan. We're going to miss him very, very much in all kinds of ways we can't even imagine right now. You know, I'm thinking of all the work in the house that Tony knows how to do better than I do, like putting up Venetian blinds, little things like that. And the big, important things. Missing his company. Missing being with him. Do you know what I missed right away? Things I don't like! His snoring. You know, sometimes, we were unable to spend the whole night together in this bed because he would snore so loudly he would wake me up. So sometimes he'd sleep on the couch or next to you. I miss his snoring. If I were given the choice of sleeping next to him every night, without another room to go to, so that he would interrupt my sleep every night, I would give anything for that. Anything!

"You know," I continued, "everybody has something that's a little annoying, something that bothers you. When they're not going to be with you anymore, you want everything back again just the way it was. It doesn't matter. But when you are living with people, it's all right to express your annoyance with them. It's like when you don't put away your Legos. It's important for you to be considerate of your belongings and other people using the living room. But if I came home one day and you were never going to live with me again, I would say, "I will take him back with his messy Legos and I won't mind at all!" Do you understand what I'm saying?"

He whispered, "No."

"You were remembering how Tony used to lose his temper with you, but that was such a small part of his personality. There are people who yell all the time, never show their son that they love him. There are fathers who yell and never play with their children, never hug their children, who never tell their children jokes. All they do is yell. But Tony only yelled when he was frustrated."

Alan squeezed his grief through his throat.

"There are fathers, they see their kid come in the door, they start spanking them."

I looked at Alan's slightly swollen face and spoke very slowly. "Tony was one of the best fathers I've ever seen, ever seen. And all our friends, when they would see you and Tony together, could not believe how wonderful a father Tony was. Because he was totally involved with you. When you were born, he was there beside me. When you needed to be cleaned, he cleaned you. He helped to feed you. He just did everything he could, to help take care of you. He was such a special father because he had so much to give. He would make you lunch. He took you to school. He repaired your toys. He always tried to buy you things that you would enjoy. He would look at you sometimes when you were sleeping and say, 'I just can't stand it, he's so beautiful!'"

"Do I have to go to school today?"

"Of course not, but somebody has to go to your school and tell Miss Weber and the principal. Maybe I can do that."

"Does she know about Tony?"

"No, dear. I'll tell her."

After breakfast I made a series of important phone calls. First came Mr. Cameris, who had been appointed as my contact person at Pan Am. I gave him my parent's phone number, told him they needed help arranging to fly to New York. He gave me his work and home phone numbers, told me to call whenever I needed to, and that he would keep me informed.

Then I called the rabbi of my synagogue. "May I come and talk with you?"he asked. "When is the funeral? I'd like to see you before then — will Sunday be all right, in the afternoon?"

After leaving Alan in Sue's care, Shirley and I set off on our errands. First, we closed out my joint checking and saving accounts; otherwise, as soon as the bank learned of Tony's death, they would freeze my assets.

The bank transactions accomplished, we walked on to Alan's school and notified the principal. When we came home, Mr. Grupp from Ethical Culture was there, waiting for us. We went upstairs to my study to be alone.

He seated himself at my desk. I sat to the side. I showed him some photographs of Tony and answered his questions while he took notes. "The reason I like to come to the home," he explained, "is because I can absorb the atmosphere, get an intuitive feeling about the person that I could not get any other way. Now, I want to ask you a very difficult question. What was Tony about? Why was he here?"

"Tony was very loyal to his family, to his friends, his employers. During these past years he was utterly devoted to his son, of course, but also to his struggle to establish his own company. He gave me absolute, unconditional love. I never found the limits to his love. Is that an answer to your question?"

"The investigation hasn't given us any answers yet. But if it is proven that it was a terrorist bomb, then that means your husband was murdered."

I hadn't thought about it in such stark terms before. He had named the crime.

He offered to give Shirley a lift to the subway and to drop me at another bank I needed to go to. Before we left, my housekeeper came to take care of Alan for the rest of the afternoon. She had been my occasional housekeeper and child-minder since Alan was a year old. She didn't know.

"Oh my God!" She struck her chest with a closed fist, lifting her face toward the ceiling. We held each other for a long time.

I joined Sue in the kitchen, put up a pot of tea, perched on the high wooden stools at the butcher-block table. I felt safe, enveloped by friendship, by continuity in my life. I would be all right. Alan would be all right. Tony was gone, but the future held no terrors for me. God help me, I felt as though I were on a difficult, dangerous but exhilarating adventure.

I talked about Tony's foibles, his procrastinating over household chores, the unfinished projects — only one unit of shelves up in the kitchen, the lack of a working sound system in the living room, and this from an accomplished furniture designer and builder, an expert in microphones and sound systems!

"It's the shoemaker syndrome," said Sue. "His children go without."

When Alan returned for dinner, he found a full house again, friends gathered 'round the table. Alan fell in love with a colleague from school who stopped by and spent most of his time on the man's lap or shoulders.

We had a merry feast, lots of punning, repartee, laughter, as though Tony was with us at the table. "Tony was the funmaster in our home!" Alan declared to us. We invented a new parlor game, "What's My Neurosis?" in which we swapped neuroses with one another for the evening, and everyone else had to guess whom we were pretending to be.

Alan fell asleep on the loveseat in the living room. A friend carried him upstairs and put him to bed. Everyone left except Sue, who slept over again

## December 24th

I woke at 3:00 a.m. and couldn't get back to sleep. Alan woke up, too, and came padding into my bedroom and crept in beside me and fell asleep. I shifted to his bedroom in order to be alone. I talked my eulogy for Tony out loud until I put myself into some kind of sleep.

Annette arrived, bringing soup and bread.

"It's pouring," I said. "The sky is weeping, too."

"The whole world mourns with you. Did you know that there was a United Nations ambassador aboard the plane? He was returning from Africa to New York, having worked out a peace agreement for South-West Africa. There was a moment of silence at the UN yesterday for him."

From the moment I had seen the flames of Lockerbie on the TV screen, I had shielded myself from any direct contact with any of the media. I didn't listen to the radio, didn't pick up a newspaper, didn't turn on the television. Friends told me everything I needed to know.

After lunch, Alan put his head down on the table and fell into a deep sleep. We transferred him to the couch, where he remained the entire afternoon. He hadn't slept like this since he was a newborn.

Leah's mother called and asked if she could come over to talk to me. We went upstairs to my study to be alone. She had been the first person to tell me that I had to tell Alan the whole truth and to tell him as soon as possible. Now she wanted to help me teach Alan how to grieve.

"I am speaking from my own experience and also as a sociologist. A child who loses a parent is changed for life. You are teaching him that some things are not going to change. He still has you, his home, his school, his friends. But everything else has changed. Don't wait for him to come to you. Reassure him that even if he doesn't cry or feel sad, it doesn't mean he doesn't love Tony, that Tony didn't leave him because he doesn't love him, that you will not also die now.

"You know," she continued, "adults come to the house, they cry with you but they smile at the child and give the child presents. They ignore the child's sorrow, the child's pain. They try to console him by diverting him. This is wrong. Children do not know how to mourn. You teach them by example."

Alan woke suddenly and asked to go over to Leah's house. He was on his way out the door when a car pulled up and my family emerged. He continued resolutely out the door and down the block, ignoring his grandparents.

My father, still in his overcoat, opened his arms to me as he walked into the living room. He wept in my arms. "It's not fair! It's not fair!"

Like my brother's response, this was utterly unexpected and unprecedented. I wept, too.

My mother gave me a long embrace. "I was so worried when you didn't come on time!" I told her. "I couldn't help being afraid."

She shook her head and looked over at my father. "I knew you'd be upset. The plane was delayed because of the holiday crowds. I couldn't help thinking, as we sat there, this is just like poor Tony was, belted into his seat, thinking about seeing you and Alan in a few hours. Do you know that Mr. Cameris from Pan Am met us at the airport with his wife and drove us here? They insisted on bringing us. They were so upset. These flowers are from them."

Then my sister and her daughter walked into the living room and gave me long, silent hugs. I was surprised to see them; no one had mentioned that they would be able to accompany my parents from Florida.

"We just had to be here," said Tamara, my niece, who had just moved to Florida with her new husband a month ago.

A few hours later, Fran, a friend from Boston, arrived weeping. "He was about love," she said.


## December 25<sup>th</sup>

I woke early to work on my eulogy. The phone rang. A young woman asked, "May I please speak to Tony?"

"Who is this please? I am his wife."

"I have sad news for him. His brother Peter died last night. Can he come to identify the body?"

I controlled my shock, my fear, "Please, who are you?"

"I'm a friend of his brother Peter. I've met Tony a few times. Apparently Peter went to the apartment of his girlfriend's mother last night and she found him this morning, dead on her couch. He must have died from a heart attack in his sleep. She got in touch with me. She didn't know how to reach Tony."

"This is very difficult to listen to," I said carefully, "I have something very sad to tell you, too. Tony was on Pan Am 103."

She began to scream, "Oh, oh, you poor woman! You poor woman!"

When she calmed down, I gave her the phone number of Peter's stepson as the next of kin to be informed. "As soon as Tony died, we tried to reach Peter through him. He didn't know where Peter was staying and could only promise to tell him as soon as Peter contacted him. I'm afraid that I'm overwhelmed with my own responsibilities right now, so I would appreciate it if you could call his son."

"Of course I will."

I tried to understand what had happened, what it meant. Had Peter died because he somehow learned of Tony's death — or was his death only a "coincidence"? There was that word, again. For all their conflicts and periods of separation, the two brothers had been very close to each other. If Tony had been asleep now, in our bed, and I'd had to awaken him to this loss, I believe he would have been shattered. The death of his brother would have plunged him into a deeper grief than had the death of either of their parents. The fact that he and Peter had been estranged since the summer, hadn't spoken since the fall, hadn't seen each other since — I wasn't even sure exactly when they had last gotten together — would have made Peter's sudden death unbearable.

I had been worrying about Peter's reaction to learning of Tony's death, dreading how he might take it. I assumed that on Christmas Day he would have at last contacted his stepson, and I would have to deal with him. We had had a very difficult relationship over the years; he was a troubled man. Now this. I shuddered. It had an inevitable feeling to it. There was some kind of cord between them. Even if Peter didn't know, he knew. And the will to live had left him.

Once again, I thanked whatever goodness there might be for sparing their parents. The shock of this double tragedy, the loss of both their sons, would have destroyed their mother and their father.


It was a rainy Christmas day. What was I going to do about Christmas? Should we have a tree as always? I felt that it was important to continue traditions but not to blindly reenact them. Christmas had to be modified to suit our sorrows. A tree without lights. A tree in mourning in the corner of the living room. I called my next door neighbors and asked them to buy a small tree for me when they went to purchase their own.

Then the tug-of-war began. Leah's mother called. She had looked at me peculiarly the day before when I mentioned finding a way to celebrate Christmas.

"I think it's wrong to act as though everything is normal. It isn't. I don't even think you should give Alan his presents today."

*Who the hell does she think she is telling me what to do?* I thought. Nevertheless, I was so lacking in self-confidence that I called back my neighbors and cancelled the tree. Then a friend who is a therapist called, with an entirely different take on the situation: "Alan has been deprived enough already. Christmas is about giving gifts to a child. Don't make him feel you are punishing him. Don't take Christmas away from him too!"

I found a way to compromise. I asked Alan if he wanted his gifts. He nodded quickly. So I gave them directly to him without ceremony, I handed him my gifts, unwrapped. He tore them open and lost himself in play.

Late in the morning, Jeff Marker, the rabbi of my congregation, came over to talk with me about the funeral and sitting *shiva*. "You must understand, Helen, that I am only telling you what is the tradition. What you are planning to do is very unusual, very unorthodox. Ordinarily, the body of the deceased is present at the funeral, in a closed coffin, and then is taken to a cemetery where it is buried. One doesn't begin to sit *shiva* until you return from the cemetery, having buried the person who died. Our first obligation is to attend to the person who has died. Then we attend to ourselves. Then we begin to formally grieve. I understand that these are peculiar, horrible circumstances . . ."

"Surely," I interrupted, "there are always circumstances when burial is impossible —someone lost at sea, in a war, in a fire, and so on."

"Yes, but then it is a certainty that there will never be a body to bury. In this situation, you do not know yet if Tony's body will or will not be found and identified. What I am trying to say is, if and when his body is returned for burial, you may need to sit *shiva* all over again."

"Then I will. That is not a problem. What I know is that it's necessary for all of us to come together as soon as possible. We need to. I cannot wait. And I need to sit *shiva* now. Since I am not constrained by adherence to Orthodox tradition . . . oh, what extra agony the Orthodox families must be going through now!"

"Tony was not Jewish and you are not Orthodox. You may do whatever feels right and necessary," he said kindly.

"Tony would want me to do whatever comforts me. That is why I am trying to create this blend, this mix. The service will be under the aegis of the Ethical Cultural Society, because that is how we were married. But I want to do everything else that is of my own tradition, if it makes sense to me, if it feels right. I know about the tearing of a garment, lighting a candle, sitting *shiva*, that is, having an open house every evening for a week. My family never covered their mirrors, but I have seen that in other people's homes."

"I will be there tomorrow at the chapel. Before the service begins, you and Alan can step into a private room and symbolically tear some clothing.

*Keriah* used to be an actual garment; now most people cut a tie. I will have some black ribbons for you and Alan to tear. The mirrors are covered for two reasons. First, the face of God is diminished whenever someone dies. And then, it is deemed inappropriate for the mourner to be concerned with personal vanity at a time like this. The candle is lit when you return to your home. It should be the kind that will burn throughout the *shiva* week."

"Annette told me that she had an extra one from the time her husband died two years ago. She's already offered to give it to me."

"It is customary to wash your hands when you return home from the grave and to eat a symbolic meal as soon as you return home. It is called the *'seudat havra'ah,'* the 'meal of consolation.' According to tradition, it should consist of hard-boiled eggs, eggs being the ancient symbol of fertility and life. The mourner is required to eat of life. As a mourner, during the week of *shiva*, you should refrain from using cosmetics, from wearing leather, from bathing, and from cutting your hair."

"Well, everything you've said feels right, except the prohibition on bathing! I don't know about the leather. And I'm not yet sure about covering the mirrors."

"There's one last important matter I need to discuss with you. Helen, do you want a *minyan* to come to your house every night, so that you can say *kaddish*?"

"Yes, I do. But why is it necessary for a *minyan* to assemble here? I thought that the *kaddish* is a meditative prayer for the dead, that a mourner is obliged to say it for the first year after death, and that you are supposed to say it at home as well as in synagogue at appropriate moments in the service."

"Yes, it is, but the *kaddish* is not a prayer that one can say in solitude. The *kaddish* is always said in public because in it, the power of God is acknowledged. Even though it is a prayer said by mourners, the word death, the concept of death, is never referred to. The prayer is an affirmation of life, for ultimate healing and redemption from suffering. In order to say it, there has to be at least the minimum number of Jews together to form a congregation."

I hesitated because Tony had been antipathetic to religious institutions, to religious practice, and had disapproved of my attempts to incorporate Jewish rituals into our home life, fearing that I was becoming religious myself. But I wanted to fling myself into my tradition and let it carry me through these frightening days. I trusted that its practices would give me a guideline to follow, to help me begin to heal.

"Yes, of course," I said. "Arrange for a *minyan* to come here every night. How long should I continue to say *kaddish* for Tony? All year?"

"You may, though it is customary to say *kaddish* for eleven months only for parents. Traditionally, the mourner comes to synagogue the first sabbath after *shiva* concludes, to say *kaddish* then. And during the year, there are four *yizkor* services in the liturgy. And there is the ritual of the *yortsayt*, the anniversary of the day of death. Each year, you once again light a candle, this time a 24-hour candle, and recite the *kaddish*. But as a widow, you're only constrained to observe social restrictions for thirty days after death. In fact, you are permitted to remarry after three months. This is to ensure the paternity of any children which may result from a remarriage. In the middle ages it was vital that the community have continuity as soon as it was decently possible."

So Alan's impulsive request for me to remarry would have been approved by any medieval Jew!

Mary arrived from Washington in time for dessert. After Alan went to sleep, I sat quietly with Mary, telling her about the last months of my life with Tony. "I'm so glad you're here . . ."

"I had to be here," she replied softly. "I was there when you first met each other. I was your maid of honor at your wedding."

"Would you help me do something?"

"Of course."

"I want to cover some mirrors downstairs."

We scooped up the newspaper from a rack in the living room and covered the mirror over the telephone in the front hallway. The mirror closed its eyes.

When we had first moved into this old Victorian house eight years ago, I had suggested to Tony that he claim the formal front parlor as his office. It had a large mirror framed by elegantly carved cherry wood columns. Mary and I worked silently, side by side, she handing me sheets of paper prepared with strips of tape on each corner. Next, the living room with its narrow mirror above the mantle piece; then the dining room and its two mirrors, one above the mantelpiece, the other set back into a built-in sideboard.

The house went into mourning.

# December 26th

The following morning was cold and sunny. I was calm, and confident that I would remain calm. I put on the dress I had been wearing when Tony first saw me. It was black, sleeveless, and didn't quite reach my knees. He told me years later, "I didn't know where to look when you walked towards me! All I could see were your legs!" A lacy black shawl gave it a touch of decorum.

Parkside Memorial Chapels sent two cars to drive us to the memorial service. As soon as I walked through the front entrance, the director told me that he had given us the larger of the two chapels, anticipating an overflow crowd. "The press called. They might turn up because of your death notice in the *Times*."

"If I had wanted the press to come, I would have invited them!"

I walked down the side aisle, heading towards the reception room where Rabbi Marker, my parents and son were, but was stopped by a line of people the length of the chapel waiting to talk to me, to take my hand: from my neighborhood, summer community, current and previous schools where I had worked, from Alan's school, family friends, my friends, Tony's friends, his colleagues from companies past and present. Each embrace was personal, each expression unforgettable.

Mr. Grupp came up behind me and whispered that it was time for me to join my family. I followed him into the reception room at the end of the chapel.

Rabbi Marker handed Alan and me the two black ribbons representing *keriah*, the garment that was traditionally ripped. Alan did not wish to wear the ribbon. He handed it back. He had carefully chosen his outfit. He was wearing on his chest the "Justice for the Homeless" button that Tony had given him the day we had walked in a demonstration, and around his waist, on a thin leather belt, was a holster with an Amnesty International badge, an organization Tony supported.

I pinned my ribbon to my black dress. "It's part of the funeral," I said, and pinned Alan's ribbon onto his leather cowboy vest, another gift from Tony.

Rabbi Marker said, and I repeated, *"Adonai natan, Adonai la-ekakh, ya-hai shaam Adonai meborakh"* (the Lord has given, the Lord has taken, let God's name be blessed).

We filed in. Alan left my side to sit next to Liam, his best friend from kindergarten. My parents sat down next to him. I found a seat closer to the lectern.

Mr. Grupp looked at us before he began to speak.

"While I did not know Tony personally, I have come to understand something of who he is, who he was, who he shall continue to be for you, the family and friends, those whose lives he touched and who touched his life. This shall be a non-denominational ceremony; he would have wanted it that way. These flowers that flank me on either side shall be symbolic of Tony's life.

"Before embarking upon this service, one cannot overlook the downing of the plane over Lockerbie. We do not yet know the reasons for this tragedy, whether structural failure or terrorism. If it is the first, that is serious enough, but if it is the second, then . . . all of us are victimized — not only the Engelhardt family and the Hawkins family. Governor Cuomo has called for the flags to be placed at half mast. The Secretary of State, Mr. Schultz, has called upon the UN for a moment of silence. The world stopped to take full recognition of the persons who gave their lives.

"I spoke with Helen and I visited the home and it is a home with books and books and more books, and it is a home filled with the laughter of young six-year-old Alan. It is a home filled with Tony — in the way the house is arranged, his office, in the quality of life. The home is unpretentious. The home is lived in, lived in by people who care about one another, lived in by people who play a lot of games. Isn't that true?

"As Helen describes him, he was an Englishman: self-contained, independent. A relaxed and easy-going man who could be depended upon in emergencies. A person there for you when you needed him. They fell in love at first sight at a New Year's Eve party. Tony was romantic. Tony was sensitive. Tony was fun. Tony was a raconteur. Tony was a bachelor when he met you, and quickly became a family man soon after meeting you, which is what women do for men!

"Tony's liberal politics were reflected in the way he lived. He was a member of Amnesty International. Alan wears their button on his belt. He showed me earlier a button on his jacket, 'Justice for the Homeless.'"

Alan stood and showed the badge and button for everyone to see, as though on cue.

"He was a fast and skillful car driver — maybe too fast! But that was

Tony! That's the way he was. He was a gifted designer, a good draftsman, artistic. He had a wonderful feeling for words. He wanted to be known as an authority in his field. The Runaround — the tape-recorder editing rack that he created for audio equipment — sold in Canada, in Australia, all over the U.S. Perhaps it didn't make a great deal of money, but it was used by professionals who understood its quality. It came from what he was as a person, from his desire to make a unique and special contribution.

"He appreciated the world of nature when Helen finally got him into it, with all of her ecological concerns. . . ."

Here Alan piped up, "And I got him into Legos!"

"Even now in our grief, Alan and Helen can think with smiles of the person who was in their life, who will always be in their life. Every day that they think about him, and every time Alan ever does anything that makes for more justice in the world, or for good storytelling in the world . . ."

Alan interrupted "Or what he did with me!"

"Alan was the one that gave him bliss. That's the word your mother used, Alan. When your father looked at you, he said, 'Now I know what bliss is.' You gave your father absolute joy . . . As for Helen, she told me that she had  never found the limits to his love or tolerance.

"The deepest kind of immortality for Tony rests in each of you, in the way in which you live out, in your own life, the best of what he wanted his life to be. You keep him alive as much as you want to have him in your life. In that sense, none of us ever die. We live in the radiations of those around us and in our wife, in-laws and in our son — who has yet to fulfill the dream, the promise of his father.

"Helen told me that Tony was not really a religious man in the traditional sense, and as I thought about it, I realized that that was true. But I would say that he was a deeply religious man. He believed in love. He believed in generosity. He believed in kindness. He believed in humor. He believed in work. He believed in his child and he believed in you. When you live that way, you live a religious life.

"This world is better because he lived in it. We are better people because we know what he stood for. We are different and changed irrevocably because we have been touched by him.

"Three people have offered to speak about Tony. After they do so, I will return to the podium. The first to speak is Eileen Brennan."

"I am Liam's mother. Liam and Alan have had three months of incredible togetherness. I talk because I am Liam's mother and because Tony, your dad, Alan, brought an awful lot of joy into our home.

"One of the very special memories that Liam and I have is driving up in front of P.S. 217 at the very last minute every morning, and somehow, ten seconds before us, there were Alan and Tony going up the steps. Alan, your father *never*, in rain or in rush, *ever* showed an impatience, which I am afraid Liam has learned too many times from me. There was a joy for him in that very act of bringing you to school.

"I think you and Liam have retold at our dinner table all of Tony's stories from the army. We now have a little Brooklyn accent, a little English accent and a little Irish accent as the stories are re-told. There is a presence in each of these stories, because each is told with excitement and exactness. The stories have become part of my dinner every evening since September.

"Tony stayed home for Alan's birthday. Tony wouldn't leave until that which was most important was completed and that was the celebration of his son's birthday. When I came to pick Liam up, I saw the game that was most important to Alan — Legos. And in the package were two little men. The other day I suggested to Alan that one man would be little Alan and the other would be little Tony, and little Alan and little Tony would continue to talk and tell the stories that Tony had told Alan.

"On your belt is a Volkswagon key. The Volkswagon has tremendous meaning because I work in a neighborhood where I cannot go to work without my car. My car broke down; I had to be towed. On a very, very busy day on a Monday afternoon, Tony dropped everything and towed me from the gas station and dropped me home. The same way Tony had time to do that for me, Tony constantly had time for Alan and Liam. And your dad always had time for a cup of tea at the kitchen table.

"I used to die and hope you were never looking too closely because the rule in our house is that you may never have more than two scoops of sugar, but he had to have three. Each of my guys can count, so we used to say that the English count just a little bit differently! . . . Having that cup of tea meant that Tony could sit quietly for a few moments. Alan and Liam both loved that cup of tea because it meant that they had more time together to play . . .

"Kahlil Gibran . . . addressed the purpose of real sorrow. Suffering carves out a hollow within us. The purpose of that carving, that hollowing, is to increase our capacity for joy. It is not meant to be filled with the emptiness of things. Helen — fill yourself with the joy of Tony's memory, with Alan and with what he is going to create with you. Our capacity for joy exceeds death, when we allow our suffering to become the vehicle through which our joy can grow. Tony didn't need the emptiness of things . . . Tony was at ease with Tony and needed nothing else — except Alan and you.

"To both of you and to Tony I say, 'Thank you.'"

Alan replied, 'Thank you!" loud enough for the entire room to hear.

"He's always going to have the last word!" Eileen smiled and blew Alan a kiss.

Dina Paisner walked to the podium and looked around the audience before beginning to speak. An actress and a singer, she had long white hair, braided like a crown around her head, giving her a regal appearance.

"When Helen called to tell me this impossible news on Saturday, I found myself on Christmas Eve doing something that I always have a great deal of trouble doing. I was throwing away papers and suddenly there was a line that sprang off the page. I was quite startled. It says, 'Death ends a life, not a relationship.' Well, Helen, you and Tony had one hell of a relationship! I mean, it was love at first sight, from the word go. It never stopped. Whenever I thought of that wonderful household and Alan, I was always inspired. They worked at it. There was mutual respect for their work, for their space, their creativity. It was wonderful.

"I was invited to Alan and Helen's mutual birthday party. On Christmas Day, Tony made a trifle. It still waters my mouth to think of it. Tony was sweet, gentle, lovely."

Dina concluded by reciting the words to two songs, the Gershwin classic, "They Can't Take That Away From Me," and Nina Simone's "Consummation."

Sue Horowitz, following Dina, needed a few moments to compose herself.

"When I remember Tony, I tend to think in images. The images are images of the senses . . . like the smell of coffee, because Tony liked very strong coffee with breakfast . . . He would make omelets, very light omelets in a shallow pan. And they would come out very delicate. I remember saying to Alan, 'You know, your father is a very good cook,' and he corrected me and said, 'No, he's not a cook, he's a chef.' I was so impressed. He couldn't have been more than four and he knew the difference between a chef and a cook. That's pretty good!

"Along with the omelets, I remember all of the wonderful dishes Tony used to make, and I especially remember the Christmas dinner he always had in his house — he would make lamb. For me, being Jewish, it was a wonderful thing to have an English Christmas, a special treat in my life — I could go to Helen and Tony's house and have an English Christmas. Besides the taste of the food, there was always this tremendous feeling that would come through, the wonderful feeling of family, home, and love.

"When I think of the sounds, I think of Tony's English accent, which of course, was very charming. He could do any kind of English accent, and would always have an amused light tone in his voice that used to cheer me up. He had a great attitude towards life that would say, 'Come on, luv, let's get on with it!'

"When I think of the sights, I think not only about how Tony looked, but certain things that we used to see together, and how he used to help me see through his eyes. One of those things were the stars. I used to visit Helen and Tony at a country place called Long Pond at Mahopac, New York. I remember walking out on the dock at night and looking up at the sky, seeing all those beautiful stars, and Tony talking about the stars. He knew about the different constellations, and I was just amazed that he knew all of that and could talk about it in a mixture of poetry and science.

"When I think of touch, I think of the feeling of really being hugged by someone who means it and who doesn't stop, who doesn't let go. The feeling is the total feeling of loyalty, of depth, of not being afraid of emotion, of 'I'm here for you,' of 'I believe in you.' And after a while, you believe in it, too, because your body believes what your mind resists. And that came through in the way he hugged.

"The final sense that we get is, of course, not from a physical sense, but from the mind, because the mind endures forever. After a while, be it through separation or death, we no longer have our senses, but we always have our memories and our feelings. I got from Tony a tremendous generosity of spirit. The reason I'm here today, is really just to say 'thank you' for all that I've been given by Tony and Helen."

Mr. Grupp returned to the podium. "In my experience," he said, "it is unusual in the extreme for a member of the family to speak and it is even more unusual for that person to be the wife. But in Helen we have someone who is sensitive, strong and able. She's going to share what is in her heart, the meaning of this moment."

I was so eager to get to the podium, I practically bounded up the steps. On the tiny platform, I felt as though I were standing on the prow of a ship. I looked out over the entire room, every face upturned towards me. Tony would have been even more surprised than I was to see how many people loved him. I looked to the farthest corner of the room, towards the doorway, through which Tony himself should have been walking, and we would all turn around and shout, "SURPRISE!" What a weird thought. I couldn't possibly share it. I tried to look at each and every face before beginning to speak, but I didn't want to tip myself over into tears. I dropped my eyes to the typewritten pages in front of me.

"Shalom. We have gathered here today in order to honor Tony, to comfort ourselves in the enormity of our loss. There are perhaps half again as many people who would be here with us, but geographical distance, previous commitments for the holiday season, or infirmity prevented them. At this very moment, his first cousin is in New York; he couldn't get an earlier flight.

"It was my special privilege to have known Tony as my lover, my best friend, my husband, the father of my child. I was his closest, his best friend, his beloved. This December 31st would have been sixteen years to the day that we met. It was a whirlwind romance. We met at a New Year's Party in Washington, D.C. We married on June 21st, 1973, Midsummer's Day, the summer solstice, the longest day of the day. He was killed on the winter solstice.

"I wrote our marriage vows: 'I choose you freely and in joy, to be my partner, my husband. To inspire you, encourage you, nourish and sustain you, to honor and cherish you. May only death separate us.'

"I wrote a sonnet for him called 'The Raft of Joy' —

'"The raft of joy, we ride on it!" you said —
here and now on this white passageway
between chamber and study in the light of day

launched on the wide mattress, our chosen bed.
We are each other's vessels. We are wed.
Now, you kneel to guide me as you may,
your singular craft under your sway.
Now, I climb your mast, reaching ahead
to set sail into unknown waters.
Below begins the rising of the flood
that carries us upon it, sons or daughters,
whatever comes about, will be good.
The flow transports us to the distant call,
irrevocably toward the water's fall.'

"At the conclusion of our discussion three days ago, Mr. Grupp asked me to try to define Tony's essence. What was he about? Why was he here? What was his purpose? Three words seem to describe him best, and they all begin with L: Love, Loyalty and Liberality.

"There are many ironies in the circumstances of his death. He had gone to England on a mission of personal mercy, to attend to ultimate responsibilities, to set things right. He went to visit his favorite uncle who is mortally ill, to see him one last time. He went to sort through and bring back with him the last of his father's things stored in his uncle's home. He went to reimburse his uncle for the headstone on his mother's grave. He went at this time of year, rather than in January, to take advantage of a free round-trip ticket from Pan Am. The offer expired December 31st, 1988. He had earned his frequent flyer status and qualified for this reward during the two and a half years he was national sales manager for Beyer Microphone, a job that required him to leave us and travel two weeks every month all across the United States.

"I told Alan that I gave Tony a blessing before he left. But my blessing was for the flight on the 20th. Once he changed his ticket to 103, I no longer had any power to protect him. Nobody did. They all walked into a trap. If it were possible for anyone to survive that disaster, it would have been him. He had courage, quick-wittedness, technical expertise, fast reflexes, determination to live. He was so *vital*.

"Tony hated violence. He loathed terrorism as much as he despised injustice. He was an intensely private person, but his death is not a private tragedy. It is part of an immense international grief. When Pan Am called me after midnight December 21st, I told them they had to guarantee me that it truly was a freak accident due to mechanical failure. Not incompetence. Not greed. Not indifference. And most of all, not terrorism — anything but terrorism — for me to accept his death without bitterness, without rage. I don't want the hideous circumstances of his death and the ugly, still unresolved controversy swirling around this event to overwhelm the memory of this man, this good man — Anthony Lacey Hawkins.

"To paraphrase Auden: We must love one another *before* we die. As he did.

"I conclude with words that are not mine but Sean O'Casey's, slightly modified. These are Mrs. Boyle's final words from *Juno and The Paycock*. She has just been handed the body of her son, riddled with bullets, another victim of the Irish civil war in the 1920's, not the 1980's.

"'*Take away our hearts of stone and give us hearts of flesh.*
*Take away this murder and hate and give us Thine own eternal love.*'"

I stepped down and walked directly to my parents. My mother enfolded her arm around me. I put my head down on her shoulder and wept.

Mr. Grupp returned to the podium. "Love. Loyalty. Liberality. Let us have one moment of silence . . .

"In conclusion, when we think about Tony, we think about our own mortality. There are three things, perhaps, that we would want for our own lives. First, that those whom we love should understand what we lived for. Secondly, we would want our lives to have made a difference, some lessening of the pain in the world, some increment for good. And thirdly, those whom we love are not confused and depressed, unable to face their future. All of us are of one life. All of us share in this life. Our task is to make life sweet, not bitter. Let the memory of Tony be with us all of our days. Let us leave this place in quiet and peace.

"The family will be at home this afternoon and will be sitting shiva this week. Helen asks that contributions be given to Amnesty International . . ."

We returned home to a house filled with guests, and with Tony's cousin to worry about until he finally arrived.

"I'm so sorry, Helen. The plane was delayed and we had a terrific amount of traffic from the airport."

I sobbed with relief and rushed to embrace him. He hadn't been snatched from us, too.

Alan jumped into his arms.

"Hello young man! And how are you?"

Rabbi Marker rang the bell promptly at 7:00 p.m. to begin a *kaddish* service. Within moments, our living room was transformed into a house of prayer, with people standing in clusters, holding books, and chanting in Hebrew. Alan sidled over to me and whispered in a voice that carried to the kitchen. "What going on here? We don't even believe in God!"

"Shh. It has nothing to do with God. It has to do with comforting me. It does make me feel better. So go and play in the other room and try to be quiet until our service is over."

I was embarrassed, amused and impressed by the sturdy skepticism of Alan's spirit and his loyalty to Tony's atheism. The prayers, the presence of my family, neighbors and friends from the congregation, the ancient familiar melodies and when we ultimately came to it —the words of the *kaddish* — gave me everything I needed to conclude this day.


## December 27th

I didn't have a chance to talk quietly and personally with Tony's cousin until the next morning after breakfast. He joined my parents and me at the dining room table. Again and again the conversation turned like a nail seeking a magnet to the only subject we were really drawn to. Tony Stoppani told us how it had been for the family that night.

"At first nobody knew if Tony was indeed on that flight. We had heard about the crash on the radio, but nobody could get through to the special numbers that Pan Am had set up. They were engaged. Nobody knew if he actually left. I think he stayed with our aunt Laura, didn't he, on the Tuesday night? And on the Wednesday he intended going to Catharine House and nobody knew for certain that he'd flown out. All we did know was that he intended going out that night. When I talked to Len, he told me he hoped Tony might have missed the plane because he tends to leave things to the last minute. Nobody could find out anything, so I got a police officer to go round to Pan Am and they confirmed that T. Hawkins was a passenger."

I asked, "And when was that?"

"I did that about ten minutes before I rang you. You can never be certain. It could have been someone else."

"What I really want to know, Tony," I said, "is for you to tell me about your visit with him last week."

"To be honest, there's not a lot to tell, because Tony — after contacting my wife — came along to visit on the Sunday morning, had lunch and tea with us in the afternoon and left 'round about 6:00. Basically, Helen, we talked about family, swapping memories. And after lunch, he and I took the dog for a long walk. We live in an area where there's quite a lot of woodland traversed by motorways, what you would call turnpikes. I know he enjoyed himself. He had a very nice day. He was talking about coming back to England, perhaps next year in the summer, with you and Alan. He was talking once again about trying to get all the family together. That really was it."

He added: "Among things I want to go back with, Helen, is a full description of the ring. I've seen it on Tony."

"I could give you a photograph of Tony to take back, too," I said.

My visit with Tony Stoppani was interrupted by the arrival of a friend. She only had an hour. I detached myself from the table and went upstairs to be alone with her in my study. Florence was a friend from earliest childhood, but ever since she had gone to live and work in France twenty-five years ago, we had been out of touch. Alan's birth in December of 1982 had brought her back briefly into my life; now Tony's death had brought her to my door. Once again, within moments, it was as though we had never been apart. We found the cord that connected us. There were details to swap, a heightened, abbreviated recapitulation of our lives to quickly fill in.

She had been unable to come to Tony's funeral, she explained, because she had to be with her daughter — whose friend had also died on Pan Am 103.

"I don't believe this, Florence! The cab driver who drove my parents here the other day knew someone who knew someone. I'm feeling that this disaster has touched everyone in this city, in cities all over the world."

We embraced, the fabric of our friendship restored. This time, I believed, we would not permit ourselves to be separated again. I was mistaken. Tony's death was an earthquake in our lives. It brought me closer to some people temporarily, separated me from others, and once the aftershocks subsided, I realized that very few of the reunions would be sustained. Every relationship I had was subject to realignment.

## December 28th

Mr. Cameris, my Pan Am contact, called early in the morning with startling news. "Tony's body has been identified. Where should it be sent?"

"Who identified him? His cousin just left for England yesterday. He couldn't possibly have gone up to Scotland yet."

"I think they received dental records, or maybe he had personal identification on him, you know, credit cards, driver's license, things like that."

"I guess you should send it to the Riverside Chapels, where the service was held."

Before I could absorb the impact of that call, Tony's uncle called from Toronto. "It was a bomb! Scotland Yard has announced that explosive remains have definitely been found in the wreckage! The FBI is still saying they have no proof it was caused by terrorism. How can they! Oh, Helen, it's so terrible, I can't take it in. And Peter's gone too!"

"Tony's body has been identified. They'll be shipping the coffin home tomorrow. I'll let you know when the burial will be."

"I want to send flowers."

"Oh, there are my parents at the door. Got to go. I'll get back to you."

But Alan walked in. He started walking up the stairs to his room. I caught up with him, put my arms around him and began to sob, "They've found Tony's body. They found him. We know where he is. Now we can bury him." I held him, sitting on the stairs, the front door still opened wide to the mild morning air. I sobbed from the pit of my stomach, from my entire intestines. I literally felt grounded. Hearing that Tony's body had been found and identified felt almost as comforting as learning that he was safe, that he was not in danger any more, that he was alive. I sobbed from a well of grief now uncapped and available to me.

## December 29th

The State Department called — a young man. "Excuse me, Ma'am, but was your husband, Anthony Lacey Hawkins, an American citizen?

"No, he wasn't. He still held a green card at the time of his death."

With an audible sigh of relief, he thanked me and hung up.

I was still so innocent to the political implications of this disaster that I didn't realize I had been treated inappropriately, indeed outrageously, by my State Department. I had not thought to respond, "But he left an American wife and child!"

In the months to come, I would learn that another widow, upon trying to retrieve her husband's wedding ring was told, "Lady, he's dead. Get over it."

The FBI called to ask, "Why was Tony in England? Could anyone have asked him to carry on luggage for them, or given him something, some gift to carry home for them?"

"Never," I boasted. "Tony was too clever, knew too much about how terrorists operate. He was very interested in terrorism."

I could hear the intake of breath on the other end of the line. "Why was he interested in terrorism?"

"I don't mean that his interest was extraordinary. He just was interested in being informed about politics, about what is going on in the world. And he paid attention to the various incidents involving terrorism that have been occurring so frequently." It was impossible to explain that Tony seemed to take terrorist attacks personally without making him sound peculiar.

## December 30th

Quiet day. Gave Alan a bath. Our time to be alone with each other in deepest trust and delight had become a ritual that sustained me through these days of pain. We made a special game out of toweling off. Alan scrambled out of the tub and curled up in a ball on my lap as I covered him with a large, thick towel. "Oh, what is this? Is this a big rock? Let's see . . ." I uncovered his heels and arched soles, the tiny pink toes curled tightly — "Hmmm, what could this be?" — and proceeded further to reveal his smooth, rosy calves. "And this? I lost my little boy, where could he be?"

"Here I am!" Alan shook his head out of the towel and smiled at me. I hugged and rocked him in my arms.

"I'm always upset," he said, "but I don't always cry."

"That's how I feel too, sweetie," I said, rubbed his hair dry, and kissed his forehead.

Mr. Cameris called with very distressing news. "They are holding the bodies indefinitely! They're being treated as part of the criminal evidence in the investigation."

"I can't believe this! I can't bear it. Withholding the bodies from us? Not letting us bury our dead?!"

I called Tony's cousin for an explanation. He was a policeman, he would know the answer.

"Tony's body is being held along with others from that section of the plane because it is critical to the criminal investigation. The earliest that they expect to be able to release him is January 10th. It's being given special scrutiny."

For the first time since Tony's death, I felt the full consequences that the criminal investigation was imposing on me. Deprived of the traditional rituals, I felt not only frustrated but fearful, and utterly powerless. I called everyone to notify them that Tony's burial was being postponed indefinitely.

## December 31st

This was the day I was required to go to synagogue to say *kaddish* publicly for the first time. "Alan, we need to go to Park Slope Jewish Center to say *kaddish* for Tony."

"I don't want to go, Mom. It's too boring," He continued playing with his Legos. I did not insist. I left him with my parents.

At the conclusion of the service, Rabbi Marker extended an opportunity for me to personally thank the congregation for their participation in the *shiva* services conducted every evening in my home. I stepped up to the *bimah* and faced the room filled with attentive faces.

"As you know, Tony was not interested at all in any formal practice of religion or to be associated with religious institutions. He didn't discriminate;

he stayed away from the church he was baptized into as well as mine. So it was particularly moving to me that so many of you came to our home to create a minyan each night, to enable me to say *kaddish* for him. Whatever else the *kaddish* is, it is a ritual to comfort the newly bereaved and Tony would have wanted me to be comforted."

When I got home, I walked Alan down the street to Leah's house. He carried a huge new black tank with the word "bomber" scrawled across it, a Christmas gift from the next- door neighbors. I couldn't believe they had selected this toy as a gift for him. But once he unwrapped it, I couldn't take it away from him.

When I returned home I called Mr. Cameris. "Please get me the names and phone numbers of some of the other families in the New York area. We need to talk to one another. Not being able to bury our dead is too much to bear alone."

"I don't have that information now, of course. I'll have to call the office on Monday and get back to you."

That evening, the last *minyan* gathered in our home. I looked across the living room at the large color photograph I had placed on the mantlepiece, of Tony and myself, taken many years ago, at the moment when the deep bond between us was made visible. I am gazing at his face, beaming love at him, and he, with a delicate gesture compounded equally of affection and embarrassment, was glancing past me, his large hand gently touching my chin.

Behind it stood a photo in black and white of Tony and me dressed in costume. He is in bowler hat and tight black jacket, striped trousers, a cane dangling from his left arm, a black velvet mustache taped across his upper lip -Chaplin's tramp fused with Mr. Verdoux. I am in a flamboyant flowered hat, long-sleeved, ankle-length patterned dress, high-laced shoes. His Girl. My left arm confidently linked through his, my right reaching across to pinch his bicep, not believing my good fortune, both us grinning to outdo the spring sunshine in Prospect Park two months before our wedding. These pieces of paper with their fixed faces had become a shrine. One tear slid out of my right eye and traveled slowly down my cheek.

Rabbi Marker lit the braided *havdala* candle and put it out in a saucer of wine. We passed around the spice box and breathed in the mixture of cinnamon and cloves, sweet fragrance of the sabbath which just ended, sweet scents for a sweeter New Year. He asked me to say a few words about the significance of this night, New Year's Eve, which he knew was also the sixteenth anniversary of my meeting Tony.

I had a quiet supper with my parents. Alan was in Leah's house, invited to be at their New Year's Eve party.

Designed to burn for seven days, the *shiva* candle expired at midnight after only six days. Midnight was the moment Tony and I first kissed each other sixteen years ago. I was shaken by this quiet coincidence. I distracted myself by removing the newspapers covering the mirrors. My father came into the room.

"Dad, something really eerie just happened. The *shiva* candle stopped burning at the moment Tony and I first kissed each other at the New Year's Eve party where we met each other. The candle symbolizes the soul of the deceased, doesn't it? Isn't the soul supposed to hover around the its body for seven days before departing for other realms. Isn't that why the candle is designed to burn for seven days? But Tony didn't die seven days ago, and we didn't hold the funeral within twenty-four hours of his death. His funeral was held five days after he died, so this *shiva* candle began burning on day six after his death, so it could no longer be a symbol of Tony's soul hovering over his body in a temporary morgue in Lockerbie, Scotland. It has become instead a symbol of our own personal history."

My father couldn't hear what I was saying. The word "soul" triggered his lecture mode, and he launched into a diatribe, dismissing the concept of soul as anti-rational, and how even if the soul actually exists — which it does not — it couldn't have any possible connection with a burning candle.

In exasperation I walked away and went to bed.

## January 1ˢᵗ, 1989

Late in the morning when I woke, I was told that my mother had slipped on the stairs in the middle of the night and hurt her back. She spent most of the day resting.

My father found me in the kitchen. He looked ill at ease. "I should have let you finish what you wanted to say last night. I should not have responded like that. I want you to share your feelings with me."

I was surprised and grateful at this gracious gesture on his part. It was most unusual for him to apologize and to honor feelings above opinions. "And I want you to share your feelings with me," I said, "your feelings, not your opinions!" I hugged him.

By evening my mother felt well enough to come downstairs and sit on the living room couch in the evening, reading the *New York Times.* She looked up at me and shook her head. "There is a vast criminal investigation going on, on an unprecedented scale. Who knows when they'll ever release Tony's body to us? It might be months."

## January 2nd

The next morning, however, my mother was in great pain. I arranged to have one of her friends drive her to the hospital to take x-rays. I called the chairman of my department. Tomorrow would be the first day of school after the Christmas break. I explained about my mother and said that I didn't know when I would be able to return to work.

"You do what you must do. We'll work with you."

I felt ready to tackle Tony's desk. He had taken over the front parlor room to be his office — the only room with an original cut-glass chandelier and a full-length mirror framed in carved cherry wood — in order to be near the living room, the TV, and the kitchen. He had never liked to be isolated. At first, sitting quietly in his chair and sorting papers was comforting. But then I discovered that he had let his AAA membership lapse — how could he have, he doted on that car — and then that he hadn't paid the $94 premium due on his International Airplane Passengers Association policy a week before he was killed. I hadn't even known about this policy! That $94 lapse had deprived Alan and me of $250,000 in death benefits. When I learned, two days after he died, that he hadn't kept up with his life insurance premiums, I wasn't angry with him. I didn't want to profit by his death. But this was different. This was outrageous. If he hadn't been financially able to pay these modest premiums, why hadn't he told me, why hadn't he asked me to help him out? Shame had triumphed over responsibility. I was furious and disillusioned with him. "Damn you, Tony! How could you have done this to us!"

My mother returned from the hospital feeling better. Her back hadn't been seriously harmed. She simply had to rest and take muscle relaxants.

"Mom, I've just learned something absolutely unbelievable." I showed her the documents I had uncovered. She shook her head and sighed. "Poor Tony. Managing money was not one of his strengths. Every window closed to you."

That night, for the first time, I dreamed of Tony's death. I woke with my nightgown drenched in sweat.


## January 3rd

Alan began crying when I handed him the wrong shirt. "Tony always put short sleeved shirts on me!"

"I know you're missing Tony," I said softly.

"No! I'm angry with you!" he shouted, and stomped out the room.

Understanding why Alan was behaving like this didn't help me feel less shaken and saddened by it. I brought him next door for his first drive to school with our neighbor. I helped my mother, and then headed out to the Pratt Institute, School of Architecture. I wanted to assure the dean that I was prepared to teach my ecology class when their new semester began the following week.

From Pratt, I walked to the high school where I worked. It was a mild, sunny morning and I enjoyed the exercise. I went first to the principal's office. He wasn't there, but the chairwoman of the Health Careers Department was, a formidable person, very stern in her demeanor. As soon as she saw me, she concluded her business, put down her papers and opened her arms to me. We cried together. Her emotion disarmed me.

"Helen, I want you to know that I'm always here, if you need me."

I moved through the halls very slowly; so many people wanted to reach out to me. When I finally made it up to the fourth floor to the science department, a colleague with whom I had quarreled my last afternoon before the holidays gave me a condolence card, shook my hand, and said simply, "I'm sorry."

On my way out, I bumped into the principal in his overcoat, his arms weighed down with manila envelopes. "Good," he exclaimed, "I've been wanting to talk to you."

I followed him back upstairs into his office. He put his hat down on the table, but remained in his overcoat. "What do you need from us, Helen? We'll help you in any way we can."

"There is one practical way you can help me. I need time in the morning to feed and dress Alan. Tony used to help me with those routines, so that I could get here by 8 o'clock. Would it be all right for me to come in at 9:00 a.m. until I can find someone to help me with Alan? It's very important for us to have peaceful mornings together."

"Of course."

With help like this, I knew I was going to make it. When I picked Alan up at school, I spoke with his teacher. "How was his first day?"

"Too good to be true. Best behavior. When I asked him why he hadn't called me, he replied, 'I've been too worried about Tony.'"

Two phone calls as soon as we hit the house. First, Mr. Paradise from Riverside Chapel. Yes, that was his name! "Tony's body is being sent home tomorrow. I'll go to the airport to meet the plane and bring the casket back with me. I've been told that the casket must remain sealed for sanitary purposes."

"Does that mean we can have a burial the day after tomorrow? That will give me time to notify people."

"Yes. You should stop by here tomorrow and see me. There are documents you have to sign."

Then Mr. Cameris called. He had an answer for me about my request to be put in touch with other families in the New York area. "Pan Am will not give out any names or phone numbers. We have to protect everyone's privacy."

"I'll deal with that issue later. Right now I have to notify everyone about a burial on Friday."

**January 4th**

As I helped Alan get dressed, he said, "We want to do the things Tony used to do."

"Yes, sweetie, that is what we want to do."

I went back into Tony's files trying to learn more about the missing AAA membership renewal and came across many documents that only deepened the mystery. There was a letter from AAA dated November 23rd, 1988, warning that Tony's membership needed to be renewed immediately and a notation at the bottom of this letter in Tony's handwriting that Check # So-and-So had been mailed November 29th. I went to his checkbook and found the stub. I hunted down the envelope of returned checks and found that the only one missing in the series was that particular check. I called AAA. Their records clearly showed that they had cancelled Mr. Hawkins' membership at the end of December, 1988 because they had never received his check. Another door slamming shut on my fingers. This one was incomprehensible. Tony was meticulous about the care of his car. He had spent the last few days before leaving for England running from the car inspection garage to the Motor Vehicle Bureau where he stood in line for hours in order to clear his tickets. If he had written a note that a check was mailed, he had mailed it. He might let every life insurance policy lapse, but never his AAA membership. I couldn't understand it. Fate was really thumbing its nose at me.

At bedtime, Alan told me he wanted to put something next to Tony "to take with him when we bury him. I want you to put in some Legos."

"That's a wonderful idea! I'll choose something to bury with him, too."

I stood in front of Tony's dresser studying the shells displayed there. In the very center was a collection of small Mexican ceramic heads encircling a miniature vase. They were primitive, unglazed. They looked like funerary ornaments. I chose two. They were Tony's originally. They would be Tony's again.

## January 5th

Alan refused to give up any of his own Legos to place in Tony's casket. "No, no! Buy him new Legos!"

I took the Coney Island Avenue bus to Riverside Chapel and met with Mr. Paradise in his office. A copy of the death certificate lay on his desk. I picked it up. "I've been told I'll need several copies of this, each one with a seal. How many do you have to give me?"

"Only this one. I'll get in touch with the police in Lockerbie and ask them to send you a batch. You're right. You will need many for various legal purposes."

I looked down at the buff-colored paper in my hand. In the upper left hand corner, a tiny lion seated on a crown held a sword and a staff in each paw. IN DEFENS. In the upper right hand corner was the code number DE 826065. Entry Number 175 in the District Number 837 in the Year 1988 a Death was registered in the district of Lockerbie. 1. Hawkins, Anthony Lacey 2. M. 3. Audio Equipment Salesman 4. Married 5. Date of Birth 1931, 11, 13 6. Age 57 years. 7. Name and occupation of spouse — Helen Ruth Anglehart. 8. Found dead 1988 December Twenty-second 1400 hours Halldykes Farm, Lockerbie. 12. Cause of death 1 (a) Multiple Injuries (b) Civilian Aircraft Accident

It was signed and certified by three different people. I swallowed and tasted vomit in my throat.

"My son wants to put some toys into the casket next to his father. Can you open the casket for this purpose?"

"No problem. But I recommend that we take care of this today, not tomorrow."

"I still have to buy the toys. May I return here within a few hours?"

"No problem. I'll be here until 5:00."

I took the next bus to the end of the line, walked down to Seventh Avenue and Garfield Place, to Little Things, Alan's favorite toy store. Tony often accompanied Alan on his shopping expeditions for Lego sets. We had been there very recently, early December, doing some pre-birthday, pre-holiday shopping. Allen and Edith, the couple who owned the store were there. They didn't know.

"You mean, I'll never talk to him again?" Allen asked, shocked. Edith could only shake her head, slowly, silently. "Is the burial tomorrow? I'd like to come," Allen said.

I found what I thought was a set of Legos appropriate for this occasion, a small box of half a dozen Lego Spacemen. "This is Alan's offering and I have money which is left over birthday money for Alan. I'll feel better paying for it." I handed over the box at the cash register. They nodded.

When I handed the box and the Mexican pottery heads over to Mr. Paradise, I asked him for one more favor.

"When you open the casket, could you just glance at the fourth finger of his left hand to see if a ring that looks like this one is on it? Nobody from the family identified the body. I'm taking their word for it that it's Tony they've returned to me."

On my way home I stopped for flowers at Newkirk Plaza. These were to be handed to each person to place on the casket before it was lowered into the earth. I selected red roses and blue miniature iris, the colors of the British flag.

I went to sleep praying for the safety of family and friends and that if it were going to snow tomorrow, it snow gently.

## January 6th

I woke to soft snow steadily falling, snow like soap flakes, without wind. The first snow of winter.

The limousine pulled up in front of my house and waited for us. I looked for Alan. I found him chatting with the chauffeur. My father held onto the railing and took the stairs slowly, one by one, while I held my mother's arm as she carefully negotiated the front steps. This was her first day out walking on her own after her fall.

The driver hadn't taken us more than a block and a half when I remembered: "Flowers!"

"It's all right, Ma'am. There's plenty of time." The chauffeur calmly turned the wheel to the right and brought us home again so I could retrieve the bouquet of red roses and dainty blue iris from the refrigerator.

The snow was falling heavily, covering the streets and sidewalks. We drove at a stately pace in the gray limousine along Ocean Avenue. We were quiet, thinking our own thoughts. Alan was on his knees staring out the back window. My parents withdrew into their overcoats.

The chauffeur parked behind the chapel and directed us to the rear entrance. Once inside, someone showed us to an elevator, which took us to the reception room upstairs. I saw Tony's nephew Steve, who wore a large white bandage over his right eye and half of his thin face. "Steve, your eye! What's happened to your eye?"

He smiled shyly. "Not to worry. I slipped on the stairs yesterday and hit my head."

Wherever I turned, people were in danger, under assault, ready to slip, to fall, to break.

The steel blue casket, silver tipped at each of its four corners, guarded by two enormous floral displays which towered over it at either end, was waiting for me in its alcove. On the center of its curving lid was a modest rectangular tray, dainty blossoms peeking over the edge. The people of Lockerbie had sent heather to accompany each casket home; his uncles had sent the great bouquets.

"There he is at last." I walked towards it, still rubbing my hands from the cold, and tentatively touched the lid.

*Thank God I don't have x-ray vision.*

"Look at Alan," my mother said softly, standing behind me, her voice breaking.

Alan had his left ear pressed against the casket, his right hand lightly resting on its gleaming surface.

"He's listening for Tony," she whispered.

I knelt down next to him and put my hand on his small shoulder. I could not let myself enter too deeply into his imagination. I had to lead him back to us. "Tony's inside there, dear."

"The Legos, where are the Legos?"

"They're inside there, too." I stood up and took his hand. "I think it's time to go now. I think everybody who was able to come today is here."

Steve came with us in our limousine. I asked him if he had any recollections of Tony from his childhood. He nodded. "Oh, yes. Uncle Tony. He always had interesting ideas, things he was inventing. He was fun." He smiled and fell silent.

I chewed over the crumb he had given me, hungry for any new details, any new facts, any new descriptions from the forty-one years of Tony's life before I met him, especially from his life in England, especially through someone else's eyes. I knew quite a lot about Tony's childhood and early manhood from Tony himself. He loved to tell stories and could transform the most ordinary incident into a vivid and amusing anecdote. He especially loved to talk about his brother Peter:

*"For a number of years, Peter lived in a large house, a stately home, really, not far from Bath. When I'd visit him, there'd always be some huge party going on, with live music. They had a resident rock and roll band living in one of the wings of this great house, helping to pay the rent. There was always plenty of food, drinks, smokes, people sitting around on mattresses on the floor. But what I remember is this: every now and then, one of Peter's four children who were running around on the huge beams above our heads the whole time, every now and then, one of them would slip and fall and bounce onto a mattress beside us and no-one took any notice. It was incredible! They'd just pick themselves up and scramble back up to the rafters and run around again!"*

Folding his arms across his chest, Tony would laugh again at the memory, then lean forward and reach for another cigarette.

I glanced at Steve's impassive face and thought, *All that I may ever know of Tony's life is only what he himself told me, and I can't remember everything.*

We drove slowly, the windshield wipers whispering, *"I will never forget this, I will never forget this, I will never forget this."* Inside the gothic gates of Green-Wood Cemetery we waited a long time before being permitted to proceed. A bell began to toll over our heads. We drove through a timeless landscape, snow sifting through boughs onto gravestones, covering the shoulders of marble angels with soft white shawls.

The cars stopped. Doors opened. We walked carefully to the graveside. A family friend held onto my father, who picked his way cautiously over uncertain ground. His eyesight was poor and partial under the best of circumstances. The lines on his face seemed deeper; he had aged during these last days. I held Alan's hand.

I didn't recognize the grave site. Two weeks ago I had been shown a patch of raw red mud. Now the ground was carpeted with snow, the grave almost completely concealed under a crisscross of poles and draped by dark green plastic turf. The steel blue coffin, with the flowers rearranged around it, was centered on this supportive structure. I had anticipated a classical arrangement of deep hole opened to the sky, coffin to one side waiting to be lowered.

We found our places a few feet from the grave. Shirley sang the opening prayers in Hebrew, her eyes hidden behind dark glasses. I took a few steps closer to the coffin and opened the green leather cover of the writing pad we had purchased during our visit to England two years ago. Green memento from green days. I faced the coffin but spoke austere and familiar words adapted from Auden's "Elegy for Yeats" to the people standing silently behind me.

"Earth receive another honored guest:
Anthony Lacey Hawkins is laid to rest."

I had not been able to write a new poem for this occasion. My emotions were in hibernation. I read an old one, "For Having Been."

"Say only it was with me
by me for wonder
for one time
Say only prayers
of Thanksgiving
Say only songs
of praise for love
and joy would only
echo psalms
sung without words
alone in grateful
silence for you
for having been
by you."

I closed the pad, replaced it in my pocket, nodded to my mother and returned to my place. My mother stepped into the center of our semi-circle, faced us and began to speak in a clear, firm voice:

"On the occasion of Tony's birthday, the year he married Helen, I sent him this card. Helen saved it all these years. What I said then, sixteen years ago, is as true today, even truer. 'Dear Tony, you have not only enlarged and enriched our family, but you have endeared yourself in our hearts deeply and securely. We love you.'"

I looked at my friends and family standing quietly beside me. It was fitting that the earth be beautiful for Tony's burial, that it be winter-white and cold, that each one of our words be inscribed in the frozen air. My mother stood silently for a few minutes before resuming her place in the circle.

I nodded to Mr. Grupp, who spoke from where he was standing. He once again found the appropriate words to say, reiterating a theme he had explored at the memorial service: "The deepest kind of immortality for Tony rests in each of you, in the ways in which you keep him alive in yourselves, the ways in which you make manifest the best of what he wanted his life to be about."

Shirley began chanting the *kaddish*. She broke into sobs. She sobbed for me. I could not. I walked over to each person and handed them a flower from my bouquet. Alan did not want to place his on the casket. I did it for him. Everyone came forward one by one, adding their red rose, their blue and purple iris, to the gleaming blue surface. I grabbed a handful of crusty, ice-flecked mud and threw it into the hole. Alan ran to me and peered over the edge. It was done.

"Tell them" — I gestured towards the grave diggers waiting patiently at a distance — "tell them that only the flowers from Lockerbie are to be lowered into the grave. The two floral stands are to return with us in the limousine."

Mr. Grupp nodded and delivered my message. I looked for the last time at the blue box that held Tony's body, and walked with Alan to the car.

Mr. Grupp leaned towards the window and extended his hand. "I've done everything I know how to do, lady. Now it's up to you to continue. I know you will."

I took his hand and pressed it — "Thank you" — and thanked him also with my eyes.

Everyone who was able to came home with us for lunch. I was overcome by fatigue and went upstairs to bed. I closed the door and lowered the shades, and pulled the quilt up to my shoulders. I closed my eyes and saw the white snow and the red roses and purple blue irises and the blue coffin. I wondered what Alan would remember of this day. The day after the memorial service, when he called a friend from school, I heard him say, "A lot of people were there who loved Tony," and then he said, "She wasn't very upset."

I confronted him. "Were you talking about me? Just because I wasn't crying, doesn't mean I wasn't upset. When you don't cry, that's okay. It doesn't mean you're not feeling sad."

I roused myself and reached for the tape recorder by my bedside. I was probably the only relative from the Pan Am 103 families who could make their dead speak again. The tape recorder and the stack of tapes were waiting for this moment.

I selected one of the tapes we had made over the years, this one recorded during an evening we sat around the dining room table with our friends. I heard him clearing his throat, his hearty laughter. He was regaling us with one of his favorite set pieces from his days as dispense barman at the London Hilton in the 1950's.

*"This time, there's a magnificent cake. Comes on a trolley. It's this wide by the length of this table and it's like, it's like a Roman set of columns. And there's some more columns and another cake and some more columns and another cake, and on top of that, there's a medallion — Marine's medallion — their badge, in chocolate icing. It's wonderful. Four marines come through and they take hold of this trolley, and one of them shakes it to see, y'know, he wants to know what it feels like and pkwhew! it breaks into three pieces on the floor. And they all stand there and I get the phone and Ding Ding Ding.*

*"Oh no, I call the patissiere. The Hilton Patissiere. What do y'do? Um, the guy comes around — I can't believe it — but this is what. Within a minute or two, the guy comes running around and he's got a black doctor's bag, he comes running around and he skids to a stop on the tiles and he looks at this thing and he gets down and he opens the bag . . . and he gets out icing and everything . . . and within a couple of minutes he's repaired it and puts it on top of the cake and he snaps his bag shut and walks off. Beautiful! He's done the best repair job I've ever seen. The patissiere of the Hilton. He made the bloody thing in the first place! So he ought to know how to fix it and he does know how to fix it . . .*

*"These four guys wheel the cake through the open doors and they wheel it off to the left, and they've got to wait in the dark until the proper moment for the flag-lowering ceremony. There's nothing can go wrong. There's no nets or anything. But they do have these huge lights which look like yellow pineapple, lots of crust, and this guy brings the point of this thing right down through the light. And this poor fellow with his light, with his lamp, what he's done is opened up a slot, now there's this full light right on him from this dim lamp . . . Spotlight! Cake! DUH DUH DUH RAH . . .*

*"And in they come and the cake is safe until one of the wheels hits one of the bits of broken light . . . The top of the cake falls into the middle bit and the middle bit falls . . . And the medallion goes scudding across the floor . . . And they don't stop! They're wheeling the remains of the cake . . . And the Ambassador's wife gets up to cut what's left of the cake. And the waiters are all falling over.*

*You've seen films of people falling over with laughter? Yeah. The waiters, their comments about it — can't remember now — so funny!*

*"And, uh, along comes the Marine sergeant again, and we give him drinks and he tells us that every year there's a disaster! Every year!"*

"Where are you Tony? I know where your body is . . . but where are you?"

# PART TWO

## CHAPTER ONE

### December 31ˢᵗ, 1972

The party was going to be a communal affair hosted by three neighbors who lived in adjoining apartments on the ground floor of a large brick house in the Northwest section. In its glory days, "2001 19ᵗʰ Street" had been the Chinese Embassy. By the time I first made its acquaintance at the end of the '60's, when my friend Mary moved in, it had long since been transformed into an apartment house with character. There were perhaps twenty residents living on its three floors, students, artists, professionals, in their thirties and forties, and they occupied one- or two-room apartments. The wide common entry hall and stairways encouraged friendliness between them. More than one single person had found a roommate within its congenial walls. Mary was one of these.

She was a tall, slender woman with very short, ash-blonde hair. Her hooded gray-blue eyes and her voice, low-pitched and musical, first attracted me to her. We met as colleagues working for a medical magazine in Manhattan in the mid-'60's. She was writing programmed instruction for nurses and I was her editorial assistant. After she moved to Washington, I continued to visit her several times a year.

During my visits with her and her companion, Senter, I got to meet some of their friends and neighbors in the building. Steve, who lived directly across the hall, was a large, bearded hi-fi salesman. He was second host for the party. Gil, was the third. He lived on the other side of the fireplace wall. He was a slim, good-looking young man who had recently become a devotee of Scientology.

Saturday afternoon, Gil invited himself over for lunch. The previous spring, when we had seen each other at a party in his place, I had enjoyed flirting with him. This time, we got into an  argument over language — the ways in which contempt for women is woven into the very fabric of English — and Scientology. He denied my description of it as a totalitarian, patriarchal organization trying to capture the minds and hearts of young people all over the world. He left in a huff.

Mary and I decided to go for a walk in Rock Creek Park. The air was so warm, the humid air so heavy with pollution, that the walk left us sweaty and exhausted. The unseasonal and unhealthy weather seemed ominous to me. I began to dread the approaching party. Late in the afternoon, we did our last-minute holiday shopping and took in a movie in the mall on Wisconsin Avenue near Chevy Chase. It was a classic, the original *Pygmalion* with Leslie Howard and Wendy Hiller, a myth with a special message for me. If I could penetrate to its heart, perhaps I would understand the secrets of my self.

Watching it, I mused on my pronounced Anglophilia, my consistent though not exclusive choice of British companions throughout the years. Englishness as such was not sufficient; Englishness for me meant a certain sensibility, a sense of humor both elegant and bawdy, an innate skepticism, a liberalism about social realities, a connection by birthright to English literature and folk music — and, let's face it, the musical accent and precise and beautiful speech simply turned me on.

As I dressed for the evening, I anticipated a probable scenario: I would resume my role of glamorous single woman from New York City, flirtatious, witty, unavailable, a role that I was only able to play here in Washington, where I felt temporarily released from the inhibitions and competitiveness that hobbled me on home ground. I selected a black, sleeveless dress, with an old-fashioned narrow choke collar and partially bared back. It showed me off to advantage. I felt both comfortable and attractive in it. I helped carry the platters of hummus and tiny frankfurters across the hall and through the door into Gil's apartment.

It was an enormous room carved out of the library of the former embassy. The long wall was still lined with books, and the ceiling disappeared into darkness somewhere over our heads. Gil's sparse furniture and the waterbed in the middle of the rug emphasized the unusual scale of the room. Gil's room was the natural choice for the party's focus, where the bar would be set up, snacks provided and sound system available for dancing. But Steve and Mary were also opening their apartments for additional socializing and inviting their own friends. The mix promised to be intriguing.

As people began to trickle in, Gil turned up the sound system to full blast. I kept strolling over and discretely turning it back down to a less punishing decibel level and he kept turning it right back up. The battle was joined.

By 11:00 p.m. I had cased the joint; there wasn't a man in the vast, lugubrious room who attracted me in the least. I was beginning to feel sorry for myself. I retired from the action and busied myself in the kitchenette, partially hidden from the main room by a free- standing wall. Steve came round the corner of the wall, and, as though putting a herald's horn to his lips, announced to everyone in general and no one in particular: "Tony Hawkins is coming, and he's bringing lights!"

"And who is Tony Hawkins?"

"He's a friend of mine, great guy. Audio salesman. He just called. He's bringing bubble lights with him."

Steve beamed at me and disappeared back into the dancers before I could find out what exactly were "bubble lights"? Probably disco stuff. Strobe lights. Ugh. Within a few minutes, there were sounds of activity near the door, furniture being scraped across the floor, the music stopping and then resuming. I walked around the rear of the dividing wall. Everyone had moved over to the doorway to dance in a shaft of colored lights being projected onto the wall behind them. Standing in silhouette beside the projector was a man dressed entirely in dark clothing, his reddish hair haloed by the light. I walked towards him. Standing in profile, smiling and talking, Tony was the only one in sharp focus. There were dim figures in the background, dancing in the swirling lights.

I crossed the room to flirt with him, because he was a new man, a new possibility; because he brought excitement into the room, enlivened a party cruising at boredom; because I liked his looks at a distance and even more so close up.

He was dressed in black, like a stagehand, outlining his trim body, setting off the reddish brown of his hair, the blueness of his eyes. He turned a face to me that was handsome, open, animated, with eyes that caught the lights. His face reminded me of Danny Kaye, the coloring, the nose and mouth, the humorous mobile expressions. But his voice was his own, and it captivated me instantly.

The accent was English, London-educated with a light touch of Cockney. I see us standing there, separated by the bubble light. We are talking. I jotted down some of what we talked about in my diary, but to memory's ear, our voices are inaudible.

I began with the obvious. "Is this a bubble light? How does it work?"

"It's a wheel of colored oils sandwiched between two plastic disks," he said with a smile. "As the wheel turns, the oils melt in the heat of the lamp shining through them. It's a projector really, tarted up!"

When he smiled, his thin upper lip all but disappeared. I liked what his broad smile did to his eyes. They curved downwards, imitating the creases drawn by his cheekbones, while the lines under his eyes curved upwards.

"It's a favorite in discos these days," he said. "People love to dance and make love in these lights. I understand it's a real turn on! I can't sell them fast enough all across my territory, which is from the Mississippi to the Atlantic, Maine to Florida."

As colors slid across the faces of the dancers, I remembered the months I had worked as a model at Cooper Union's School of Art in the early '60's. Images of paintings were projected onto the skin of my back and onto shawls the instructor draped over me. He told his students to try to draw what happens when two dimensional designs are projected onto a three dimensional surface. I shared this memory with Tony, so that he would imagine what I might have looked like naked with beautiful designs patterning my skin.

Tony grinned. "Well, I've never been an artist's model, with or without my clothes on, but I did take drawing lessons when I was a child. I was permitted to remain in the studio for the life drawing class. My parents and brother are artists. I'm not. I didn't continue my formal studies, but I can still draw fairly well."

And then, somehow, we went from life classes and lights to our mutual love and nostalgia for the radio plays of our childhood years, and he confided his dream to me: "I want to produce radio drama like the BBC!"

A few seconds before midnight, the energy in the room altered, people began preparing themselves for the big moment. I abruptly said, "Bye," and walked away. I did not want to be kissed by a man simply because we happened to be talking to each other at the stroke of midnight. Besides, Tony was too attractive and too fraught with inherent disappointment — a traveling salesman, for God's sake! — to continue this flirtation one minute longer. Heartbreak City. I sought Mary and her companion at the other end of the room and embraced them.

Two large hands on my shoulders turned me around and gently cupped my face. Tony's clear blue eyes slowly scanned my face, from forehead to chin. The look in his eyes traveled directly into mine. "I know you. I've found you. I like you. I want you." He brought his face close and slowly kissed me on my closed mouth. "Would you like to go for a walk?"

The air was still so warm, so heavily laden with moisture, we didn't need any coats. We strolled out onto the deserted sidewalk and wandered up 19th street, noisemakers and calls of "Happy New Year" reaching us from the distance. Tony smoked as we strolled, his puffs blending into the misty air. He did most of the talking.

He told me about his childhood, growing up in London during World War II, the excitement of it, the daily adventures: the prisoners of war fenced into internment camps on Wimbledon Common; the schoolboy positioned as lookout spotting buzz bombs from the chapel towers of his Jesuit school; how the daily lessons resumed as soon as the "all clear" sounded; coming out of a movie theater to see a real life dogfight overhead, planes trailing smoke as they crashed beyond the rooftops; his father working for J. Walter Thompson as an advertising man all through the war, never missing a day.

He told me the story his father had told him of an ordinary night, when the men gathered to drink in the pub until the quantity of plaster raining down and the explosions of the bombs falling in the street outside forced the publican to announce closing time. Then the men picked their way carefully through the debris to the bus stop, waited for the bus that came along, diverting, when necessary, from streets that were now burning, and brought them home to their families, who were hiding in their Anderson shelters in the backyards of their little house in the suburbs. Having finally gotten to sleep at 4:00 a.m., they would rise again three hours later to return to the city for another day of work.

We returned to 2001 and didn't want to go back into the party. So we sat down in the hallway, on the carpeted floor, the plastic runner between us, contemporary equivalent of the medieval sword between unmarried lovers.

Mary found us like that, on route back to her apartment, and invited us to follow her and make ourselves comfortable in her living room as she returned to the party still going strong at Gil's place.

As soon as she closed the door behind her, leaving us alone, Tony was at my side, arms opened wide, no longer shy. I backed away. "Wait. I am only beginning to know you."

"Fine." He smiled, reached for a cigarette, found an easy chair across the room and sat down, crossing his legs. His kiss had been the seal of his acknowledgement, and this demonstration of self-controlling ardor was proof positive that he was for real. I chose the couch.

"So tell me more about your work. I know you sell bubble lights!"

"My expertise is really in microphones and tape recorders. When I was store manager of Teletape, a very well known hi-fi shop in the center of Piccadilly, rock stars like Donovan used to come in all the time. Once I had to throw Peter Sellers out of my shop, but that's a long story, for another time. I get to travel around a lot — as I mentioned, my territory is everything east of the Mississippi. That's one of the things I love about this country, it's so big! Last time I was in New York, I met a journalist and arranged to interview him in the home of a friend of mine in Brooklyn. Do you know Brooklyn? Park something."

"Park Slope?"

"Yes, that's it!"

"Where in Park Slope? It's a pretty big neighborhood. I live there."

"You do? How wonderful! Garfield Street, I think I have it written down in my address book at home."

"Garfield Place, and it's about two hundred feet from my front door." I enjoyed the expression of surprise and delight that lit up his face.

"I would love to see you next weekend."

"So would I."

The door suddenly burst open and Mary, Steve, Gil and the remaining revelers, joined us. Gil glared at Tony and me. Tony sat quietly and calmly at the side of the circle, watching and listening with a bemused expression on his face.

There is a snapshot that survives that evening. Mary took it. She stood behind me, a little to the right. Only the back of my head is in it and one shoulder. Gil is the focus of her picture, his striped shirt loosened at the collar, his arm gesticulating, his mouth open. Tony is nowhere is view. He is off right of the frame. If only she had included him, the most important actor at the sidelines. If only I could see him as he was at that moment, through the camera's dispassionate eye.

Gil managed to get to his feet. He was trying to leave. I offered to walk him to his door, as much as to expedite his safe and speedy exit from our midst, as to show him a little warmth and understanding.

"That guy is trying to make time with you."

Tony was standing anxiously by his chair when I returned to his side. "I thought you might disappear without my getting your telephone number." He wrote his down on a slip of paper. "May I see you again tomorrow?"

"I'll be leaving early, I'm afraid, probably right after breakfast," I said.

"I'll call you then, in Brooklyn, about next weekend." He left reluctantly, along with the last of the guests.

Mary and I curled up on the couch, sipping cups of tea. "Tony is the first man I've met in over two years who is even a possibility for me," I said.

She nodded. "Yes, he's very special."

The next day was too beautiful, too spring-like, to rush back to New York. I delayed my departure to picnic with Mary and Senter along the Potomac. I thought about calling Tony, but decided not to. I wanted him to call me first.

## CHAPTER TWO

### January, 1973

Tony called mid-week, confirming his visit to Brooklyn the following weekend. He turned up Saturday, early afternoon, expecting first to interview the journalist at the home of his friends two and a half blocks away and then spend the rest of the evening with me, but the journalist cancelled. Tony was not disappointed, since it gave him more time to be with me. "We've both been invited to dinner," he told me. "George and Sally would love to meet you. They have two children, Adam and Laura. Come over as soon as you can. I miss you."

I changed into a full-length woolen skirt and a long-sleeved, high-necked, ruffled blouse. Walking past the elegant rows of brownstones between Polhemus and Fisk Place, I felt as old-fashioned as the architecture. I should have arrived in a horse drawn carriage.

Sally met me at the front door and welcomed me, leading me up the stairs to their apartment. She had a round, friendly face and long, dark straight hair. She immediately put me at my ease.

"They're all in the living room." She opened the door and we stepped inside.

Tony was sitting in a large upholstered chair, his attention utterly absorbed by the two children, a boy to his right, a little girl to his left, who climbed up into his lap. A fire flickered in the fireplace on the left wall, a couch with other easy chairs was in an alcove to the right, and large, original, contemporary paintings were on every wall. Tony held his right arm out to the side of the chair to keep the cigarette smoke away from the children. I felt grounded in the certainty that here, at last, was the man for me. This was the man to be the father of my children.

"Hello, luv!" Tony looked up, smiled and held out both hands towards me. "Let me introduce you to my friends. This is Adam and this is Laura. Laura's been painting some terrific stuff on her easel today."

"And I'm George." A tall, broad-shouldered man with closely cropped dark hair gave me a firm handshake.

At dinner, seated on benches around their plank table, I learned that George was an artist's agent, representing Tony's brother Peter. He was trying to place Peter's sculptures at the Museum of Modern Art's gift shop. While we were still working our way through Sally's home-baked dessert, the bell rang. It was Peter, unexpectedly stopping by for a visit.

As soon as Peter came into the room, Tony brightened. He obviously regarded his brother with enormous affection, even awe. Peter was taller and leaner than Tony, his face craggier, his eyes hooded like Mick Jagger's. He had just returned from a visit home to England and told Tony the latest news about their parents, whom he called by their first names.

"Clare is thinking about selling her house and trying to return to

Brighton again. She says she was only ever happy living in Brighton, after Lacey left her. And Lacey is working on a new invention to help illustrate a book on optics. He seems to be getting steady employment as a freelance artist with these science books for children."

"Is he still painting watercolors?" Tony wanted to know.

"Yeah. He showed me the latest street scene. He only does actual places he has seen in Devon. He takes snapshots first, and then works from them."

At the end of the evening, Tony walked me back to my place and asked if he might stay the night.

"I only have this room, this convertible couch." I grinned at him. He was flustered.

"But I really thought . . . isn't that another room, another bedroom in there?"

"It's the size of a bedroom, and the tub is as large as a bed, but it's a bathroom." I showed him the great claw-footed tub in the spacious tiled room.

He reddened. "What should I do? Will you be too uncomfortable if I stay? Shall I go? I don't want to."

I had made up my mind. "It's all right . . . but is it possible for you not to smoke so much while you're here? It bothers me, and I don't want you to bother me in any way."

He gave me a melting look and came forward to hug me.

"That means you want to see me again, and that's good!"

He undressed, folding his clothes neatly over the chairs near the kitchen table, while I removed the pillows and pulled out the mattress. I didn't like the way he looked with his socks on; they emphasized the shortness of his legs. After he removed them, the ribbed pattern was still impressed on his ankles. I undressed in the bathroom. He was in bed waiting for me to join him.

We made love immediately, shyly at first, then with a rush of urgency. Tony left me behind. I gasped in pain. He was mortified when he saw the tears in my eyes.

"Oh, luv, I'm so sorry! That's not like me at all. I just stopped thinking. I wanted you so much."

It wasn't like him. It never happened again in our years together. He comforted me and we fell asleep in each other's arms. He had to leave early the next morning. When I awakened into his absence, the warmth and scent of crumpled sheets and discovered his ring beneath the pillow, I held it between the fingers of my right hand and examined the turquoise and silver work of the broad band.

"Well, that was lovely. At the very least he will have to phone me to get his ring back."

When he did call, a day or two later, it was from some place on the road. He wanted to see me the very next weekend; he hadn't realized that the ring had slipped from his finger.

"That's never happened before. Well, we were a bit . . . active! Take good care of it, luv, it's a favorite of mine. And so are you."

In his Monthly Minder for 1973, Friday, January 12 has a business appointment neatly crossed out. January 13, the words, "V. Customer B'more," that is, "visit customer in Baltimore." If he kept that appointment, he drove straight on to New York in time for dinner at The Cookery on 8th Street and University Place, where he quietly said to me, "I believe I'm falling in love with you," from across a candle-lit table.

The following weekend, I returned to Washington, this time to stay with him in his apartment. During the previous nine years, I had made the trip frequently, to be part of the enormous demonstrations that were held every season of the year, civil rights giving way to anti-Vietnam War. Now, I was headed towards a reunion with my lover, but also to be a witness with him at the symbolic validation of my nation's political process. Tony first stepped off the plane onto American soil the day of Nixon's first inauguration, a day Tony regarded with dismay. Four years later, Nixon's second inauguration was backdrop to our burgeoning love and the weaving of our lives together.

I expected to see him waving at me behind the gates, but I crossed the train's platform and walked towards the cavernous waiting room without him. Suddenly, he was grinning at my left side, having sneaked up on me. "Welcome to Washington, luv!"

"Tony! Aren't you cold?" He was wearing only jeans and a jeans jacket. "You did say, 'Welcome to Washington,' not Waikiki!"

"Cold? What cold? I've got my love . . ." He put his arm around me as he reached for my luggage cart with his other hand. "You need help with this, missus? Always a pleasure to be of service for a pretty laidy." Instantly the Cockney porter.

As he loaded my luggage into the back of his orange Datsun hatchback, he pushed aside the bundles of laundry. "Just picked up the sheets up from the cleaners," he said with an apologetic smile.

"Should I assume you don't do this for just anyone?"

"Only for royalty. And this" — he pointed to his car — "is Thunderpussy. Va va va vooom!" — and turned the ignition key.

Tony drove with flair, passing everyone and obeying all the traffic laws except the speed limit.

"Does the law ever catch up with you?" I asked, glancing at the speedometer.

"Now and then," he grinned. "I've got a modest collection of speeding tickets."

He took me to dinner at a favorite local place, and then home to one of the older apartment houses in Washington's N.W. section. Its front entrance featured brass doors with an Art Deco brass-edged overhang.

He lived on the highest floor. The door opened into an L-shaped living room. What would have been the dining room table was piled high with papers, stationery boxes, magazines, paperback books. Cartons were stacked on the floor underneath. Two chairs faced a wall of loudspeakers flanking an impressive sound system, a small collection of tapes and records. That was it. Tony saw the room through my disappointed eyes.

"I don't really live here, luv. I'm always on the road. I just pack and unpack my car, check my mail, hit the sack and I'm off again."

I had wandered around the bend of the "L" into the kitchenette. Prominently displayed on the table was a large framed portrait of a young woman with straight, sun-bleached hair, a pale, plain, friendly face.

"That's Kay. I guess I should have put her picture out of sight."

"You obviously wanted me to see it."

"I've known her for two years. She lives in Ohio. She's a school teacher, elementary school. She was with me, Christmas Week. New Year's Eve she got food poisoning or something, and was sick in bed, too ill to go to the party."

"Tony! Do you mean, when you came to the party, she was here waiting for you to return?" I turned around and glared at him.

"Yes, but it was her idea that I should go, at least. She didn't think it made sense for me to stay with her. I couldn't make her feel any better."

"That's not the point. You asked to see me the very next day!"

"But she was going home to Ohio. Am I very bad?" He came over to me and put his arms around me. "Helen, as much as I like her, it's not the same as it is with you. Things aren't going well, haven't been for a long time. We're in a rut. I met you — I want to be with you. Don't you have any other boyfriends?" He looked very worried, and puzzled.

I shook my head.

"What's the matter with the men in New York?" he murmured, and melted my consternation with a kiss.

"I've brought something for you to hear," I said to change the subject, and went to retrieve a cassette tape from my shoulder bag. It contained two songs of mine. My voice teacher and I had worked on them so that Tony could hear me singing them to her piano accompaniment. We sat side by side in the two separate chairs, facing the sound system. The equipment enhanced the quality of my voice and the songs themselves.

Tony leaned back, resting his head on his arms crossed against the top of the chair. "I can't tell you what a privilege it is for me, for you to be here with me. This is beautiful."

The bedroom was down a short hallway to the right of the front door. It was a good-sized room, with only two pieces of furniture in it: a chest of drawers in front of the windows, a single bed at right angles opposite.

"Don't worry, it opens up!" Tony bent down and pulled out a cot from under the bed, which lifted up and locked in, to create a reasonable facsimile of a double bed. He took the freshly pressed sheets out of their brown paper wrappings and quickly made up the bed.

"How long have you lived here?" I wanted to know, because the room had less personality than a motel's. Usually there is a direct connection between a person and his place. You can read a person through his home. But not a whiff of Tony's vivid personality, playful energy, colorful speech, wit, or love of art was present in this indifferent clutter of his possessions, the bare walls of his bedroom. Only his meticulous care for his sound equipment, that was all.

"About a year. But I'm seldom here. I'm constantly on the road. Sorry, luv, I should have done all this before you got here, but I've been working all day."

"It's all right. It doesn't matter."

And it didn't. We made love all night, sleep overtaking us in the gray light. This time we took ourselves into a deeper realm. No gestures or phrases remain with me, just the memory of fulfillment, of peace.

We awakened to a fiercely cold and clear Inauguration Day. Breakfast in his apartment was hopeless. The refrigerator was stark except for containers of milk and orange juice. "This really is a bachelor's pad. Don't you ever eat in?"

"Not if I can help it. I don't enjoy eating by myself."

After his requisite cup of coffee, with its requisite three teaspoonsful of sugar, we were on our way to join Senter and Mary at a mock inauguration. We found a place to eat along the way, and met our friends and everyone else who had been invited to the event, upstairs in the host's apartment. It was much too cold to stand around outside until the performance was ready to begin.

A sizeable group of us laughed and cheered the spoof, a rather good impersonation of Groucho Marx as master of ceremonies, a plucked chicken being lowered by a rope from an upstairs window every time the secret word was uttered, and a decent impersonation of Richard M. Nixon himself, jabbing the frosty air with his fingers in a V. FBI men in their trenchcoats photographed us, scribbling things in notebooks. At one point, the police drove up and stopped the proceedings, demanding if we had a license to do this sort of thing. It made us feel most important.

The party moved on to "Henry's," a nightclub in Dupont Circle. Tony left me to pick up some money, and missed the entire party. He returned just as Mary and Senter were arranging with me to meet us back at their place. I was miffed at him for being so foolish, what was the urgency? We weren't planning to spend any significant sums of money the rest of the weekend. But Tony didn't feel comfortable unless he had money in his pocket.

"Returning to the scene of the crime, eh?" Mary smiled as we walked through her door into the embrace of her living room at 2001.

After a drink and a natter, Senter and Tony both nodded off as Mary and I talked quietly on her couch. That I owed this happiness to Mary's friendship was perfection, and entirely appropriate. Tony woke easily and in good humor. After a cup of coffee, he was able to drive us the few blocks home.

Sunday was dedicated to ourselves. There came a moment when I needed to hear him put into words what he had been telling me by touch.

"How can I help but love you, Helen? Of course, I love you. I love you!"

"And I love you too, Tony."

I returned on the last possible train, arriving home well after midnight.

The next morning, the phone rang before my alarm clock went off. It was my mother, anxious to find me because I hadn't been home all weekend.

"Mom — I've met the man I'm going to marry!"

"Oh, Helen!"

"I didn't mean to shock you like that. I didn't know I was going to say that until I heard myself. But it's true. I've met the most marvelous man. He's for me. He loves me, he wants me, he's right for me. . . . I don't know what his marital status is, actually. There's a girlfriend in the picture. He may be engaged to her, but I don't think so. She is more involved with him than he with her. But he might be married to someone else and separated, or divorced. He might have children. It doesn't matter. I know that I'm going to marry him, I just don't know when."

For the first time, I was in love with a grown up. I didn't have to woo him, free him from the enchantments of his fears, heal his unhealable wounds. Tony was all of a piece, mind and heart and body, he gave himself to me without reservation.

Sometime during the same day I told my mother about him, Tony wrote a letter to his mother:

*January 22nd*

*Dearest Clare,*

*So long since I wrote. I must have had four letters from you in the meantime. I've been through some changes. For Christmas, I went with Kay to her mother's place in Iowa, about a 1,000-mile drive each way. Very pleasant, quiet time. When I describe a holiday as quiet or peaceful what I'm really saying is that nothing happened. But that's a nice change. Kay came back to Washington with me, and we were invited to a New Year's party, but she took ill and I went alone. And there I met a scintillating creature called Helen. Now it's not possible that at any time, anywhere near Helen, nothing would be happening. She is a writer, songwriter, composer, singer, actress, and she teaches school. But she lives in New York City. Between Helen and Kay, I'm going through some changes.*

*I'm interested in reviving an old art form here, which would not be strange to the English — the Radio Play. Just talking about it produces amazing effects. I've been approached by actors and playwrights offering me their work or services. I remember when, in England, I had nothing to do. Now I could be occupied for the next two years with what is in my head at this moment.*

*I expect to come to a turning point in June. That's when I shall take a month's break and come to England. I do think about you all the time. Maybe we'll be able to sort things out. Remember I'll be home in June.*

*Love*

The facts were: I didn't teach school. I worked as a lab assistant in the biology department of a New York City high school. I wasn't an "actress, singer, songwriter, composer, writer," just someone who enjoyed and participated in these arts. But extravagance is the province of new love.

## January 1989

Janus: two-faced god of all going-out and coming-in, to whom all places of entrance and passage are holy. Guardian of the gates to the New Year. January: month of the perilous crossing over the chasm of our loss. Alan and I holding hands on the narrow swaying bridge, hour by hour, day by day, walking away from our old life.

It didn't feel that way in the living of it. We walked out the front door towards school, towards work, towards our daily tasks. We returned each afternoon to our home and as the door closed behind us we returned to the presence of Tony's absence.

In January I responded to the repercussions of what had happened to us and created new routines, accepted new responsibilities, reached out for people to assist me in my new status as single parent, widow and litigant. At the beginning of the month, I didn't have anyone living in the house who could help me with Alan. I didn't have a lawyer. My income, limited to my salary and the rent from the apartment unit in my home, was inadequate to meet my old debts and new burdens. By the month's end, I had pieced together a patchwork of care for Alan, chosen a lawyer, stabilized my debts and registered with Social Security to receive a widow's monthly benefits for my dependent child.

My neighbor Diane agreed to include Alan when she drove her daughter to and from their school. I arranged with my housekeeper to be there for Alan every afternoon when he was brought home.

Eileen, the mother of Alan's best friend in kindergarten, thoughtfully offered to have Alan brought to her home on the one day each week I taught an afternoon college class. She not only made it possible for me to continue with this new job, she ensured that her son and mine would continue their friendship.

So now there were four of us doing what Tony had done by himself. Tony used to bring Alan to school every morning and pick him up every afternoon. He also made the sandwiches everyday. Those elegant and humorous designs created out of strips of cheddar cheese and red pepper (a motorcycle, a vase of flowers on a table) were the wonder of the class. The children used to gather around to see what Alan's daddy had created that day. Alan would have to settle for peanut butter and jelly or tuna fish on rye from now on.

One night Alan asked, "Who said they were going to be a father to me?" I told him the names of the men — my brother, a neighbor, a friend in another city — who had offered, in the spontaneity of their grief, "to be like a father to Alan." Brushing his teeth, he reached for Tony's toothbrush and said, "It's not too sad that Tony's dead."

I fell asleep beside him in his bed. He woke up weeping in the middle of the night and clung to me. I soothed him back to sleep, silently crying along with him. In the morning he sniffed, "I have the flu. I can't go to school."

I didn't believe him. I insisted that he go. He hadn't been to school in three weeks. Mid-morning, while at work, I received a call from his school. "Alan has swollen glands. Can you take him home now?"

I had already made plans to meet a lawyer in Manhattan and it was impossible to cancel the appointment. The school secretary thought that Alan was well enough to be kept in the general office until Eileen's housekeeper could pick him up and bring him to her house. I promised to retrieve him by early evening. I was amused and perturbed by my woefully inaccurate diagnosis of Alan's symptoms. Real illness was still possible in the midst of mourning.

Each day's efforts were cause for tears. If things went badly — Alan and I slow to wake, out of sorts, disorganized — I wept because everything was such a mess. It was worse when things went smoothly, if Alan and I hummed along without a hitch, and everyone played their part; we shouldn't be able to do so well without Tony.

Every morning, as soon as Alan was safely delivered into Diane's hands, I could give myself over to my longing for Tony. While I walked the seven blocks to the subway station, I talked to him. I discussed the responsibilities that awaited me, reviewed what had happened the day before. At Prospect Park, I left the station, crossed Flatbush Avenue and walked through or around the perimeter of the Brooklyn Botanic Gardens. Except for Mondays, when they were closed to the public, or when the weather was daunting, I headed for the Gardens.

Once I was beyond the turnstile and the rhododendrons, the traffic of Flatbush Avenue became inaudible. I could begin to hear other voices, could listen to my own, could listen for Tony's. This was my time to tell Tony my feelings, to walk on my words towards him. I talked out loud, in a low voice. I didn't put words in his mouth, but I felt connected to him, protected by him.

This time-out-of-time lasted until I reached the herb garden and the Washington Avenue gate. Then my school swallowed me up. The first day back, I walked into my chairman's office to say hello. He took one look at me, gently closed the inner door and handed me a box of tissues.

"I thought I was doing okay. This doesn't compute, damn it! This doesn't make any sense. This really can't be happening!"

My colleagues eased my way. People were eager to talk to me, people I already knew, others who approached me for the first time. The Italian teacher, who once translated a long letter for me from one of Tony's Italian cousins, sought me out in the cafeteria. He reminded me of Tony in his short powerful build, his round face, his warmth.

"They told me the other week. I couldn't believe it. The slim woman, I said, her husband?"

He had lived through World War II in Italy. I told him about Tony's childhood in England during the war. I told him that I had dreamt about the possibility of Tony's death.

"Dreams are funny things," he said. "My father-in-law came to me in a dream. I thought I didn't have to go back to school the day after Labor Day for sure. That night, when I go to sleep, I see my father-in-law standing in front of me. He is wearing a suit, shirt, a tie. He is holding my briefcase in his hand. I went towards him, but he walked around a corner and disappeared. In the morning I think, why is he holding my briefcase? He was coming to tell me to go to work today! I rushed to school and got there late. I was supposed to be there! We have to study the dream more."

People came over to offer their condolences. They came to give me information — they knew someone who knew someone on the flight — or they wanted to talk about their own losses. Conversation suddenly cut to the bone.

"I still talk to my daddy," confided our school's supply secretary. "I still want to pick up the phone and call him when something happens to me."

Only once did someone say something stupid. In the school bathroom, a woman I had never spoken to, never wanted to speak to, hesitated as she watched me splash water on my face, then blurted out, "Maybe God wanted it to happen!"

I whirled around and screamed at her,"Don't you ever say that to me again!"

She took cover in a stall. I ran out, trembling, thinking, *It's as though I've become fair game for anyone to say whatever comes into their tiny minds. Does she really believe that God is a terrorist?*

Walking the halls felt like walking a gauntlet of caresses. At the end of the day I was both energized and exhausted. Alone at last in the Botanic Gardens, I shouted across the frozen lawn: "Tony, Tony, come home to us! Just come home to us! No, you can't stay one more day. I don't want all these new friendships with my colleagues! I don't want to feel closer to them. I don't need to have my friends from high school calling me up. I don't need all these reunions. I just need you!" I sobbed and sobbed, my cries turning into puffs of steam in the frosty air.

On the first Friday morning after I returned to work full time, I found a phone in a quiet place and placed a call to Tony's favorite radio station, WBAI. They were in the midst of a membership drive and as part of their fundraising efforts, were offering their listeners an opportunity to call in and speak on any topic for two or three minutes. Mine was the very first call.

"I want to talk about my husband."

"Hey, this lady wants to talk about her husband!"

The radio host was amused and unprepared for the direction his show was about to take. I spoke into the phone, trembling, my eyes fixed on the typewritten sheet of paper in my left hand.

"My husband was one of the 270 people killed one month ago on Pan Am 103. He had two strong and enduring connections to this radio station. First of all, he was a loyal listener-sponsor for sixteen years. This station was his university, his adult-education seminar, offering him courses on jazz, history, health and nutrition, and his first and abiding love — radio drama.

"Secondly, as a salesman of microphones and other radio equipment, he was well known to many of the 'techies' at your station. In his memory, I am going to donate $57 in a matching fund. He was 57 on his last birthday two months ago."

There was silence for a few minutes, then the announcer said, "Well, sometimes up, sometimes down. Never know what you are going to hear."

At home, I tried to mention Tony's name naturally, to let a situation or activity prompt my memory. Alan's powers of recollection never ceased to astonish me. He could describe not merely the event, but the gesture, the tone, the color. He had inherited Tony's gift of mimicry, too. "This is how Tony would crack his knuckles!" He folded his right hand over his left, bending the knuckles of his left hand in a downward bow, then snapping each fingertip as hard as he could against the palm of his right hand.

Alan, who was marvelously cooperative and obedient all month, spoke freely about Tony whenever he needed to. He called any plane he saw, "Pan Am 103."

"Can they put the plane back together again?"

"Yes, they're trying to. They are trying to learn as much as they can about what happened."

"Too bad they can't put the people back together again. Too bad there isn't a super magician who could bring Tony back to us."

"We have to be our own magicians to keep Tony alive in our minds."

"I try not to think about Tony too much."

"If we don't think about him, he will truly die forever. Do you remember what Mr. G. said at the funeral? That people live as long as we let them live in our thoughts and the things we do? So many people loved Tony and will never forget him. But we knew him best of all and loved him most of all. And he loved us best — especially you.”

“I know that.”

One night, Alan said something very powerful to me. He asked, ‘Whatever happens, Tony will always be my father, right? And he’ll always be your husband, right?’”

Of course! Of course! Alan had solved our terrible dilemma with one brilliant insight. Whatever happens, I was not afraid any longer. Tony will always be central to our lives, without ever becoming a barrier, without preventing us from opening ourselves to other people.

Tony had been snatched from us. His spirit could not be reconciled to his death, nor should it. And I should not let him go. My obligation was to keep him close, to keep him vivid, to strengthen his spirit by recalling him as clearly and accurately as possible. Perhaps talking about him, talking to him, was like clapping for Tinkerbell.

Mid-January I received a letter from Cardinal O’Connor’s office. Typed on the Cardinal’s official stationary, beneath an intricate logo that displayed the Cardinal’s hat hovering over a banner on which was written, “THERE CAN BE NO LOVE WITHOUT JUSTICE,” the letter was gracious and to the point:

“Dear Mrs. Hawkins:

“Along with every individual of good will I share in the grief that must be uniquely yours. Anthony’s death has no doubt left an immense void in your life and at the same time filled you with an infinite number of thoughts and feelings.

“While there is so little that any one of us alone can do to take this burden from you, I thought it appropriate to have all the members of the Archdiocese of New York mark a Day of Prayer for the victims of the tragedy. Sunday, January 29th has been designated for this. I personally will be celebrating the 10:15 Mass at St. Patrick’s Cathedral in New York City on this occasion. If it is possible, I want you to know that you and your family would be most welcome to join me on this occasion. As death does not differentiate among religious creeds, so God is Father to us all. It is in this conviction that we turn to Him in our need.

Faithfully,

John Cardinal O’Connor

"(Aware of privacy considerations. I have asked the representatives of Pan American to mail this letter to you. They have graciously consented to do so.)"

At last! I would see their faces! What I had been unable to do on my own, to pry loose the names and addresses of the other families from Pan Am's grasp, the Cardinal had accomplished for me. Each of us, isolated in our private desolation, was to be assembled in one place at one time. We could begin to know one another, perhaps to help one another.

I filled out the enclosed card and returned it the next day. But should I bring Alan along with me? Would it upset him too much to attend another service?

"Wasn't Tony raised a Catholic?" Eileen asked me the following Tuesday night when I came to pick up Alan. We were standing in her kitchen, and she looked up at me from the sink where she was rinsing vegetables under a stained glass pendant of an Irish harp.

"He left the church as a young man."

"This Mass is to honor his father. Don't you think Alan should be there?"

"I don't know yet. I have to think about it some more."

"Aren't you and Alan in therapy yet?" (Eileen was a social worker.)

"No. I don't feel the need for therapy myself, and I believe I am giving Alan what he needs now."

She looked at me sharply. "He tells me he's not eating with you every night. That isn't good. Family time at the table is most important for him, especially now."

I carried my anger all the way home. I didn't want to feel angry with Eileen. She was helping me in such a committed, generous way, opening her home to Alan every week. Nevertheless, I resented her feeling free to tell me what to do, how to behave.

Merle, a practicing therapist herself, supported me on the therapy issue. "I don't believe that you and Alan automatically need therapy. I think you are coping very well and it seems that for now, you are all Alan needs. You'll know when you will need to seek professional assistance."

But Leah's mother, a Jewish sociologist, contradicted Eileen on the Mass issue. "Alan shouldn't go to the Mass. It's not for him."

It was the Christmas tree tug-of-war all over again. I didn't know what to do. The dilemma was resolved when I heard for the first time from another Pan Am widow. We had many friends in common, but we had never met before this disaster, nor spoken, until she called me late on the Wednesday night before the Sunday Day of Prayer.

For the first time I heard that my story was not the only story and that every story was the same story, differing only in the details. As I listened to her deep musical voice, with its Canadian lilt, its rapid rhythms, I pulled the comforter up to my shoulders, turned off the bedside light and relaxed into the friendly darkness — and Pat's breathless monologue.

Her husband Martin, also an Englishman in his 50s, had flown to England to attend a college reunion with classmates at Cambridge University, in spite of universal disapproval from colleagues and family. He was still recovering from a serious heart attack.

"I begged him not to go. I never do that. He used to travel all the time. But this time it didn't feel right. It wasn't really necessary for him to go. But you could never tell him what to do. He always had to have his own way.

"I had just returned from shopping. I was still standing in the hallway when my brother Tom told me, 'Something's happened to Martin.' I just assumed it was another heart attack. I was just standing there in the doorway with the packages in my arms when Tom said, 'No, it was the plane.' I couldn't understand it."

"You were lucky to have someone from your family with you, Pat. I was all alone except for my son and a boarder. I was up all night. I never felt sleepy. How about you?"

"I don't remember when I slept, when I woke. I was so exhausted, so drained. When I went to sleep it was as though someone hit me on the head. I slept the sleep of the dead, like a stone." Her voice sounded flat.

"Are you having any nightmares?"

"I never dream," she said, "or else I never remember dreaming."

We were living through the same loss so differently.

"When did they tell you Martin's body had been found?"

"Two days after, I think."

"Two days! They didn't call me until the day after Christmas and then they held his body for another three weeks!" At that moment I was angry that she had been treated better than I had been. "So when were you able to bury him?"

"Right after Christmas."

"I wasn't able to bury Tony until January 6," I said.

"I was in Lockerbie then.

"Lockerbie! Tell me about Lockerbie! When I try to imagine it, all I can see are those burning houses, that gaping hole in the ground. A nightmare in black and white."

"Oh, it wasn't like that at all. It was dark and cold and crowded. People came from all over Scotland to help. It was very organized. I remember, all the families waiting in the airport were very quiet. I can't remember anyone talking. We were given a place apart to be by ourselves. They flew us from London to Scotland and then provided us a free bus service to take us to stay in towns nearby. There weren't any rooms to be had in Lockerbie. A free bus service was arranged by the volunteers to take us back and forth each day.

"They also set up a round-the-clock cafeteria in the Town Hall. That's where I spoke to an Indian woman, whose daughter died. According to Hindu law you must bury your dead within a day or two of death, otherwise you are excluded from participating in the necessary rituals. The police would not release her daughter's body for burial. Her religion was very important to her. I cried for the first time, talking with her. I hadn't been able to cry. I was so numb. I still am.

"The social workers and the police were completely at odds with each other. The social workers kept insisting that the families be allowed to view their dead, that it was vitally important for them,  and the police refused. They would not be swayed."

She said that the police had taken her to see the place where her husband's body was found. She and her daughter walked around the pasture strewing flowers and sticking them into hedgerows and fence posts so the cows wouldn't get them.

I imagined the two women, their arms cradling long stemmed flowers, moving in straight lines across a stone-walled, snow-filled pasture, slowly and gracefully removing a stalk at a time from their arms and carefully releasing each flower into the air, the flowers floating to the ground: dancers in slow motion. I listened quietly, trying to take all of this in. I glanced at the clock.

"I really have to try to get to sleep now. But I need to ask you something.

I assume you've received the Cardinal's invitation to the special Mass this Sunday. Are you planning to go?"

"Yes, yes, of course. My children are coming, but there will be plenty of room in the car. Please come with us."

"I'd love to. I'm going to bring my son. Where do you live?"

"On Garfield Place between Seventh and Eighth Avenues."

"I don't believe this! That's where I lived when I first moved back to Brooklyn about twenty years ago."

"We have so much in common, Helen, so many friends. We should have met before. Tony and Martin should have met before . . ."

"I know. I know. We have to find the others too. The main reason I'm going is to see who we all are. I think we ought to try to form our own bereavement group."

"That's a wonderful idea!"

"I'll write an open invitation letter and distribute it at the Mass. Will you help me with it?"

"Why don't you read it to me after you write it?"

I slept easily and deeply that night. I had been able to get to a deeper place of sharing with this stranger than I had with my closest family and friends.

On the morning of the service, Alan balked. "I don't want to go." He was sitting on the floor of Tony's office playing with his Legos.

"I've already explained why you should come with me, Alan. I'm not leaving you behind.

"But I'll miss all my cartoons."

"You can watch them until the car-service arrives."

He nodded and turned on the television. I felt reassured whenever I was able to find appropriate ways to respond to his turmoil.

The car turned into Garfield Place, and pulled up in front of the house where the Garfield Place Block Association used to meet when I was a member in 1968, twenty years earlier. Pat's twenty-year-old, red-headed daughter opened the door and welcomed us through the vestibule and into the grand hallway. It was as I remembered, this spacious and beautifully detailed house: the carved staircase, the hall leading straight back through the dining room, the country kitchen visible at the top of a short flight of steps.

"Make yourselves comfortable in the living room. I'll tell my mother you've arrived."

I studied the portraits on the marble mantle piece — a close-up of a man and a woman, Martin and Pat, smiling wide, warm smiles, faces pressed cheek to cheek; the entire family lined up on the sidewalk in the summertime, hands on each other's shoulders, Martin with a jacket over his free shoulder. He reminded me a bit of Tony, the easy bulk of his body, the pride and pleasure in his family radiating from his open, fair face.

"Hi there. Sorry I'm late." Pat came into the high-ceilinged living room with quick, nervous movements. Her short grayish-brown hair trimmed into bangs, framed her round face. We hugged each other.

Alan and I sat next to Pat's daughter in the back seat of the car. Pat's son drove. On route, Pat let me read a pamphlet that the social workers had distributed in Lockerbie, "To The Newly Bereaved." I found it obvious and beside the point.

The steps of St. Patrick's Cathedral were crowded with people distributing their fliers. I joined them and began offering the one-page invitation to form a bereavement group, which Pat had helped me edit during several phone consultations. Someone handed me a flier signed by Paul Hudson (father of Melina), Bert Ammerman (brother of Thomas) and Richard Hartunian (brother of Lynn), announcing "the preparation of a general newsletter by and for the victim family members." An open letter from Victoria Cummock, who lost her "husband, best friend and father of her three very young children," announced the formation of a support group and information network for the family members only, "since we all have very many questions and have gotten few answers, if any answers, from Pan Am or any of the U.S. government agencies." Victoria had already been in contact with several congressmen and independent air safety consultants.

I guided Alan into the vast interior of the cathedral, found seats in the third row, claimed them with our coats, then walked around handing out our flyer. At the last moment, a thin woman with a baby in her arms and a four-year-old boy by her side  squeezed in beside us.

Alan shifted to my right side to make room for them.

"Where's Daddy?" the boy asked.

"Daddy's in heaven," she whispered.

Her husband was a businessman who had gone to Lockerbie for the weekend. He had tried to return as soon as his meeting concluded, buying his return ticket at the last minute. So many seats were available on flight 103, the plane took off only one-third full. "I'm going to return to my family in Missouri. I'm too alone where I'm living, now, out in New Jersey. I don't know anyone there. We just moved there recently."

One of the ushers walked up the aisle asking for a child to carry the "gifts" later on in the ceremony. I volunteered Alan, without knowing what exactly he'd be asked to do.

The cathedral was filled, every seat taken. To the right, behind the pillars, under the glare of their spotlights, men and women were standing pressed closely together behind the unblinking eyes of their cameras staring at us. A thin red velvet rope held them back.

Even the mighty organ could not entirely cover the whirr of movie cameras turning as the procession of altar and choir boys, and priests in full golden vestments filed into the sanctuary. Cardinal O'Connor was the last to enter, dressed in emerald vestments, golden crosier in hand, golden mitre on his head. Alan was impressed — as was I when the Cardinal did not ascend the pulpit to deliver his sermon, but rather stepped to the center of the first row at the beginning of the aisle and spoke to us directly. I had accepted the Cardinal's invitation in order to find the other families; I had not expected to be moved by the ceremony or his words. He spoke softly and thoughtfully and, from his very first words,  directly to me.

"I have no answers for you. Many of you are probably thinking: 'Is this the best God has to give me?' For those of you without faith, this is a meaningless tragedy.

"In August of 1965 in Vietnam, a tank accidentally drowned all its men while crossing a river on maneuvers. I had nothing to say to the grieving families. I had no answers for them. But I must believe in the power of suffering, to reflect on the universality of suffering.

"I received a letter from a man named Eggleston. He lives in Glens Falls. His son was coming home to be with his mother before she died in the hospital. She died on the 22nd of December.

"I received a letter from a woman. Joan Dater, who lost her only daughter Gretchen. 'Now I know how Mary felt when her child died. Her heart and her womb ached, as mine does now.'

"You know, I had never realized until that moment that men and women might grieve differently. That a woman's womb might ache as she grieves the life she brought forth. I had never understood this before."

I was astonished that the Cardinal would confide in us so intimately, share his imperfect humanity with us.

"What can we make of our suffering except to deepen our capacity for compassion?"

Indeed, what other good can we make of this crippling pain? The vast interior of the cathedral was filled with people listening in rapt attention. I could hear the quiet breathing all around me. Then the Cardinal continued: "Christ was killed by terrorists. He was killed by men whose ends justified their means."

*No!* I thought, *he's wrong. Terrorists kill anonymously and don't care who their victims are.* I resented the Cardinal for appropriating what had happened to us and applying it to the religion he represented, rewriting his story to create a nonexistent similarity. But then he returned to speaking deep emotional and powerfully relevant truths:

"They loved us far more than we ever realized. Some of you may be feeling guilty because you did not love them enough. Be gentle to yourselves with this one."

I began to weep.

Alan was bewildered. "Why are you smiling and crying at the same time?"

"That's the way listening to the Cardinal makes me feel, many different feelings at the same time."

"Today we are offering Communion because it is the most beautiful healing ceremony we know. We offer it to everyone who has been invited here, whatever your faith or background."

The usher whispered, "It's time for Alan to carry up the gifts."

Alan took his place with the group of priests and other boys who walked up the aisle towards the Cardinal where he stood at the altar. Alan was given the tray with the golden dish and ciborium. He held them out to the Cardinal, who solemnly accepted them, then extended his hand. The two figures stood in a nimbus of light, the tall man in the golden hat and the emerald gown bending over to shake the hand of the small fair haired boy in a blue suit.

Alan returned to me glowing with pride. "Did you see me?"

The aisle began to fill with the congregants lining up to receive Communion.

"Let's go mom! I want to do it!" He jumped up and joined the line assembling in the aisle.

I stood up to take my place in the line with my son. The usher stepped over to my side and whispered, apologetically, "Only Catholics can receive the wafer."

"But I thought . . . I don't understand. I thought the Cardinal invited all of us to participate. The Communion is being offered on behalf of all of us."

The usher was embarrassed. It was a difficult moment. "The Communion is being offered on behalf of everyone here, but unless you are a baptized Catholic, you can't receive the Host. Even if your son were Catholic, he still couldn't because he's too young. Children have to receive instruction before they are entitled to make their first Holy Communion when they're eight years old."

Alan looked back towards me, puzzled why I wasn't on the line beside him. I made up my mind. "I'm not going to disappoint Alan. I hope you won't either." I sat down and told Alan to walk down the aisle without me. The usher did not stop him.

"Though I live in a palace," the Cardinal said when the Mass was concluded, "I cannot invite all of you to be my guests. I can, however, invite the families to join us now for some refreshments in the area below the stairs. We would also like to meet you. The Bishop and I will be standing behind the altar."

I took my place in the slow moving line to shake the hands of the Bishop of Scotland and the Cardinal and then joined the others for an hour of socializing.

Afterwards, Alan and I walked over to Rockefeller Plaza and snacked on hot chestnuts, dried fruit and pretzels. He fed the sparrows. I was exhausted to the bone.

That night we watched the Cardinal featured on the TV evening news. The camera came in for close ups as he claimed that Christ was killed by terrorists and pulled back to show tear stained faces in the crowd. We didn't see our faces. We didn't see the Cardinal shaking hands with the brave little boy in blue.

# CHAPTER THREE

## February, 1973

Tony put his right hand on my knee, and gave it a reassuring pat. He had just passed three cars, tucking back in the lane seconds before a truck bore down on us. Tony drove like a cross between a cabbie, a racing car competitor and a state trooper. That is, he prided himself on always knowing the best routes to follow, couldn't bear not to pass everyone on the road, but followed regulations scrupulously (except the speed limit) and scolded others for their infractions. While he gleefully drove rings around every other car, he was the first to come to anyone's aid, setting out flares, or uncoiling the jump-start cables — whatever was needed.

"You've got to trust yer 'awkins, luv. You've got to trust yer 'awkins!"

And not just for breathtaking maneuvers on the highway. He meant me to understand I could rely on him in any circumstances we might ever find ourselves. I could and I would, "trust my 'awkins."

We were on our way across the Potomac Bridge to take a look at his dream house in Annapolis, the one he had selected for himself before meeting me on New Year's Eve. It was late Monday morning, Lincoln's Birthday, the last day of our second weekend together. To give us the longest possible day, I planned to take the air shuttle home at 9:00 p.m.

During the two weeks since Inauguration Day, he had been constantly on the road visiting dealers in Pennsylvania, Maryland, Ohio. He called me late at night from motel rooms. That's when I learned the essential answers to the basic questions: He was a 41-year-old bachelor who'd had numerous long- and short-term relationships but had never been married. For the past two years, he had been involved with a teacher who lived in Ohio. She loved him and wanted to marry him. All of his British friends thought he was a fool for refusing to: "She's a ticket to a green card, mate!"

"But I can't get married just for a green card!"

"What's that?" I asked, "some kind of 'open, sesame' passport?"

"You better believe it! I'm an alien, you see. A Brit. I'm able to work here, in your wonderful country, because Revox is sponsoring me. The catch is, I can only work for them and for their wages. And they pay us as though we are still living at home! But, if I had a green card, then I could work for anyone, live anywhere I please. Several people have made me some very nice offers, indeed. Thing is, a green card is almost impossible to come by, but you automatically acquire one when you become the spouse of an American citizen. You still retain your alien status, but you acquire financial freedom.

"I have all kinds of love for that girl, but not the kind that's right for marriage. For one thing, she never wants to have any children, though that's not really it. I don't know. Until I met you, I knew I was continuing to see her out of loneliness, because she loves me, but I didn't realize how dissatisfied I was, and that what was wrong was not my fault. It is just what happens between her and myself. And it will never be any different."

"You have to tell her, Tony. It's not fair to her, otherwise."

He promised to. But when he called me on his way home to Washington after his visit with her, he confessed he hadn't been able to. They had spent long, silent hours driving around, and made love. I was angry and disappointed in him. He had promised me, he had promised himself. I didn't resent the fact he had made love with her, not even exactly that he had told me. It reinforced my trust in his honesty, in his need to tell me everything he considered important. It also seemed to have been rather sad and dutiful, something to do instead of talking.

"I do love you," he said, reassuring himself as well, "though I'm not sure I'm capable of being in love anymore. Why does someone always have to get hurt?"

I can still hear the fatigue in his voice, the discouragement, the doubt. "Maybe because we lead such complicated lives," I said. Most of the time, I had been the "other woman," the one ultimately rejected. It felt odd, unfamiliar, to be the one chosen.

I told him about the man in Canada, of the incredible parallel in our lives, the temptation that had been given to each of us to resist. Just as, for the past two years, Kay had offered Tony the possibility of marriage, and the possibility of a green card, liberation from his status as indentured servant to Revox, and he had refused her offer, so had I met a man, while traveling through Saskatchewan in August, who also offered me a proposal of marriage that would have lifted me out of my rut — and I had refused him. In fact, he might very well have accompanied me to the New Year's Eve party, as Kay might also have come with Tony, and then . . .

"We would have met at the party anyway, Helen. We would have found each other. I would have found a way to call you. Listen, I will tell her. I have to go out there again in two weeks on business. I'll tell her then."

But he blurted it out over the phone within two days. "It just happened. I began telling her about the Inauguration and then about you and that I, we, would probably marry . . ."

"And then what happened?"

"She was furious! She called me bastard, hung up on me, and threw my tires out of her garage!"

"Well, you didn't really discharge this delicate responsibility with finesse!"

Still, it was done; the air cleared; the way prepared for us. And I could return to Washington to be with him for Lincoln's Birthday. It was a holiday for me, but a working weekend for him. The annual Hi-Fi Show was being held at the Hotel Washington, and Tony had to set up the Revox equipment and be there every day, demonstrating it for all potential customers. We would have the evenings and the mornings for ourselves.

Weather and labor troubles conspired to keep us apart: Penn Central custodians were going on strike at midnight Thursday, and a snow storm was promised for Friday. I took the bus, and the snow changed to rain.

Tony was there to meet me at the bus station, looking very worried. "I thought you'd never get here! Listen, luv, I want you to come with me to England this summer! I want you to meet my mother and father and stepmother. I want them to meet you."

"And I want to meet them!" This went beyond any fantasy I entertained to get me through the dreary bus ride. I was going to embrace his family. Tony couldn't have given me a greater gift.

He took me home via the hotel, to show off the exhibit room. This was my first Hi-Fi Show, and it was very classy. Instead of a pandemonium of booths under an echoing roof — with which I would become all-too-familiar in the near future — several floors had been set aside. Each exhibitor rented a suite of rooms, and attendees walked down the corridors, going in and out of the rooms, listening to the nuances of the state-of-the-art equipment in a controlled, comfortable environment.

Tony brought me into the room he had designed, named the banked walls of loud-speakers, tape recorders and turntables, and turned some knobs to envelop me with the power and fidelity of the sound system. Our casual embrace quickly changed mood, caught the crescendos, took us both by surprise.

"I love you! To come down here and bring me such joy!"

"I did actually, bring you 'joy' — wait 'til you see my Valentine's gift."

"You are my gift, Helen. I don't need any others."

Back home, in his bedroom, I presented him with a first edition of Comfort's *Joy of Sex — A Cordon Bleu Guide to Lovemaking*, with an inscription inspired by John Donne: "Tonio mio, 'we sought each other long before we met . . . we found ourselves so mutually taken with each other, so acquainted and so endeared betwixt ourselves, that from thence forward nothing was ever so near to us as one another . . . begun to late, there was no time to lose.'"

I had added a poem of my own:

"O let us lichens be!
We shall survive
where all others fail
where we alone would fail.
We shall entwine so
we seem a singular growth
though we are always
two together.
Everything that is
bare
inhospitable
we shall make our home
on boulders
and the trunks of trees
in the fiercest cold
on the mountain's peak
at the farthest pole
the earth can reach
and the sea drenched rock."

Tears gathered in Tony's eyes. "I'm speechless. No one has ever given me such a gift before."

His emotion made me shy. "I also brought you this," I said, and handed him a cassette of Ewan MacColl's "The Great Hewer," a radio documentary with the voices of coal miners interwoven with MacColl's original songs.

"There's an anomaly, here," Tony said tenderly, as he turned off the tape recorder. "I want to listen to this marvelous music, but it's taking my concentration away from you." And so we went to bed without consulting the book.

I had known intimacy; I had known intensity; but for the first time in my life, they were inseparably fused. If I am asked to date the moment our marriage began, I return to the three nights and days of that weekend in February. There was never a formal proposal; there was mutual recognition to follow our impulses all the way.

"Are you sure it doesn't matter, won't matter, that we are from different backgrounds, that I am Jewish and you were raised Catholic?" I was leaning on my elbows, cupping my chin in my hands, looking down into his blue eyes.

"Of course not! How could it? We wear our religions lightly. We're intelligent people. There isn't anything we can't discuss." He caressed my face.

"And children?"

"Oh Helen, I hope so!"

The next morning, he shared his fantasies about what married life would be like with me, wherein I spied, though entwined with flowers of affection and camouflaged very prettily, a suburban prison.

"No, Tony, I don't work to amuse myself, to fill up the hours of my day, nor from dire necessity. I will not cease and desist as soon as you support me. If you free me from the necessity of continuing at my present job, wonderful! Then I will be free to seek work that is more fulfilling, more creative. But don't expect to come home every evening to find a warm meal bubbling away on the stove and me knitting you another sweater in front of the fire. As for children, I haven't met a better man to have them with, but don't rush me!"

Tony put his arm around my waist. "In all my references, my employers always say about me that I'm very flexible. Besides, after waiting so long to find you, I'm not eager to turn us into parents right away. I want to be with you, live with you."

But where to live? Tony had his eye on a house in Annapolis, Maryland. I agreed to at least take a look at it. Late on Monday morning of our last day together, Tony drove us in his sporty orange Datsun 240Z — nicknamed "Magnolia Thunderpussy" — across the Potomac towards Annapolis.

I knew immediately that Annapolis was out of the question for me. Without access to public transportation and the stimulation of congenial people, I'd be around the bend within months. The dream house would become my padded cell. And it wasn't even that dreamy. The District would be it, then. Or Brooklyn. Wherever we could find the best situation, a better house. His job, as travelling salesman covering the entire Southeast and Midwest, and parts of the Northeast as well, could be done from a Brooklyn base, whereas mine was tied to New York City. I could, of course, leave my job, but I wasn't sure I wanted to jump over into the Washington public school system. From what I had heard, that was rather too much like leaping from the proverbial frying pan.

We missed the 9:00 p.m. shuttle to New York by four minutes. That was the first but it wasn't to be the last time I would see how Tony needed to arrive, or try to arrive, under the wire.

I had not flown since the new security regulations had gone into effect in response to the epidemic of hijackings sweeping the world. I assumed that these new procedures were only enforced on international flights, not on a shuttle between Washington and New York.

I was the only passenger on the 10:00 p.m. shuttle, Tony the only person beyond the barrier. I prepared to open my bag, placed my suitcase on the moving belt. The security guard shook his head. "Are you carrying any weapons, guns, bombs?" he inquired in a bored, mechanical voice, without lifting a hand to examine my luggage.

"A bomb, of course," I replied, my sarcasm provoked by his boredom.

He snapped to alarmed attention and signaled to an armed guard who stood in a far corner of the room, who quickly came to take charge. Tony, alert to what was happening, rushed over to the gate, preparing to vault it if necessary.

The armed guard stood directly in front of me, his hand hovering over his holstered gun and said in a low even voice, "Why did you say you are carrying a bomb?" His eyes never left mine.

"Do you think I would announce I was carrying a concealed weapon if I were indeed doing so? Would anyone? I was offended that this man" — I gestured with my head toward the security guard — "was too lazy to actually examine my luggage or even to put it through the machine and check the screen. If he is really here to protect the plane and passengers, why doesn't he examine my luggage?" I was feeling self-righteous and very frightened.

"You must never joke about carrying concealed weapons. You could be arrested just for lying about that," the armed guard answered, straightening his arm.

"What going on, luv?" Tony called out to me, leaning on the gate. That's one of those snapshot moments, where I see us as we were then, freeze-framed. Then the shutter button is released, and we move and speak again.

The guard released me. "It's all right. Let her go on."

I rushed over to Tony, quickly explained what had just happened, hurriedly kissed him good-bye, and ran to make the plane. They never did check my suitcase.

It was a crystalline winter night, visibility sublime, the stars phosphorescent pins in black velvet. I thought: *The bastards. Once this system is in place, it will never be removed. Those lunatics have taken us all hostage.* The cab I hailed at La Guardia had a thick meshed bulletproofed shield separating me from the driver. The weekend euphoria was over.

## February, 1989

In less than two weeks after the Mass, I spoke at our first press conference, was interviewed on the radio, and my photograph appeared in two New York newspapers and innumerable others across the nation and the world. The Victims of Pan Am 103 had found their voice and their mission, and I had ceased to be a private person.

Betty Capasso called a week after the Mass to notify me about the press conference. I learned about her from an article about her eldest son Gregory, which a colleague had clipped from a Brooklyn newspaper and placed in my mailbox the week I returned to work mid-January. It was headlined, "Scholarship to Keep Tragedy Victim's Name Alive."

*"A scholarship fund has been established at the University of Buffalo in memory of Gregory Capasso, the 21-year-old Marine Park resident who was*

*among the 259 passengers that died aboard Pan Am flight 103 last month . . .
'I want to keep his name alive forever,' Betty Capasso said last week. . . . Gregory
Capasso was an aspiring film director . . . he was supposed to graduate this May."*

Using the article as a guide to find her phone number, I had called Betty
the night before the Mass, hoping we might meet at the Cathedral. She was
loquacious, intense: "I believe everyone has a spirit, good or bad and when
they die, it is released. They are all here with us and everyone they've ever
touched is feeling their presence. I feel Gregory is here with us, and all his
friends who come to see us and write to us, they're feeling his presence, too."

I had agreed with her. "Tony was trying to come home to us. He's still
trying."

"Hi, Helen," Betty said. "I saw you at St. Pat's but it was too crowded for
me to get over to you. Listen, Paul Hudson has called a press conference at
the Hyatt tomorrow morning. We're trying to get as many of us over there as
possible. It should be a big thing. Can you come?"

"Probably. But what's the reason? Has anything new happened?"

"No. It's that we have so many questions and we don't like the way we're
not being given any answers. All those empty seats on the plane four days
before Christmas, and that warning the State Department posted for its
employees in Moscow. Listen, bring a picture of Tony. We're all bringing
pictures to make it real to those bastards. It wasn't just numbers that blew up
in that plane. By the way, has the President sent you a letter of condolence?"

"No, of course not. Why should he?"

"Why not? It wasn't just an accident, you know. It was an act of war
against our country. I mean, as far as I'm concerned, it was not different
than the bombing of the Marine barracks in Beirut."

I hadn't thought of it like that. She was right. Suddenly, the silence
from the White House and the State Department seemed ominous, and
that fellow from the State Department who had hung up on me with such
audible relief when I told him that Tony was not a citizen of the United
States was no longer an overworked employee but perhaps part of a
coordinated attempt to sweep this embarrassing mess under the rug as fast
as possible. Yes, nothing would keep me from the press conference, even if
it meant missing a day of work or defying my lawyer.

My principal gave me permission to take the morning off, but my
lawyer tried to discourage me. "Go if you want to, but don't say anything,"

he said. "I don't think it's a good idea to draw attention to yourself with a lawsuit pending."

As soon as I walked past the large placard in the corridor and into the carpeted room, already filled with dozens of people milling around in front of two cloth-covered tables placed on either side of a lectern with a large microphone, I knew I had come in order to be seen, in order to be heard. If I sat at that dais, I would be seen on television and then, perhaps, I'd be seen by some of the people I could not otherwise notify about Tony's death. These were people who had once been very closely entwined in our lives, but whose current whereabouts were now unknown to me. I also needed to say something, but I didn't yet know what it would be.

A woman dressed entirely in black, with long black hair loose upon her shoulders, was walking up and down the aisles, introducing herself, handing out labels. She called out to us, "I am Eleanor Hudson, mother of Melina. Put labels on. Introduce yourselves. Name whom you've lost. Let's meet one another. Show your pictures. Hold them up for the cameras."

I went to the back table, wrote my name/wife of Tony Hawkins, and stuck it on my blouse. I introduced myself to a handsome, full-figured woman who had two pictures pinned on her suit. One was a snapshot of a young man, the other, much smaller, of a young woman inside a locket.

"Oh my God! Did you have two children on the plane?"

"No," she said with a gentle smile, "only my son Christopher. But my daughter died a year ago while working in South America. Her funeral took place almost to the day that Chris died."

I was speechless. She was so poised as she calmly told me of this unimaginable double loss: "My children have taught me so much. My son was fearless. He believed in living to the fullest, not to live with regrets."

Someone called out to Paul Hudson, who was standing at the lectern, "What are our goals?" Someone else responded, "To call for stricter security so that such a disaster will never happen again." A tall, very thin woman said sharply, "I'm only concerned about my nephew. They told me they only found part of his hand to bury . . . I'm not interested in anyone else."

I shouted out, "How can you say that! Not to be interested in anyone else!"

The woman next to me murmured, "She's in pain," and touched my arm.

"We're all in pain," I replied, "but not everyone's pain has opened them to the pain of others."

A woman stepped to the microphone and took charge. "Hello. My name is Sherry Price. I'm from the National Victims Center. Whoever wants to make a statement, come to the dais. We have about an hour to ourselves, then the doors will be open to the press."

I did not hesitate. I walked to the front of the room and found a seat between Paul Hudson and a very young, very attractive woman with thick chestnut hair in a tumble around her pale face. Beneath her name, Wendy Giebler/wife of Jay Giebler, she had pinned a large snapshot of herself standing to the left of two men. I placed the large framed photograph I had brought with me, of Tony and myself looking at each other, in front of me at the edge of the table. I introduced myself to Wendy and pointed to her picture. "Which man is your husband?"

"This one." She touched the figure on the far right. "The other man is John Ahern. He and my husband began working for the same company within a week of each other in 1986 and became close friends. They worked together in London for two years. This picture was taken last summer at a Christening we all went to in London. He was on the plane, too, sitting next to Jay. I would have been sitting with them except we decided that I should return a few days earlier to get a head start on our Christmas shopping."

"How long were you married?" I asked softly.

"Nine months."

"Wendy . . . I'm so sorry." I felt burdened, suddenly, by the gift of sixteen years I had been given.

"Please let me have your attention." It was Sherry Price. "I want to explain the format of the press conference. We only have an hour to prepare ourselves for them. Anyone who wants to make a statement has come to the dais, is that right? Okay. Your statements have to be brief, they have to be focused. The press will be impatient with tears. What we're going to do now is to give each one of you an opportunity to practice giving your statement. We're going to skip you for now, Paul, because you'll be reading from your prepared press release."

I had two different ideas that seemed equally appropriate: one was to talk personally, to tell how Tony had found himself on this flight, able to transfer his ticket at the last minute; the other to focus on the media itself, what they knew and when they knew it. I began to talk about Tony.

Sherry cut me off impatiently. "That's much too lengthy. You'll lose them."

*That's it,* I thought. *I'll speak about the media.*

After everyone had had their turn at the microphone, Sherry glanced at the clock and nodded her head. "It's time." It was 10 o'clock.

The doors were opened, and a mob rushed in. Instinctively, I leaned back and straightened my arms against the edge of the table. I was as far as possible from the front doors and protected by the table's width, but it still felt as though a dam had burst and I might drown. They filled the room in a rush, all the aisles, the back seats. Within seconds, the wall on my right was being folded up like the accordion it was, giving the press half again as much space as they needed to fill with their tripods and tape recorders.

Paul Hudson walked to the microphone, and the lights began flashing. They are ravenous, I thought. They are feeding on us. Well, we are feeding on them, too.

This was my first opportunity to look closely at the man who had organized this conference. He was thin, balding, bespectacled. He could be a lawyer or an accountant. He began reading from his neatly typed statement in a thin dry voice, not a flicker of emotion betraying his face. On the front of his suit was a label with his name/father of Melina Hudson. "We are relatives of some of those innocent persons murdered in this wanton attack, the most massive terrorist attack in history aimed at American civilians," he said. I was astonished to hear it described in this way. "We have had the support and sympathy from grieving relatives, friends, members of our communities, individual airline employees . . . The outpouring of sharing has been a great comfort to us. There has been one quarter from which the response has been utter silence. We have received no condolences from the top officials of Pan Am nor the leaders of our national government. Unlike the British government leaders, neither President Reagan nor President Bush, nor our Vice President, Secretary of State, or Secretary of Transportation have attended any of the memorial services that were held. Not even second-level U.S. officials have been present. . . . Can it be that the U.S. government policy is to ignore the 103 bombing by doing little or nothing?"

Hudson then opened up the heart of the matter, the reason that he had called a press conference. "In the immediate aftermath . . . we were shocked to learn that the FAA had issued written alerts of a terrorist threat to bomb a Pan Am flight originating in Frankfurt during the pre-Christmas holiday period. These warnings had apparently been sent to U.S. embassies, the airline, British officials and the U.S. military personnel in Frankfurt. However, the warning alert was not available to passengers or crew of Flight 103."

He was referring to the so called "Helsinki Warning," based on an anonymous phone call made to the U.S. Embassy in Finland two weeks before Pan Am Flight 103 was attacked. The State Department had taken it seriously. It had posted notices in all its European embassies, forbidding its employees to fly Pan Am home for the Christmas holidays. A photograph of one such notice in the cafeteria of its Moscow embassy had appeared in the *New York Times* on December 22nd. I wondered when the *Times* had acquired this picture, before or after the plane blew up.

"President Reagan, when asked about this policy of keeping warnings, even high-level alerts, secret from the public, asserted that so many threats are received that to make them available to the public could stop all air traffic. The FAA's own reports show a relatively small number of threats to aircraft (400 to 500 out of 6 million flights), and a positively tiny number of high-level threats (twenty-two to twenty-four in all of 1988). This threat to Pan Am flight 103 after December 5th was apparently classified as such a high-level threat. While the number of people who knew of the FAA terrorist alert is not known at present, the 168 vacant seats on this usually crowded pre-Christmas flight indicates the possibility that the alert was more widely known than has yet been reported."

So that's what Betty meant about "all those empty seats." Her son had been able to switch his reservations at the last minute, and when she questioned him, he had just taken it as personal good fortune: "I got lucky, Ma!" I had never even thought to wonder how Tony hoped to find a seat on another flight when he decided to delay his departure by twenty-four hours.

"The anger felt by many of us about suppressed warnings has been heightened by revelation that the airline security measures cannot detect plastic bombs in the checked baggage. While the FAA and the airlines have apparently known of this massive security gap since 1986 and the FAA has ordered new equipment to detect such bombs, no interim measures to detect such bombs were undertaken, apparently for reasons of commercial convenience . . ."

Then Hudson turned to some sensitive, personal concerns, the handling of the remains of unidentified victims and the indefinite delay in the return of the personal effects of property . . . A funeral service had been held last week in Scotland for a number of victims whose bodies had not been fully recovered or identified.

This was new information. In the earliest moments I imagined everyone being blown to bits; when Tony's body was recovered and returned to me, I assumed that everyone had died intact. This assumption was supported by the graphic photographs appearing in *Newsweek* and *Time* magazine in January, which I had forced myself to look at. The grieving aunt who had been given less than a hand to bury was not the only victim.

"While family members were originally told in the week after the crash that personal effects would be returned to the next of kin with the bodily remains, and other property would be identified and returned by Pan Am, Scottish authorities subsequently ruled that they would handle these matters." But now, Hudson went on to inform us, the Scots were going to turn over the effects to the U.S. State Department because these items might be needed in the criminal investigation of future criminal cases. Believing that there might be good cause to hold some luggage found near the bomb blast, he hoped that the rest of the personal items would be returned to us within the next week.

This was not an issue that particularly concerned me.

"In conclusion, we call on President Bush to act on the ideals he has championed. Please, Mr. President, break your silence and exercise your leadership to redouble the efforts of the federal government to identify and apprehend the perpetrators of this, the worst terrorist attack in history on American civilians . . . End the government's present immoral policy of providing selective warnings and alerts to certain favored persons while keeping the public and airline employees whose lives are at risk in ignorance.

"To the Congress, which will decide the degree to which it will investigate the Flight 103 bombing over the next several weeks, we urge you to conduct a full and complete investigation. Unlike most accidental air crashes, where the role of the FAA itself is not at issue, this case demands a full independent investigation of the FAA's actions on the security and warning issues . . ."

Paul gathered his pages off the lectern and Sherry motioned to me with her hand. I began walking to the lectern before Paul took his seat next to mine. I glanced down at the notes I had scribbled on the Hyatt stationery.

"My name is Helen Engelhardt Hawkins. My husband, Tony Hawkins, died on Pan Am 103. I did not learn of the disaster through the media. I learned by a phone call from England at 9:00 p.m. that night.

"If I had read every paper, listened to every program from October through December 20th, I would never have learned that a bomb threat had been made on a Pan Am flight leaving Frankfurt during December. We only learned of this threat the next day in the *New York Times*.

"If we had been informed through the media, or directly by Pan Am to any prospective customer during the holiday season, my husband would never have left home at this time to visit relatives in England. He would never have flown Pan Am. People in Moscow were warned. Why not us?

"Why did the *Times* wait until December 22nd to print that photograph of the State Department warning its employees to stay away from Pan Am? When did the *Times* acquire that crucial information? What did they know and when did they know it? I want to know what we are still not being told!"

I had not quavered; I had not cried. I took my seat. Wendy went to the microphone. One by one, we each spoke. Many people told horror stories about the State Department. One sister received her first official communication a month later, when she was told that she would not be getting a body to bury; Wendy had been challenged because she had flown home a week early, was told that she and her husband were probably estranged, therefore she wasn't entitled to either information or personal effects.

Then two men captured the microphone and dominated the rest of the conference. The first held up a newspaper into the glare of the cameras. "This is today's issue of the *Washington Times* with a banner headline declaring that the terrorists have been identified. President Bush — this is an act of war! What are you going to do?"

"My name is Bert Ammerman. My brother Thomas was on Pan Am 103. I went to Lockerbie immediately and spent ten days there trying to bring my brother home. Our government was a distant, last presence in terms of assistance and support to the families. It was Pan Am and the police from Glasgow who mobilized caring people."

Then another man was at the microphone, tossing his black hair out of his eyes. "My name is John Root. My wife died on Pan Am 103. This threat was taken seriously. The State Department and Pan Am cannot claim ignorance. I call for revenge against the men who killed my wife!"

*What am I doing here? We have nothing in common except for the coincidental fact that someone we love died on that plane.*

The press began bombarding us with questions, most of them aimed at Bert Ammerman and John Root. "What should President Bush do next? What kind of retaliation do you want to see happen?" I noticed one woman who looked distinctively different. She was dressed very informally in a long sleeved polo shirt and blue jeans, and her long hair hung freely. She asked one of the last questions: "How would you say Pan Am has treated you?" Everyone on the dais began shouting out their grievances. She took notes on her pad.

As soon as Sherry announced that the conference was over, I walked over to this woman. "Excuse me, but in the interests of truth, I want you to know that Pan Am has treated me very well, indeed. I could not say so in front of all the others. Apparently their experience has been very disagreeable, but Pan Am not only provided me with a most sympathetic 'contact person' to help me during the first weeks, but since then, their insurance company has agreed to cover the costs of almost everything I ask them to — postage, phone bills, funeral expenses, burial expenses. That doesn't mean that I'm not in a lawsuit against them or that I do not blame them for not warning people as soon as they were warned, but I have to give them credit for what they have done right."

Something about this journalist seemed familiar to me, but I couldn't place her. "Who do you work for?"

"NPR," she replied.

"What's your name?"

"Margot Adler."

"Margot! My husband loved to listen to you on WBAI! And so did I. I mean, so do I."

Margot had her own program on WBAI every Monday night at midnight, which she kept even after she began to work as a radio journalist for National Public Radio. I was surprised that I hadn't recognized her distinctive, low-pitched voice.

"Your husband used to listen to me on 'BAI?" She looked uneasy, almost frightened.

"All the time. He was a very loyal listener-sponsor for sixteen years. I turned him on to the station when I married him. He worked at home a lot, and always kept his radio tuned to 'BAI to keep him company in his basement workshop."

"Helen, would you like to be on my program this evening? I would like to interview you."

"Of course, I would love to. Wow. I don't know if I can arrange child care at the last minute." My head was whirling.

"You should arrive by 11:30 so we have a chance to chat a bit before going on air. Just call the station and leave a message as soon as you know — about 10:00 p.m. would be good enough. I had another program planned for tonight anyway; this is a really spontaneous change of plans for me, as you know! So I can always fall back on my original material."'

"I'll do my best to be there. Now excuse me, I have to rush back to work." I gathered up my things and made for the door.

"Helen!" A slender, attractive woman standing next to a thin man with glasses, mustache and a shy smile, had called to me. "I'm Betty Capasso, and this is my husband Sal."

I went over to hug her and shake his hand. "You look so much younger than I imagined you. For some reason, I thought you would be so much older. Not just because your son was 21 years old. You sounded so mature."

"Well, I am, but I'm just not old! That was a strong statement you made." Betty hadn't gone up to the dais, but she had placed a photograph of her son prominently at the edge of the table next to mine.

"Thanks so much for telling me about this event, but I have to get back to work now. Listen, Betty, Pat Simpson and I have started a bereavement group. We're holding our first meeting this afternoon at her house in Park Slope. Can you come?"

"No, not today. Let me know when the next meeting will be."

I was back at work in the bio prep room at my high school in Brooklyn within an hour. I set up the orders for the next day and left for my next responsibility. I was flying!

Pat's house was a short walk from the school. Pat and her daughter Rachel were there, of course, and a diminutive woman, who was grieving the loss of her nephew, Jerry Weston, a highly gifted entrepreneur. We agreed that we needed to find a professional counselor to guide our future meetings. Pat would try to find someone. "If you're still up at midnight, I may be on the radio tonight."

And on to my next assignment at the Prospect Park Environmental Center, a brisk walk from Pat's house. I had been associated with the Center from its inception ten years earlier. The entire staff had come to Tony's memorial service. I stopped in to thank them and to bring them up to date on the latest developments in my situation.

"You've chosen anger," said John Muir, the Center's director. "I'm impressed."

The program director drove me home. I told her my ideas for a new walk to lead in the spring through the gardens of Flatbush. As soon as I arrived home, I asked the young man who had come to live with us, if he would be able to take charge of Alan that night after 10:00 p.m. He agreed.

We couldn't find the press conference on any of the major channels at 6:00 p.m. Alan fell asleep on the couch while I worked on my lecture for my college class the next afternoon. Eventually I found coverage of the conference: Paul Hudson and Bert Ammerman were highlighted, and John Root, calling for revenge. I was in the background, glimpsed in a group shot. I called a few friends, notifying them about the radio interview. Alan woke up long enough for me to put him to bed, reading him a story before I left at 10:00 p.m.

Throughout this long, productive day, I was preternaturally alert on adrenaline overdrive.

The subway train halted at Church Avenue for almost a half hour because a kid had thrown something on the tracks that had to be cleared. I was frantic. It was after 11:00 p.m. when I ran up to the street at the West 4th Street station, and hailed a cab to drive me up to 34th Street.

Margot welcomed me warmly. We still had several moments to ourselves before we went on air. She told me how she planned to open her show. She wanted me to hear, first, what her listeners heard shortly after midnight, as her theme music, "Who Murdered the Minutes," faded out.

"It's really interesting how things happen," she began. "I was going to do a totally different show tonight. This morning, I was at a press conference, called by thirty or so family members, relatives of people who had died on

Pan Am 103.

"For me, the most amazing moment came when a woman named Helen Engelhardt, who's with me tonight, came over to me and told me that she listens to WBAI and that her husband, Tony Hawkins, who had died on Pan Am 103, was a listener, had been an ardent listener of WBAI. For me, at that instant, the world changed. Because I realized that all my life, I had looked at all those people who had been part of those tragedies — the Iran hostages, the people who died on Pan Am 103 — as separate from me. They were not 'radical outsiders' like me. People who listen to 'BAI do not get on flight 103 or get to be taken hostage in Iran! When she said that, it was, 'Oh, my God! People who listen to 'BAI get killed on Pan Am flight 103! So I immediately said to her, to come on the program and welcome! Why don't you start anywhere you want."

I began with what had happened to me when I called in my tribute to Tony to the station in January, and how hurt I had been by the inappropriate way I had been treated by a 'BAI staff member. "I couldn't tell if he was so moved, he couldn't show it — or if he felt nothing at all. My feelings, in any case, were . . . surprised."

Margot suggested a possible reason the staff person had been so rude. "I think that the tendency is to shut one's self off and to not really believe that this is you, that we could have been on that plane. It's particularly true, when you are so involved with political commitments, that you stop thinking about the individual life."

I wished to focus on the personal, not the political. My listeners had been inundated with the political. I talked about how Tony found himself on that flight, how I learned of his death, how I informed my friends and family; about the decisions I made regarding the memorial service, how the Jewish rituals of mourning had taken me through that time.

"I chose not to listen or read or look at any media that week, and in fact I continued that until very recently. This decision evolved. I couldn't do anything else at first, except deal with my friends and family. And then, as people came to me, they told me what was going on, they were listening, they were reading. I was getting phone calls from Pan Am. Within two days I was given a personal contact, who kept me informed. He happened to be an exceptional human being. I was told everything essential.

"This world is crazy and horrible, and the news that is being selected for us reinforces that sense. I had a lot more energy for myself and my friends when I wasn't scattering it. I have judiciously returned to listening and reading the news about this event. I'm learning more than I'm able to handle about what happened."

I described how I met other family members. "I began hearing about people. The cab driver who drove my parents to my home had a daughter whose best friend's fiancé was on that flight. When I went back to work, I was told that there were colleagues of mine who knew people who knew people. I began collecting these names and leads so that I could meet these people. At Cardinal O'Connor's Mass in our honor, I began to meet some of them."

I spoke about the power of talking to another widow. "Something happened between us. We connected in a way that nobody else can, except those who are going through this."

Margot asked me to summarize the main concerns expressed at the press conference. "The government is not reacting strongly to this," I said. "And they should. When you lose somebody, suddenly, to a violent act, you want action. I'll just speak for myself. If it was a bomb then we can do something. If it is a Palestinian group, then Israel and the PLO can sit down and make peace. If it is the IRA, then Ireland and the English can sit down and make peace. They can say, we won't be intimidated. You can't stop us from reaching a political settlement. The airlines can make flights safer. It wasn't lightning that struck the plane."

Margot opened up the show to phone calls. The first call came from a man who told me that people who lost loved ones should join hands and work for world peace.

I agreed. "The last thing in the world I want is for a bombing in revenge. That's not going to bring anyone back to life, and only perpetuates the cycle of violence." I went on to express my opinions about how best to deal with terrorism, how getting to the root causes takes time but in the immediate future we can protect ourselves better. "If El Al can protect their passengers, any airline can."

The second call was from Odetta, the internationally revered singer of folk songs who had been a favorite of mine since she began her career in the 1950's. "I was listening in January and that's when I heard you and I was touched to the core of me, and called in to the station and joined again to match your $57. None of it makes any sense, but looking towards a positive, this, your loss, seems to be our gain. You're so clear — the day that you spoke on the phone that morning, and this evening and the sense that I get from you. And I bless you and I do thank you."

I could barely speak. "Odetta . . . many years ago, when you first began your wonderful career as a singer, I heard you sing and went to your concerts, and have your albums from that time. I can't tell you how meaningful, how wonderful this is for me, to have this connection with you."

In June of 1993, I introduced myself to her at a folk music festival and she enveloped me in her large embrace.

The inevitable crazy call came next. A man shouted "Heil Hitler!" before Margott could cut him off. She shrugged and rolled her eyes.

A man called to remind Margot and inform me that Leo Cawley, one of the producers at WBAI, had lost his brother on Pan Am 103. "We never know when we'll last be here. So you'll remember the good and you'll take care of your son and you'll carry on."

The next man found it strange that I support a station that has been most sympathetic to Palestinian terrorists. "I know what you mean," I said. "There are people I can't listen to on this station, because of how they are saying what they are saying. I don't mind having my sympathies stretched. Even the people who are sympathetic to the Palestinians, have things to say, to teach me what I don't know. It's very clear to me what terrorist activity is: When innocent people are deliberately singled out to be killed. 'BAI still does stand for free speech and the possibility of learning what the other media are keeping from us, just in terms of politics. It's why Tony listened to the station so much. He listened to people I couldn't stand, because he wanted to hear what they had to say."

Margot added, "I think it is important to say to this caller, that there are many people who are called terrorists in our society who are, in fact, not, who are dealing with the liberation of their own countries. You cannot say that the entire Irish Republican struggle is terrorist; you cannot say that the Palestinian struggle is by nature terrorist. There may be elements within each struggle that are. But we have a tendency in this country, to label everybody."

The next caller was Jane Smiley, the author, who referred to Konrad Lorenz's *On Aggression,* about the apparently innate quality of every living creature to kill another living creature. "Lorenz concludes that the only answer is to get to know each other. The response of the survivors of that airplane crash bears that out: to reach out to each other, to help each other. Even more astonishing is to hear you say that you hope it was somebody with an agenda, because then something can happen. That is the only feeling that ever will possibly bring any peace. I don't think that I could ever bring myself to feel that way. I hope I could. But it's extraordinary to hear you. It's redemptive. Thank you so much for talking."

I replied, "There's a web of sorrow and joy that binds us together. In this case, it's sorrow. We all are touched by this, here in New York City and other large city centers where many people came from. Everyone knows someone on that flight: a neighbor, or someone who lived down the block or around the corner. Everyone who works in the schools where I work, everyone who is a 'BAI listener is now connected in that way. Terrorists don't understand this truth. It's madness not to make room for one another on this crowded planet. There aren't any other places to go."

Smiley responded, "At the same time, I admire that you are all demanding as much as can be found out. There are too many dark corners not to have light cast into them."

I replied, "The total political situation is frightening. I think if we knew what was really going on, we would barely be able to get out of bed in the morning."

A man called who asked me to comment on a rumor that it had been a CIA agent who unwittingly carried the bomb on the plane. Margot reminded us that many stories that have appeared in print are not trustworthy.

The last call we took was from a woman who brought us back from political speculation to the most personal dimension of this event. Speaking very slowly, she said, "I had never really mourned the death of my father, when I was four, nor the death of my mother with whom I had a lot of difficulties, and who I didn't see the last few years of her life. But the way you spoke about the way you mourned his death was very important. For some reason, I started to cry. I appreciated what you were bringing out, because there was some level of energy that you were letting come out of you that was so real and connected so well to me that all of a sudden I just cried."

I could barely speak. "The one thing that has made this bearable, has been the love, the extraordinary compassion, the outreaching from friends and now from a stranger, and that is a very powerful and real force — and it is the only answer we have."

Margot left the station with me, and hugged me before getting into her cab. I told my cab driver where I was coming from, what had happened to me. Talking to him became an extension of the experience. He was an ex-cop.

"They never tell us the truth," he said. "Do what you have to do."

I was totally wired, unable to sleep, and a zombie in the morning.

I decided to go in late with Alan, who could barely open his eyes. People had seen my picture in *Newsday*. I ran out to a local store. Two articles dominated page 8, under the headline, "Handling of Lockerbie Denounced." Under the words, *"'Wall of Silence' Angers Kin,"* was a picture of me, wiping a tear from my right eye. Naturally, that's why the picture had been printed. Sherry Price had been wrong; perhaps reporters are impatient with tears, but photographers aren't.

I winged it through my ecology class at Pratt. The dean stopped me in the hall; he had seen me on TV. I began to weep as I walked to the subway. The anesthetic effect of the non-stop excitement of the past thirty-six hours had suddenly worn off, leaving me to deal once again with throbbing pain. I picked up a discarded copy of the *New York Post* from the subway seat and saw my face, alone, in close-up, on page 4, under John Root's words, "Let's Mete Out Punishment!" The caption read, *"Still mourning: Two months after the Pan Am disaster, Helen Engelhardt Hawkins of Brooklyn weeps behind picture of her and her husband."* Actually, I was blowing my nose because I had a cold. I was now Exhibit A in what was becoming a freak show.

## CHAPTER FOUR

### March, 1973

"We're on the raft of joy," Tony said.

We were on the new queen-sized mattress on the floor between our bedroom and my study. The mattress was waiting for the convertible couch that had served me so well in my one-room apartment to be removed from the bedroom wall and the box springs to be put into permanent position beneath it. In the meantime, we were exploring what it had to offer us.

"But now, luv, as much as I don't want to, we have to get ready to leave. I don't want to be late the first time I'm to meet your family."

Tony had come up from Washington this first weekend in March, to be with me in the new apartment I had found for us. My family was gathering to celebrate my father's birthday and, as a surprise gift, we were planning to announce our engagement, three months after we'd met.

We stopped to pick up my younger sister Alice, who lived a few blocks from me. "I can't believe this man," she said, shaking her head. "Three-piece suit and tie and cuff links! Where did you find him?"

"I think I'm marrying a clothes horse," I said with a grin.

Tony even had on his black shoes with the heels that made him those critical inches taller. He was self-conscious about his height; in his stocking feet, he was slightly shorter than I am.

We joined my parents, my mother's twin sister and her husband, my father's brother and his wife, and my brother, all seated around the table. Before dessert was served, Tony cleared his throat and asked for attention. "I'd like you all to be the first to know, besides ourselves, that Helen and I are planning to be married."

There was a lovely explosion of noise, congratulations, embraces. Then I saw my brother, sitting at the edge of the couch in the living room, where he had gone, with tears in his eyes, leaning his head on his hand. I went over to hug him, surprised by his emotion. Tony followed me.

"Everybody loves you so much, Helen! They are so pleased for you." Tony cupped my face in his large square hands.

"Yes, of course they are, but I think all this fuss is because they can't believe that I'm finally getting married — and to such a charming guy."

We had chosen the wedding date during his visit to Brooklyn a week after Valentine's Day. We were with Adam, the 10-year-old son of Tony's friends on Garfield Place, who adored Tony and tried to spend some time with him whenever Tony came to Brooklyn.

"Why don't you get married on my birthday, June 21st?" he said. "That's the best day I can think of."

"June 21st — that's Midsummer Day. That's perfect! That's it, luv, that's it!" Tony's imagination was immediately and profoundly engaged by the mystique of this day. Years later, when he formed his own company to design and manufacture  products for the sound industry, he named it The Midsummer Sound Company and created a logo inspired by the sun rising over the heelstone at Stonehenge. He was enchanted at the idea of celebrating our wedding on a day resonant with pagan fertility rites and Shakespearean overtones, whereas I was somewhat put out at the prospect of becoming just another June bride.

True to our agreement, Tony considered the possibility of moving to Brooklyn. We looked at half a dozen apartments in Park Slope that weekend, each one having to fit the requirements of conversion to a recording studio as well as being a suitable candidate for our future home. On the back landing of a floor-through with a southern exposure, we looked over the tiny garden and hugged each other, envisioning a baby crawling on the grass.

Monday morning, Tony had an appointment with the manager of the Revox home office out in Long Island, and was told that he was being recalled from Washington to New York. Revox wanted him to be their man in New York and environs. So that settled it. Park Slope it would be. Tony stayed with me to the end of the week, working at the New York office every day and looking for apartments in the evenings.

I found us a beauty — half a house on Sixth Avenue and President Street, with basement, ground floor, first floor and backyard for only $350 a month and a two-year lease. The long front room, with its burlap covered plaster walls, could do very nicely as a recording studio.

I moved in on the last day of February, and Tony called me that night from Washington, and as we talked, he recorded our conversation. He wanted to preserve a particular story I had previously told him, but left the recorder running as we continued to talk. Although I was aware at the time, I never listened to it, and totally forgot its existence until the winter of 1990/91, when I went searching through Tony's unpacked cartons, which had been sitting unopened in our attic for ten years. I was hoping to find letters, mine in particular, that I had written during our courtship and his traveling salesman days, has well as his diary calendars — anything that would help to connect me to our life together. Instead I found back issues of *Scientific American*. But I did find a box of tapes. Most of them seemed to be programs recorded from the radio, the House Judiciary Hearings on Watergate which occurred during summer of our honeymoon. I piled all these cassettes on the top shelf of a bookshelf unit on the landing outside my bedroom door. On the first week in June, 1991, on my way to spend another day of lying in bed nursing a back spasm, I glanced at the tapes. One suddenly caught my eye. It said, in Tony's handwriting: HELEN ON LINDSAY./TONY ON CAROL. I put it in the recorder by my bedside, and turned it on.

A gift. Pure magic. Tony's voice close-up. He was talking to a woman, whose voice was slightly distorted over the telephone. I did not recognize her as myself at first. Tony was discussing with his bride-to-be whom to exclude from the guest list.

"Let's decide one thing between us. Among the guests, there will not be Governor Rockefeller or practically any other politician!"

"Oh," the woman sighs, "but if Mayor Lindsay wants to come, let's let him. I'm very fond of him." And then she begins to reminisce about a benefit for the Brooklyn Academy of Music she attended the previous December, during which Mayor Lindsay told some very funny jokes. "He's very beautiful and he's very exciting to listen to because he's witty, ironic; he works against his looks, he disarms you. Right away he puts you at ease. 'I feel like Zsa Zsa Gabor's 5th husband,' he said. 'I know what I'm supposed to do, but I don't know how to make it interesting!'"

Finally I recognized the woman as myself, and heard Tony explaining that he was recording me in order to get down on tape the story about the time I first saw Lindsay when he was a congressman testifying against renewing the budget for the House UnAmerican Activities Committee during the early '60's. I was there with other members of the anti-HUAC group, lobbying against the budget appropriations.

"We got down to Washington early in the morning. What you could do is walk into the Congress building, walk up the stairs, down the corridors, open a door and there you were! I don't think it could happen any more because of the lunatics running around killing people. We were barely frisked by the guards. They did not know what group we were representing. We came in, quietly took our seats a few feet from an enormous table, about thirty people sitting around it. They all looked like who they were! They were grotesque. The head of the Rules Committee was an ancient man who looked like a toad, no, a lizard. He had a gavel.

"The House UnAmerican Committee was still formidable. It was years in the future before the Women's Strike for Peace laughed them out of business. It was still a difficult political stance to come out against them. John Lindsay was still only a congressman from the Silk Stocking District. It was 1962, I think. He was a white knight. I had never seen anybody so beautiful so close. Glamor. The patina of the very rich and the very famous. He was sitting there and saying that he didn't think that this committee should be given any funds because he didn't like what they were doing politically and there were other committees that could handle their work. It was a courageous thing for him to do, it was not politically popular. Lindsay was not radical. He was just consistent on civil liberties. He really meant it."

"It's down, it's on tape," Tony said. "I just wanted to hear you tell that story. You told it differently."

"Well, I knew I was being recorded!" I said with a laugh. Tony was the only other person I had ever met who enjoyed interviewing people informally, collecting voices. I had bought my first tape recorder when I was 28 years old — a Craig reel-to-reel to carry with me, along with my camera, as I backpacked through Europe. I learned how to use it by interviewing my friends and relatives.

"Can you see the moon from where you are?"

"No, it should be a very new moon."

"It's little more than half. Right now the clouds have covered it, mackerel clouds scudding by and the moon is phosphorescent, lopsided."

That was how I was able to date this conversation. By going to the Farmer's Almanac and looking up the phases of the moon in February and March, 1973, I learned that the evening I described a gibbous moon to Tony was either near February 24th or March 24th. But by gibbous moon March, Tony was with me in Brooklyn. So the conversation had been recorded in February.

There is one other clue. Towards the end of our talk, I mentioned a piano in the room. So I was in our new apartment, not my old one. I moved on February 28th, a Wednesday. Tony came to Brooklyn two days later. It pleased me to play detective with this extraordinary find.

"Got to ring off now, luv. This makes about an hour and a quarter. Terrible!" He was in no hurry.

"Nobody believes we could have so much to say to each other for so long." Neither could I.

"I'm afraid that's how it is."

"I was reading recently that people who really get along very well, who've been married a long time, talk to each other thirty minutes a day, or a week, I forget which. Apparently people don't talk much when they are communicating in other ways, when they've been together a long time. You do most of your talking in the early days — and in the last year before divorce!"

"I bet you do, too!" Tony laughed.

"It's still very new, very exciting to be speaking with you, hearing from you, knowing what you're feeling, hearing your reactions. I don't feel that if I don't speak with you every day that your feeling is going to lessen, but I want to speak to you, you know . . ." My voice became very soft.

"Mmm. Yes, much the same."

"You mean it's not exactly the same?"

Tony burst out laughing. "Are we going to have a row? Are we going to have a row?"

"Nooo. You sound eager for one!"

"No, not a bit. I don't know if we ever will. Probably we will. In fact, I already know what it's going to be about."

I was really intrigued by the matter-of-fact certainty in his tone. "What?"

"Something I haven't done and should have!"

I giggled. "It could be something I have done and shouldn't have."

"Possibly." He laughed. "Not so likely. Really, statistically, it's a ten-to-one chance that it's an omission of mine."

"I just flashed on seeing you opening the door and ducking as I start flinging things at you from down a long corridor."

"Do you fling things?" He sounded positively eager for the affirmative.

"Actually, I don't fling things."

"Did I ever tell you about the fight I had with a girl I called Cow? That's what I called her behind her back. Her real name was Carol. She sublet a room in the flat I rented. She was short, fat and very rude, never said please or thank you."

"No, I don't think so."

"Cow didn't throw anything, but she hit me over the head with a chair, which I could hardly lift. The bloody thing came crashing down and I very nearly broke my arm protecting my head. It was a very beautiful fight in its way." He was lost in the story; there was no way he was saying good-night and hanging up the phone now.

I fed him an encouraging line, "Was that a worthy punishment for your . . . crime?"

"Do you remember I told you that in our kitchen in London, we used to go up and wash the light bulb every now and then? That light bulb never did burn out, and it was on for four years! What did happen was that the lead wire, what we call the "flex" over there, burned out and shorted. All the grease and grime and acid things in the kitchen rotted away the insulation. So I got fully prepared and I made up a new lead, including a new lamp holder for this bulb, and all I had to do was switch off the electricity, slip the wires out of the rose in the ceiling, and put the new wires in. Just prior to going up the ladder, I had arranged a candle for myself and switched all the lights out. I'm half way up the ladder when this banshee comes whirling out of her room and says, 'What are you doing? Put the lights back on.' Television you know. She had this fantastic television program on. So I said, 'Just a minute, Carol, I have to do this, it will only be a minute.' It would only have taken, what, three or four minutes.

"So while I'm up there, she switches the bloody thing on again. I probably had my fingers in there. 'You could have electrocuted me!'

"'I don't care if you're electrocuted!' she shouted at me.

"So, if she didn't care whether I were electrocuted, then I didn't care if she saw her bloody program or not! I switched them off again. This time she came in and knocked over the ladder and started swearing and cursing and everything. So I stood there for a little while, and then I leaned forward and gave her a stinging four and backhander across the face. And she was dumbfounded, and then she started kicking, gouging, scratching, everything! It was a fantastic row. And then she hit me with various things. She got a chair and brought it down over my head! It was a solid oak chair all beautifully carved, it was incredible! It must have weighed fifty pounds — and she swung it like a sledgehammer."

I interrupted Tony for a second. "How tall was she?"

"Just about my height and a little over my weight. Anyway, the fight sort of flagged a bit, so I did it again."

"You hit her again?" I couldn't imagine my Tony hitting anyone, let alone a woman.

"Yeah. Well, I didn't think about it. She had knocked over the ladder I was sitting on. She was behaving like a man; I treated her like one. And so it started again and all I did was defend myself and except for those two times, I didn't hit her otherwise. Thirty-forty minutes, it lasted altogether. I was a bit distraught and het up and everything, but she was just indescribable, she had made herself into such a physical wreck mess! Then she phoned up three of her friends and said I'd attacked her. So I stood there while she said this. She put the phone down, and I said, 'What are they going to do now?'

"You'll see!"

"So I got up the ladder again and I was just replacing the bulb when her friends burst in like the police and they found her in this wrecked state, honestly, a woman couldn't look worse if she had been raped. And there I was sitting on top of this tall ladder just putting together this light. And they started shouting at me, 'What do you mean by hurting Carol?' And I said, 'I didn't touch her,' and I showed them the bruises on my arm where the chair had fallen. Anyway, it all calmed down. That was on a Friday night.

"This girl was famous because she never said please, never said thank you, the words just weren't in her vocabulary. She had no use for those words. The following Monday night, she waited for me to come home, and she apologized. And that was heavy! That was more important than the row itself. She said she was very sorry, her work had been getting her down and made her get into rages and one thing and another, and she told me she had resigned her job that day, which was a good job, you know, she was in the publicity department of the BOAC. So she decided to be a musician instead and I found myself about two weeks later actually helping her transport a piano across London which is another story and not for tonight."

"Save it for when you come to this room — and hopefully not find this piano still here!" I had moved into our new apartment, and the bedroom contained an upright piano that was good enough to keep. The piano was still there when Tony next came to visit me, and he helped to move it down the front steps, having roped it and provided the planks on which to slide it with a minimum of friction. He was still wearing his suit and tie while he stood at the top of the stoop releasing the rope little by little to the waiting arms of the guys on the sidewalk.

"We've just filled up thirty minutes of a sixty-minute cassette," he noted with approval.

"Bring it with you so I can hear it, too."

"Okay. Good night, my darling."

"Good night."

He should have turned the tape over and recorded the piano story, because even though he did tell it to me — I'm sure he did — I can not recall it, any more than I can recall listening to this tape when he came to Brooklyn to be with me in our new home two days later.

## March, 1989

March came in with a phone ringing in each paw. London called first. It was David Leppard, a reporter from the London *Sunday Times* who was doing an article on the unreturned property of the Pan Am 103 victims. Tony Stoppani had given him my name, because of the wedding ring.

"Do you know when it will be returned to you?" Leppard asked.

I didn't. Next a friend called to say she had given my name and phone number to Douglas Martin, who wrote human interest stories for the *New York Times*. "He wants to interview you."

"Fine. Set up an appointment with him. Anytime will be okay with me."

Ten days later, as I was preparing for bed, the phone rang. It was Sherry Price. She was coordinating a meeting of our group and the Lockerbie police. They were supposed to meet with us the next morning to discuss the unreturned property. I had not been planning to attend. I was too preoccupied planning my second tribute to Tony, a gathering of friends scheduled to take place the next day.

"But you must come tomorrow morning. The Scottish police have something to give you," Sherry insisted.

"Tony's ring! But why didn't anybody tell me?"

"It was going to be a surprise. They assumed that everyone in New York area would come. Then I learned through the grapevine that you weren't going to be there."

"Don't worry. Nothing could keep me from going! Thanks, Sherry."

Alan and I arrived at Police Plaza in downtown Manhattan and made our way through security and the polished halls to the corridor outside the auditorium. Two police officers from Scotland were waiting for us there.

"Mrs. Hawkins? And this must be young Alan. Please sit down on the bench. I'm terribly sorry, but this is the best way we could think of to return this to you."

He was so handsome and his accent so charming. He reached into the pocket of his dark jacket and took out a small package. Visible through a clear plastic sealed bag marked 107/A.L.H. 94 was a tiny blue box. He opened the bag and the box for me. I glimpsed the golden band. It was the closest I ever came to seeing Tony's body.

"Of course it's the ring!" I snapped the lid closed and looked away.

"I'm very sorry, Mrs. Hawkins. We all are." He left the bag in my hand, stood up, and slowly walked towards the auditorium.

"I'll design our ring, luv." Tony had sketched a band with eighteen small squares in three rows of six on the curved surface. In the top row, second from the right end, a tiny chip of lapis lazuli, my birthstone, filled the square. This touch of asymmetry was a Hawkins' hallmark. Over the years, almost all the rings he gave me as gifts had this characteristic of one stone set off to the side.

A jeweler friend in Washington made them to our specifications. She ended up making three versions for me, because the chip of lapis lazuli kept falling out. The first time it did so was four months after our wedding. I took the ring off my finger intending to have her reset the stone. But before I could do so, our home was burglarized and the ring stolen along with all the rest of my jewelry. The second time, seven years later, a few months after we moved into our new house, we were burglarized again, and the ring was snatched along with other precious items. When it happened a third time, I refused to remove the ring. It remains on my finger with an empty space where a piece of blue stone should be.

Tony's ring remained intact and he never removed it from his hand. I took it to be symbolic of his loyalty unto death.

"Excuse me, did you just come from the Pan Am 103 meeting going on inside with the Lockerbie police?" On the steps outside the building, a young black man, with camera slung around his neck and a notepad in his hand, approached me.

I glared at him. "What paper do you work for?"

"The *New York Post*."

"I never give interviews to the *Post*. Find a better paper to work for!" I grabbed Alan's hand and strode off, surprised by the intensity of my fury. "*New York Post*" had set off the image of me blowing my nose over the caption, *"Widow still grieves after one month,"* on their front page. At three months, I was still a babe-in-the-media-woods. I still believed that one paper was significantly different from another, that tabloid journalism was more exploitative than mainstream. By the end of the month, I would know better.

When Douglas Martin of the *New York Times* interviewed me for hours in his apartment, his wife and baby son wandered in and out of the room. It felt like a conversation with a sympathetic person rather than an interview. Even though I could see him taking notes on a pad, it never occurred to me that everything that tumbled out of my mouth was "material." And so, when it appeared in print, on Saturday, March 18th, 1989 in his column, "About New York," with my photograph under the headline, *"Mother Struggles to Fill Void Left By Bombing of Flight 103,"* I was dismayed by what I read.

The article began with the moment I told Alan that his father was dead. I had described that moment exactly as it had happened, but Martin altered my account in two subtle but significant ways. Alan and I often referred to Tony as Tony as well as Daddy. It depended on context or mood which name was used. I know I had said, "The plane that Tony was on was in an accident," but Martin had decided, perhaps, that it wasn't believable for a mother to call her child's father by his first name, and so he had substituted "Dad." That didn't bother me as much as the second modification. Alan had pressed his face into my right breast, and when he said, "Well, you can get married again," the words were muffled by my shirt. Martin has him *"shoving his head hard into a pillow. After long moments he looked up and said, 'Well . . .'"* This is more than editing for clarification, conciseness, for pacing — this is rearranging reality in order to "improve on it." In the "paper of record," this false version has been there on microfilm in every library of the world.

Perhaps it was naïve of me not to realize that Martin would report any of the truly intimate things that I had shared. *"We had a difficult year of confrontations and challenges and my testing his love, but we had a wonderful fall and it was just getting better."* But the worst breach of confidence, from my point of view, was Martin's including the fact that Tony had let his three life insurance policies lapse, *"but had apparently been embarrassed to tell her."* What was the point in gratuitously revealing that detail?

The interview was picked up and excerpted in many papers abroad. One quotation came back to confront me when I finally made the pilgrimage to Lockerbie the summer of 1989. *"The representative proceeded to ask if Helen would like a free trip to Lockerbie. The reply: 'There isn't a place in the universe I'd like to go less.'"* When the people in Lockerbie heard my name, they smiled and said, "What made you change your mind, then?"

The day after the Lockerbie police returned Tony's wedding ring, Alan and I drove with friends to the Ethical Culture Society of Brooklyn. I thought it would be comforting to create a more informal, inclusive opportunity to gather together in Tony's memory. I reserved space and time in the building where Tony and I had been married and invited friends and family to join me. We looked at a selection of photographs that Tony had taken expressing his varied interests: children, architecture, dancers, fire-fighting, wall murals of the Lower East Side. Then we sat in a circle in the sun room and shared our recollections of him.

I called on people in chronological order, beginning with Mary at whose New Year's Eve party I had met Tony sixteen years earlier, and concluding with a man who was one of the last people to have seen Tony and me together on my birthday three weeks before he died. Alan wandered in and out of the room. The gathering was relaxed yet focused. I had asked each person who wanted to speak to share a particularly vivid or significant memory. That afternoon, I listened to the same story told twenty times.

When someone dies, you can walk all around them and see them whole for the first time. You either discover you knew the central truths about them, or learn that they gave you only a partial glimpse of themselves. Tony was so coherent that everyone who met him met the same person. He did not take any secrets with him when he left us.

Mary: "I know Tony best in relationship with Helen and Alan. We used to go and visit Helen's friend at her farm in western Virginia. Alan, who hadn't seen Tony for several days, insisted that Tony come into the living room and play trucks with him. And I was really struck how patient and how loving and how much pleasure Tony got out of playing with Alan. He had a wonderful sense of play and they were terrific together . . ."

Hillary: "We were involved with a small theatrical group in Brooklyn. Tony was donating his time and equipment to their production needs. He was terrific at sharing his 'toys.' We worked on several projects together.

"Tony taught me to drive, actually. You think Tony was a wild man in a car, but in reality he had incredible control over that machine. As a teacher, he was remarkable. He took me down near the Brooklyn Bridge and he took a piece of wood and leaned it up against the bumper of the car and said, 'Okay, as soon as you can put the car in first and move forward and then put the car in reverse and move backward without letting the piece of wood fall, you can drive my car.'

"Tony had a tremendous impact on my life . . . I'm still involved in audio today because of Tony, clearly because of Tony . . . He talked me through two promotions and four boy-friends. He was a terrific friend."

Annette: "Tony was going to pick me up at the corner of 66 Street and Second Avenue. He telephoned me before he came: 'By the way, luv, I've a splitting headache., would you bring down two Tylenol?' And just before he hung up, he said, 'Oh, bring a glass of water with you, luv.'

"Now that may have sounded to Tony like a perfectly simple request, but I live on the 16th floor. How am I going to get this water down to Tony without spilling it all over, without making a spectacle of myself? So I found a plastic cup, filled it, wrapped it in aluminum foil and put it in a plastic bag and carried it out to Tony on Second Avenue. He unwrapped it without any comment, said, 'Oh, thank you, luv,' and drank off the water and the Tylenol. I realized at that point that Tony was a very self-possessed person. He had a sense of himself. When he offered you a favor, he offered it with his whole heart and soul, and when he asked a favor, he expected you to give it with your whole heart and soul."

Syeus: "The Great Spirit — something that you know is there, you can't put your finger on it but it somehow affects you — and that's always the feeling I had about Tony. . . . There was an immediate sense of interest in what you were involved with, what you were doing, how you were feeling. And it was always an interest in the other person, which I always found somewhat beautiful and telling in terms of his quality and his contribution."

Michael: "One of the things that most impressed me about Tony was his enthusiasm . . . and ability to disarm. There was this story about coming home one day and somebody pulled a gun on him, some drug addict looking for money, and Tony yelled out, 'Watch it, he's got a gun!' and confused the guy so much, he ran off."

I read a letter from a friend in Prague. We had been her guests during our honeymoon and she had visited us in Brooklyn two years ago. "My mind is in 1986. He was so kind and sweet to me when he took me to the airport on my way to Los Angeles. We talked about Alan's possible religious affiliation. He said, 'We will let him decide when he'll be able to make decisions.' This was his philosophy — utter respect for another person's view . . . And the real milk he brought me for me while you were bathing, Alan, how I appreciated it. How he waited for me late at night at the airport . . . He was a very beautiful human being — or is . . . If there is an 'after,' I might meet him."

That afternoon, I understood for the first time since Tony's death that he was gone and never coming back. Until that afternoon, I hadn't known I was in thrall to magical thinking. Oh, I knew Tony's body was dead and buried, but Tony himself was so vivid, still so palpably a presence, I didn't feel bereft. He was just searching for a new body to dwell in, and when he found one, he would find me again and I would recognize him and we would be reunited. I didn't think these thoughts, I felt them. They supported me. They were the reason I traveled each day's trajectory with energy and optimism. Hearing one person after another describe this man, I realized that though I could find the same qualities again in other people — generosity and wit and warmth had not been buried along with him — I could never find him. The man whom everyone referred to familiarly and affectionately as Tony, named Anthony Lacey Hawkins when he was born on November 13th, 1931 in Mitcham Surrey, England by his parents Henry Lacey Hawkins and Clara Alice Stoppani, was unique and irreplaceable.

Then it was time to go, but we couldn't leave immediately. Alan suddenly doubled over with severe stomach cramps and lost control of his bowels. Two friends stayed with him while another drove me home to get him a change of clothes. He had wandered in and out all afternoon, mostly playing the garden and so we thought he hadn't heard what people said about Tony.

"I could talk about Tony forever," my friends exclaimed. "That was wonderful. Let's do it again!" But we didn't, because in the days that followed no one was eager to reminisce about Tony. No one except Alan:

• "I remember so many things about Tony! I remember he told me that the news people never tell you what you need to know. They tell you all this junk."

• "I wasn't expecting Tony to die yet. The people who put the bomb on the plane, they should understand that they killed people we want! They should go to jail for a year! If they've killed some of our people, we should kill some of theirs."

• "There should be new rules in the airports. Like, if you find a bomb, take it away immediately and detonate it. The police have special people."

• "Why did they put the time devicer on it so it blew up in Scotland? Why didn't they make the plane blow up on the ground and then some people wouldn't have been killed, like Tony."

It took a month for Alan to weep for the first time. We were standing between the mirror and the coat rack in the hallway, when Alan said quietly, "I don't know how to say this, but I want you to read the magazine article Tony read to me on the astronauts . . . It reminds me of Tony. It memorizes Tony."

I dropped down to his height and we wept in each other's arms. "You are squeaking like a mouse!" he said, and patted my shoulder.

"Let's go upstairs to the nursery," I said, "and I'll read you the article. Would you like to listen to Tony's voice too?"

"No," Alan replied, "I want to forget this upsetness! It upsets me too much to hear his voice. He should never have gone to England! . . . So we'll never see him again, our genius Tony. He *was* a genius, you know. He was our hero," Alan declared.

One night, while I was at the kitchen sink, he paused in the doorway and said offhandedly, "I miss Tony, but not that much. I do say to myself, when is Tony coming home?" He looked at me expectantly, waiting for me to say the magic words: It's all been a mistake. Tony is coming home tonight!

Another night, as I was putting him to bed, he suddenly said, "I want to sleep with Tony tonight."

"When I feel that way, I listen to his voice."

"Let's listen to his voice," he agreed. This was the first and only time he asked to hear a recording. After we listened to a tape I had made when Alan was two and a half years old, so he could hear himself as well, I asked him,

"Are you enjoying this?"

"Sort of. Let's just lie quietly for awhile. I don't know what I want."

When I showed him a photograph of Tony as a young boy holding a cat in his arms, he asked me, "How old was Tony when he died?" "Fifty-seven." "Too young. He was much too young! Wouldn't it be wonderful if the magician who could bring Tony back to life could bring him back as a boy and he'd still be your husband, with that cat?"

"I remember so many things about Tony!" he continued. "He used to fall asleep with one arm up over his head like this." Alan lay down on the bed and lifted his right arm at right angles to his body as though saluting. "When he was in the army, the other soldiers used to tell him he did this.

"We went to bed once after 1 o'clock. You were asleep. We had milk and cookies and then he read to me. I minded Tony 'sloping off' (Tony's term for falling asleep while sitting on the rug reading out loud, leaning back against Alan's bed).

"Tony used to say, 'Toe sandwich! Yum Yum! And make believe he was going to eat my feet with lettuce and tomato and butter."

Sometimes Alan would spontaneously mimic Tony's voice. Driving in a car, he would point to the slowpoke driver directly in front of us and say, "Get along, Swifty, move along Swifty!" Or he would reply in an exaggerated accent, "You're velcome," quoting the punch line of a joke Tony used to tell.

A few weeks before Tony's death, I had found the two of them on the couch in front of the TV, Alan in tears on his father's lap. Tony explained that the film they were watching about a dog had made Alan sad. While watching *Dr. Zhivago* with me two months after Tony died, Alan had become extremely agitated when the doctor became separated from his family on the train. "He's got to get back to them! He's got to get back to them!" And when, at the film's conclusion, Dr. Zhivago was not reunited with Lara, Alan had sighed, "He never saw his family again and never was with any lovable people again."

During a thunderstorm, he was fearful of being alone. He insisted that I stand outside his door. "I feel safer."

At Easter time, he wept bitterly when his eggs cracked. He sobbed for a long time. "They are my eggs. Nothing will make me happy!"

A few days after the "memory circle" at Ethical Culture, we went up and down the streets of our neighborhood, distributing petitions about aviation safety and security on behalf of the new group which had just formed, "The Victims of Pan Am Flight 103." Alan asked me if Tony knew about the Construx toy he was holding in his hand.

"No, I don't think he does. But you can tell him anyway. I talk to Tony every day."

"What's the use? He can't hear you."

## CHAPTER FIVE

### April, 1973

It rained all day the first day of April, the day Tony moved to Brooklyn. I awakened to its insistent rhythms and lingered in bed, luxuriating. In slow motion for hours, I did some errands, returned home, and resumed sleeping. He woke me in the late afternoon when he arrived, letting himself in with his key. He rushed up the stairs to the bedroom, opened the door and stood in the doorway looking at me before he took off his jacket and kicked off his shoes. He lay down beside me and took me in his arms.

"My darling, we are together now!"

The rain subsided to a drizzle. We unloaded the van in an hour. "Let's leave the unpacking for tomorrow. I have a better suggestion." I took his hand and led him up the stairs, through our bedroom, into the bathroom and pointed to the tub. He grinned. This tub, filling almost the entire width of the tiny bathroom, was deep enough for the two of us to bathe in simultaneously, wide enough for the two of us to float side by side.

"I'm going to keep you well loved and content and all to myself!" he said. We sat facing each other, slowly soaping one another. "You're pretty, a good cook, writing a book and sexy too. How can that be?" He grinned at me and slid his hand under my knee.

"My wife."

"My husband."

We fell asleep in each other's arms listening to a broadcast of "Under Milk Wood," Tony's favorite radio play, blessing us on the beginning of our life together.

It rained for five days. Every morning I woke to kisses, every afternoon and evening we made love. He embraced me at supper, when I was washing up at the sink, loading clothes into the washing machine. He came home early one afternoon, found me snoozing on the couch with the cats, and joined me there.

"Oh Tony, we'll wear ourselves out! I keep creeping into the back room of the lab to doze in order to get through the day!"

"But you're irresistible! We deserve this joy." He silenced my feeble protests with kisses.

Our desire was inexhaustible. By the weekend, bright breezes blew the sun back into town. After breakfast, we walked to the Botanic Gardens across the broad boulevard of Eastern Parkway, which was softened by lime-green blossoms on the maple trees. Magnolias circled the bronze sundial like brides, daffodils clustered beneath pine trees on the hill. Weeping cherries let down their cascades of pink tresses at the edge of the pond's green water. We hurried home and made love. By night's fall, I could not tell where I ended and he began. We were living at the center of the world.

"To wake in the morning and find you here! I'm in heaven with you, Helen." He floated into me and remained, almost motionless. He cupped my eyes, making a private stereopticon of his large hands, shutting out everything but his blue eyes. When he could speak, he said, "I don't know a moment with you that hasn't been a joy."

His boss wanted him to swing south for a week and visit dealerships in Virginia. Tony arranged to have it coincide with my spring break, which began mid-month. We headed straight for Washington and a reunion with Senter and Mary.

We drove through Washington's flowery arcades of sugar maples and pulled up in front of 2001 19th Street. Senter and Mary, were standing on the sidewalk, waiting for us. "So," said Senter curling his mustache, "you're still together!"

Tony put his arm around my waist. "We're inseparable!"

The next day we drove west out of Washington on Route 66, turned left onto 340 at Front Royal, followed it over the Blue Ridge mountains south to where it joined 81 below Staunton, and then cut over to Raphine on 252. That route, which we had carefully chosen, enabled us to be aware of the geology of the Appalachian Valley, formed by ridges and valleys, wave after wave laid down in a northeast-southwesterly pattern. When we paused for lunch at wayside picnic tables along the Blue Ridge Parkway, Tony stretched out along a bench, smiling in private reverie. In a mischievous mood, I grabbed a camera and bent over him for an extreme close up.

He murmured, "You'll get used to me, I suppose."

"I should hope so!"

"I mean, my propensity for going horizontal. Horizontal is best!" He grinned at me. "Horizontal is good!" He said the phrases as though proclaiming them from a stage.

"That's what I'm going to write on your tombstone: "Tony Hawkins — Horizontal At Last!"

In Charleston, I detoured into the 18th century at Jefferson's home Monticello for two hours while Tony did some business in town. Late afternoon, he picked me up and headed towards Lynchburg. As we drove through the George Washington National Forest and descended to the Piedmont, we noticed that many more trees were in new leaf than the red maples and tulips along the Blue Ridge. The spring comes earlier to the valley floor.

We turned on the TV in our motel room to watch the evening news and caught President Nixon's address to the nation. The Watergate scandal was unraveling rapidly. About a week after we met, the trial of the Watergate burglars had opened. At the beginning of February, the Senate had voted unanimously to set up a select committee to investigate charges of corruption in the 1972 elections. By the end of March, one of the burglars had said that politicians had approved plans for his crime. Now here was the President himself, after months of denying that anyone in the White House or the Committee to Re-Elect the President was involved in this 'very bizarre incident,' as he referred to it, telling us that he was withdrawing his claim to executive privilege.

Nixon was a man we loved to hate, and in some peculiar way he was punctuating the rhythm of our lives. Tony first set foot on American soil the day of Nixon's first inauguration, considering it an unfavorable omen.

Four years later, he was laughing with me at the Mock Inaugural of Nixon's second opportunity to uphold our Constitution. Maybe it was because Tony lived in Washington D.C.; maybe it was because he took such a personal interest in the scandal as it developed that Watergate became entwined into the fabric of our lives.

Three days later, we arrived back in Washington and had our very first "row." We went to a carpet shop to choose a covering for the bare boards of our living room floor. He left to buy some liquor for the wedding, assuming I wouldn't wait for him to return. But I waited the two hours, believing our arrangement required me to be there for him, and growing angrier and angrier at his thoughtlessness. By the time the low slung orange Datsun pulled up at the curb, I could barely speak.

We sat in the car until I calmed down. I began to laugh. "You were right, Tony. Our first quarrel was about something you should have done and didn't!"

## April, 1989

Two weeks after the press conference in January, less than two months after we had buried our dead, one hundred relatives gathered in Hackensack, New Jersey and organized themselves into The Victims of Pan Am Flight 103. I missed this very first meeting, but I attended the second one, held on March 5th in Tony Roma's, an Italian restaurant in Queens. A reporter from the Scottish press was there to cover the event. He was a quiet, respectful man who seemed to be completely professional, but I couldn't trust him until I read what he was going to write about us. I would always be wary of reporters after their treatment of me at the press conference in January. Thirty people sat around a horseshoe table and identified themselves by their own names and that of the person they had lost. It was the second opportunity to get to know these people in an intimate setting, away from the glare of lights and a predetermined format like the High Mass at St. Patrick's Cathedral or the press conference at The Hyatt. We had mingled after the Mass, so some of the faces and names were familiar, but others were new to me.

Bert Ammerman was there, the man who had emerged at the Hyatt as a natural leader, all but upstaging Paul Hudson, who had organized the press conference. I hadn't approved of his tactic of holding up to the cameras a copy of the *Washington Times* with its headline claiming knowledge of the perpetrators of the Pan Am bombing, and challenging President Bush to respond to "this act of war!" — but standing in his shirtsleeves, arms folded, leaning back against the wall, bringing us up to date on the February 19th meeting of our new organization, he was impressive. He spoke rapidly, without any notes, seeming to have the gift of total recall. He outlined the four goals of The Victims of Pan Am Flight 103: to provide support and information to family members, to lobby for an independent investigation of the bombing and actions of the FAA, Pan Am and State Department, to identify and provide specific recommendations for long-term improvements in airport and airline security, and to demand that the U.S. government implement a more aggressive policy towards terrorism.

The Victims Pan Am Flight 103 had formed committees to implement these goals. People had already begun contacting their respective Congressional representatives in a massive letter-writing campaign to alert both Houses of our existence and to push for an independent investigation. A delegation was planning to go to Washington on March 14th to testify before the Senate Subcommittee on Transportation Appropriations.

The rest of us might still be stunned, reacting in post-traumatic slow motion, but Bert was wired. He identified our problems and issues and a course of action to follow. As long as he was in charge and radiated confidence, I felt safe. I knew what to do and knew I could do it.

By the time Douglas Martin's feature on me appeared in the *Times* on Saturday, March 18th, a major breakthrough had occurred in the Pan Am bombing, and my interview became a close-up, personal piece of the larger political picture.

"Suitcase Shards May Offer Clues to Identities of Pan Am Bombers" was the headline on page 1. *"Investigators believe they have recovered shards of the suitcase that contained the plastic explosive that destroyed a Pan Am jet over Scotland, two Bush Administration officials said today . . . But . . . they haven't found whose bag it was . . ."* On page 5 was a photograph *"of a radio-tape player containing a bomb that was confiscated from suspected Palestinian terrorists last October. It is believed that a similar device was used to destroy a Pan Am jetliner in December."* Why the choice of the indefinite article, I wondered — *"a*

*Pan Am jetliner"* — as though there were others. By squinting, I could just make out the brand name: Toshiba and model: BomBeat 453. Was that a coincidence or a pathologically sick pun?

Beneath the photo of the BomBeat radio-tape-player bomb was the third major article that day, "Bomb Victim Relatives Urge Tighter Security." Bert Ammerman was described as *"leader of the Victims of Pan Am 103, which was formed recently by families of the Americans who died on the plane."* He voiced our outrage: *"I've had relatives of victims calling me from all over the country, hysterical,"* not about the radio-tape-player bomb or the suitcase shards, but enraged about what they had read in the papers and heard over TV and radio the day before — namely that the "Airlines [Were] Given 3 Warnings Before Pan Am Jet Bombing."

It seems that on at least three occasions in November and early December, the airlines had been specifically warned about a bomb being hidden inside a radio-cassette player: the first warning went out on November 10th from West Germany and included a photograph of the bomb recovered from a Palestinian terrorist group arrested in Germany in October; the second warning came from a FAA directive to U.S. airlines; the third from the British Transport Department, also with a photograph of the bomb. Pan Am had been alerted each time. None of these warnings had been made public.

*"On the one hand, our government is telling us it can't protect us from terrorism, and on the other it's saying it won't tell us of the threats — that doesn't make sense,"* Mr. Ammerman was quoted as saying. *"If you can't protect us, then give us the opportunity to make a decision on whether we want to go on the plane."* Speaking as the leader of our group, he demanded toll-free telephone hot lines so passengers could learn whether their flights had been threatened. He called for full mandatory notification of the twenty or thirty threats each year that were considered extremely serious.

Senator Alfonse D'Amato, Republican of New York, who had just introduced legislation requiring that serious threats to airlines be reported to passengers, was now calling for an inquiry into how the warnings to Pan Am had been handled. What we the survivors said to each other in private was now being talked about in the halls of Congress and was front-page news in the *Times*.

Mr. Ammerman had announced that *"hundreds of relatives of the American victims and supporters from all over the country would gather outside the White House at 2:00 p.m. on April 3rd for a prayer vigil, to be followed by a large lobbying effort on Capitol Hill. A meeting with President Bush has also been requested.*" This was how I learned that a demonstration had been planned for the 103rd day after the bombing of Pan Am 103.

After visiting my parents in Florida, Alan and I arrived in Washington on Amtrak. The train was sold out, and I met several colleagues and friends of friends aboard; we weren't the only ones choosing to spend two long nights in an uncomfortable seat and to lose two days out of spring vacation time rather than board an airplane.

The day before the demonstration, I went to the Folger Library for an afternoon of poetry. I met a woman I had known who was widowed at a young age. We had never spoken about the impact her husband's death had had on her. Now I needed to. I asked her what it had been like for her when her husband died of cancer. Much of what she said was what I was experiencing, the choices I was making: She, too, used to wear her husband's clothing, found traveling worse than staying at home. But she also had "freaked out," going through a phase when she would tell one friend she was going to be with another friend, then slip through the lie into her own solitary wanderings.

"My friends would take turns monitoring me like detectives working for an agency; they told me later that someone was always keeping tabs on my whereabouts just in case I came to real harm. I never knew. I was out of my mind for a long time."

I thought that perhaps being responsible for Alan and needing to keep my job were keeping me from sliding into that state.

And now? Where was she twenty years later? "Continually filled with joy and gratitude for what I had with him. The same memories trigger different reactions, though. And even though the raw feelings are covered over, they're still there. Recently, I came upon a portrait of him unexpectedly, and it took me right back to where I had been."

So this is what lay in wait for me: memories to ambush me the rest of my life.

The day of the demonstration, a white sun glared down on Lafayette Park. Alan and I walked towards it with a young woman who didn't know anyone on the plane, but had nevertheless traveled down from Syracuse to be with us because, she said, "It could have been me or my friends."

She reminded me of the students who used to come to Washington to demonstrate against the war in Vietnam or for civil rights.

Lafayette Park was ringed by television cameramen photographing the large crowd. People were wearing new blue buttons I hadn't seen before: "Pan Am Flight 103 — The Truth Must Be Known." I was wearing a white-on-black button: "Pan Am Flight 103 — Their Spirit Lives On." Many had pinned photographs of their dead to their clothing. People carrying masses of white carnations wove in and out of the crowd handing long-stemmed flowers to each family grouping.

Bert and Wendy, the young widow who had sat next to me at the press conference, and several other people were on a platform at the end of the park, taking turns talking into a microphone to describe their private meeting with President Bush. News of a demonstration on the 103rd day to be held across the street from the White House had shamed him into finally meeting with representatives of our newly formed organization. It was the first time since December 21st, 1988 that he had acknowledged in any way what had happened to us.

At 2:03, a bell tolled. The people on the platform began intoning the names. As each name was read, someone stepped forward and placed a white carnation in an enormous wreath mounted on a stand in front of the platform. Each was a relative or someone designated to take the place of a relative. The cameramen pushed forward and encircled the wreath, hiding it from us. I had never heard all 270 names read aloud before. I knew that people of many nationalities had been on board, and that three or four households in Lockerbie had been vaporized when the wing laden with fuel had crashed and burned on Sherwood Crescent.

Alan and I got caught in a crush. I began hyperventilating. People were weeping. It didn't feel like a demonstration, it felt like a memorial service, a second funeral, being held in the predatory glare of camera lenses. I kept my head down to evade the cameras, and, protecting Alan as best I could, found a way through the crowd to the wreath when I heard Tony's name called. I found Pat and Rachel Simpson and went to stand near them. When Martin's name was called, mother and daughter sobbed in each other's arms.

Bert was on the microphone urging us to march to the Capitol to lobby our congressmen for an official investigation into 103 and to increase airport security. People began to disperse. On my way to the Hill, I saw a group converging on the gates of the White House. They were carrying flowers, white carnations and small bouquets of varied blossoms. Some of these flowers were being handed through the narrow opening in the gates to men in suits on the other side. The gates began to close in the face of Eleanor Hudson.

Eleanor's hair was a dark cloud around her pale face. Her eyes were wild. She began screaming, "No! No! The flowers are going in. All the flowers are going in! Everyone, hand over your flowers!" And she thrust her flowers through the gates to the men in suits, and everyone behind her pressed forward with their flowers. The gates remained open until the last flower had reached its destination.

"Either she's really crazed, or she's doing a powerful imitation of a crazy lady. In any case, she accomplished her goal," I said to Alan as we walked to the Capitol.

The lobbying was well organized. Each of us were given particular Senators and Congressmen to see. To take advantage of the large number of people who volunteered, we were not necessarily assigned to our own representatives. We traveled in small groups of three or four. The group I was with actually sat down and talked with Senator Daniel Moynihan's assistant, who listened respectfully. But we didn't get further than Senator Robert Dole's life-size poster portraits of himself, or Senator Sam Nunn's wall of caricatures. Senators Frank Lautenberg from New Jersey and Edward Kennedy from Massachusetts made their offices available for our belongings.

We rushed to Union Station to make the 4:20 train to New York. We found seats near a family who were friends of the Cokers, whose twin sons had died. Alan played with their boy as I talked with his father. He was troubled that he was feeling worse than he had in December.

By this time, I knew differently. "From now on, things will only get worse for us."

Alan fell asleep in the cab from Penn Station. When we arrived home, he collapsed on the couch. The next day, he begged me to stay home, but I dragged myself to work and sent him to school. I was chewed out by my chairman. "Everyone is complaining because you are not filling all the orders. When are you going to get back to a regular schedule? It's three months already! And another thing, people resent that you are apparently doing work for your group; they see you at the xerox machine."

I had to get my act together. If I fulfilled all my professional obligations, no one could rightfully complain about me. It wouldn't matter if I continued to use the machine on my break-time.

When I returned from work on Friday afternoon I found Alan asleep on the bathroom floor. I barely had enough energy to get to my own bed, and slept instantly. It was dark when he woke me, crying, "Who will play with me now?"

"I'm sorry, sweetie, I'm just too tired to play."

He said, "If you had let me talk to Tony, I would have told him to come home. I would have known to warn him." He crawled in beside me and we both slept again.

The next day I arranged an appointment with a therapist. "It would be best if we could find him a male therapist," she said. "I'll see what I can do."

# CHAPTER SIX

## May, 1973

"That's Charlie Chaplin! I know."

"No it ain't. You wrong."

The two children sitting on their stoop on Garfield Place, midway between Fisk and Polhemus Place, stared at the spectacle strolling down their street. First came a man with a movie camera on his shoulder, walking slowly backwards, his lens pointed at a man who twirled a cane, a man in tight striped trousers, black jacket, black bowler hat on his reddish brown hair, a black velvet patch pasted under his nose above his grin. Two other people — a man wearing a khaki jacket and smoking a cigarette, and a woman wearing a long-sleeved dress which reached to her ankles, an old-fashioned hat bobbing on her head, and a 35- millimeter camera slung around her neck — completed the group.

When the children left their stoop and began following "Charlie" down the street, other children joined them, rather like a silent spontaneous reenactment of the Pied Piper. The group walked slowly and solemnly around the entire block. By the time, they returned to where they had first spotted Charlie's double and stood in line to have their portrait taken with him, the children looked like a 1970's version of "Our Gang."

"Charlie," the cameraman, and the other two grown-ups walked up the street and into Prospect Park, where "Charlie" and his "Girl" posed for a portrait in front of a clump of bushes. Tony and I were making a short film inspired from a phrase by Gertrude Stein that had seized the imagination of Frank Kuentsler, a poet friend of ours: "Charlie Chaplin walking around the corner forever and forever." "When I met Tony, I knew I had met my Charlie," Frank said.

The film has long since disappeared. What remains is the photograph of Tony and me that is prominently displayed in my living room.

The very next evening, one month before our wedding, Tony drove to the airport and took off for a cross-country business trip, leaving me alone for three weeks.

"I wish I could take you with me." He loaded his suitcase into the hatchback and reluctantly drove off to the airport, leaving me to cope with all the details remaining for our wedding and honeymoon. His boss, a married man with a woman in every major city coast to coast, was having a hard time accepting the fact that his chief salesman was no longer a bachelor married to his job. If he had known that Tony was already engaged to a woman living in Brooklyn, he would never have asked him to return to the New York office. Perhaps Tony was the only man for this job that had to be done a month before our wedding, perhaps not. But neither of us questioned the necessity at the time.

Before he left, Tony designed our wedding invitations and wrote out the original in his fine, calligraphic hand. I brought it to a printer, and then distributed them to three of our friends who were artists; they handpainted or printed original works of art on each one of them. My mother and I enjoyed a peaceful afternoon addressing them. Both of us were people who find it a challenge to be content in the moment, but we spent those hours addressing envelopes side by side, loving each other's company, loving the task.

We met with the leader of Ethical Culture Society. Mr. Box thought that ninety people would be more than the mansion could comfortably hold. That's when the idea of two wedding parties evolved, the first for family and city friends to be held on June 21ˢᵗ, the second to include friends and neighbors up at my parents' country cottage on Sunday afternoon, three days later.

While trying to record a soundtrack for that afternoon's background entertainment, I burst into tears, my technical ineptness highlighting my resentment. Why was I forced to struggle with this task alone instead of working as part of a team with Tony? Where was he?

He was on his way to California calling home every night to an increasingly frustrated and resentful fiancée. He called from Denver. "I'm very lonely and miss you very much. An air hostess approached me, but I refused her."

"Then why did you tell me about her?" How immature was that!

A week later I had fallen asleep listening to his tape-recorded voice. He woke me at 1:00 a.m. "I love you and want you now!" When I slept again, I dreamed of a woman trussed up like a chicken, turning slowly on a skewer.

The next day I woke to a chill November of the soul. It was overcast and cold. Tony hadn't called me. But a note from him was in the mail. It disappointed me. He didn't speak of his feelings or reflect on what this separation was doing to him, to us. I felt heavy, leaden. Tony now seemed a stranger. He had been gone twelve days. Who was he really? He called the next morning, apologizing for missing two nights. "I fell asleep. I'm having a hard time out here without you."

The next night, Tony called around midnight from San Fransisco. He had spent the evening with Laura and Judy, my cousins, who wanted to meet him before the wedding. "I miss you very much physically."

"And I, too. I also am very angry at you for going on this long trip at this time. Why didn't you find out if it could be postponed to August, after we return from our honeymoon? Maybe it didn't have to happen now, or to be for so many weeks. You accepted orders without consulting me."

"Yes," Tony agreed. "There's an important lesson here."

A letter arrived from Tony's mother. "You are the right girl for Tony and the right daughter-in-law for me." She was visiting from England on May 30ᵗʰ, to live with us until the wedding. She would sleep on the cot in my study, next to the bedroom. She had sent me a small snapshot of herself, the sort taken for passports. It showed a determined face with a prominent jaw. Tony said his mother was a difficult woman.

It rained all the next day. Tony called from L.A. "I didn't know what to write you. I'm so uptight. Listen, luv, they've asked me to stay another week. It would be neglectful of me not to stay as long as I'm needed."

"No, you listen, Tony," I said, trembling. "I've about had it. You didn't take anything I said the other night seriously, did you? Your mother is arriving here in a week, for Christ's sake! What's more important, your job or me? Who are you really married to, Revox or me? If you do not return early tomorrow night, you will not find a home waiting for you."

"I guess I better come home," he said softly.

"I guess you better."

"At this point I don't think I can get home much before midnight, but I'll do what I can."

"You'll find an angry resentful woman."

"And you, a frightened man."

He called back a half hour later to tell me that he had booked a flight which would bring him into Kennedy at 9:00 p.m.

"I'll be there."

A colleague of his, an Englishwoman whom I suspected had a crush on Tony, called and offered to be my chauffeur, to pick me up at 8:15. At 8:30, she called to say that she'd been delayed and would instead go directly to the airport, pick Tony up, and drive him home.

My reaction surprised me. I visualized Tony walking through the gate looking for me, and seeing her instead. I was flooded with possessiveness. *I belong there, not you! Yeah, I bet you were "delayed," I bet you planned this cute little maneuver.* I said, "I'll take a taxi," called a cab, and was on my way within fifteen minutes. The plane was delayed. I was standing at the gate when Tony finally emerged and walked into my arms.

"I almost lost you!" he murmured into my shoulder.

"And I, you."

His colleague, waiting at the baggage claim, refused to look at me. We found Tony's car in the long-term parking lot and drove home. Years later, I apologized to her for completely misinterpreting her generous offer.

Over supper at Snookey's Pub, he showed me the fortune he saved from a cookie in a San Francisco restaurant: *"You will marry the girl of your dreams."*

"I love you very much, Helen. I never want to be parted from you again."

Home to total, enveloping reunion. We had the weekend to ourselves, to repair the damage. "For five years I've been my own boss; for forty-one years, unmarried. I have to learn to think differently. I have to stop saying, 'I,' start saying, 'we'. It will be better, luv, I promise! Our vows will affect our lives for years to come. I am intending to be married forever. I've had all the girlfriends I've ever wanted."

On the last day of May, a hot, humid New York Special, Tony's mother arrived at our doorstep. Nothing Tony had said about her prepared me for the tiny, neatly dressed woman by his side who talked a streak as blue as her handmade coat. With her small eyes and powdered, pale cheeks, her pillbox hat, white gloves, and handbag, she was a Cockney version of the Queen.

Utterly absorbed in her own world, she appeared to have the attention span of a child. Within five minutes, I heard her unsolicited opinions about Indians and Pakistanis (nasty people going where they're not wanted, unable to feed themselves, always begging the world to take care of them). I learned that she had visited Italy — the most beautiful country in the world — several years ago in order to meet her Italian cousins. She seemed to have no curiosity about the city and the country she was in right now, actually, for the first time in her life. She barely had any curiosity about me.

"Do you have any Squash in this country? She finally turned to look at me. "I'm very thirsty after that long flight."

I was bewildered. "Of course we have squash in this country. I don't have some right now, but I could buy some at the market up the street. We thought we would take you out to dinner tonight at our favorite air-conditioned restaurant. But if you're thirsty we have orange and apple juice, water, milk, or beer in the fridge."

She stared at me. "I'll have some water now, thank you very much. But I'd very much like to buy some Squash at your market." I later learned that Squash was the brand name of a fizzy orange drink, and that the word the English use for zucchinis and squash was "courget."

We showed her to her room where she unpacked her suitcase and gave us her wedding present, a clock with four brass balls that moved in a halting motion. It was going to be a long month.

## May, 1989

May was the month I came unglued. For months I had been SuperWidow: volleying interviews with journalists in the morning, teaching ecological succession to college students in the evening, working at a full-time job, shopping, cooking and clearing up after dinner, all before tucking my son into bed and falling into my own. Suddenly, I had no energy any more, and my live-in support system, such as it was, collapsed overnight.

We've always had boarders as well as tenants in our house — tenants in the apartment on the second floor to pay the oil bill, and boarders because we had more rooms than we could reasonably make use of by ourselves. The fellow who was renting a room at the time Tony died was not able to relate to Alan. I asked him to leave, and within two months of Tony's death, I had found someone to help out with Alan. He was an ambitious actor, very personable and responsible. I couldn't have managed without him. But on the first day of May I found a note taped to my bathroom mirror informing me that the new job he was starting required him to be at work at 6:30 every morning, hence no more help with Alan, only rent money from now on.

I couldn't cope. I was barely discharging my duties as lab specialist; I couldn't meet the demands of my ecology course; Alan was crying himself to sleep at night. My mother called and said matter of factly, "Take a leave of absence. Now. This is just too much for you. We can help out with a loan. Alan's well-being is at stake. You can't collapse." She was right.

The next day, I told my co-worker that I was going to apply for a leave of absence without pay. She wasn't surprised. She'd been very concerned about me. Once I applied for the leave, I felt a weight lifting from my shoulders that was almost tangible. My chairman told me then that he had wanted to suggest that I apply for a leave, but felt it wasn't his place to do so.

"First things first. You are Alan's world," he reminded me.

And I was no longer capable of being Alan's grief counselor and father substitute. I brought him to meet a therapist, Maryann Santora. He was shy at first, then didn't want to leave when the hour was up. Maryann said that when asked what he wanted, Alan had replied, "Someone strong with a loud voice." Maryann's voice is very soft and feminine. "I will do my best to find an appropriate male therapist for him."

Alan wasn't the only one who needed therapeutic support and guidance. When Rabbi Goldberg first called me in April, I didn't believe his eight-week bereavement counseling program was meant for me. Other people might require such assistance. I was a pillar of strength; I inspired others, I provided a shoulder and an ear. No longer. I called the rabbi and made an appointment.

May 5th was the last day of work until September. I found a thoughtful note from the principal in my mailbox wishing me peace, understanding that I needed to do this for myself and my son, hoping that by September I'd be able to return to work full-time again.

I went for a walk in Green-Wood Cemetery, not to visit Tony's unmarked grave but to acknowledge the spring before it took off into summer. The weather was tempestuous, heavy clouds threatening to burst open, scudding across the sky, the wind tossing the trees. The azaleas and dogwoods were in vivid bloom.

I resented the thoughtless parade of blossoms luring a new generation of insects and birds into the dance. The fact that in a corner of this ground, Tony's body was turning inexorably into earth, nourishing this busy life, was not only not a comfort, it was an outrage. He belonged at my side, enjoying the black-crowned night heron hunched on the stone wall, the red-winged blackbirds — his favorites — swaying on the plumes of phragmite reeds in the marsh. Had it been in my power to do so, I would have waved a wand and restored the world to ice and snow.

Maryann found a good male therapist for Alan. Peter Marsh was as gentle and soft-spoken as he was tall. Alan was delighted. I think his request for someone with "a loud voice" was code for "man." For one hour a week, he had a man to talk to and with whom to play games. He no longer cried himself to sleep. His spontaneous recollections of Tony were sweet to savor, but pricked too.

"Do you remember when we used to hug, we called it 'family hugs'?"

"Tony and me used to steal soap from our hair to wash our legs and we used the rough brush on our fronts and we'd cheat. We'd use it on our hair. I didn't like to use it on my back, it was too rough."

"It's a good thing Tony put in the special shower before taking Pan Am 103. If Tony were here, we'd be laughing so much!"

"I didn't want to say good-bye to Tony and now he's gone away for a long time."

"Why are we talking about this? Let's read. Why did he have to go to England?"

My friend Annette invited Alan and me to spend Mother's Day weekend with her. She lived on the Upper East Side of Manhattan, and taking the subway train was like taking Amtrak to another city. We carried our overnight bag up and down the steps; it took almost two hours and three transfers to emerge at East 86th Street.

Alan, who had complained of not feeling well while on the subway, slept for several hours on Annette's couch. He woke feeling himself and enjoyed a simple supper with us, then made up a new game to play with his Lego pieces — he positioned them on the authentic Victor windup Victrola and watched them ride their own merry-go-round. He and I both drifted off to sleep in the cool lavender guest room. Alan woke once, trying to vomit, couldn't.

In the morning, he woke with a sore throat and bloodshot eyes. He sat in a stupor in front of the TV set. I thought I'd prepare a special treat for him, frozen bananas put through a blender and mushed into the texture and taste of ice cream. I had forgotten to remove the skins when I placed them in the freezer the night before. The knife slipped off the icy surface and plunged into the palm of my left hand, to the bone.

I removed the knife and looked at the wound. Clean, bloodless, and painless.

"It's really serious," I told Annette who was equally alarmed. "It's deep but it doesn't hurt."

"I think you'd better get to a hospital as quickly as possible. New York Hospital is only a few blocks away. Don't worry about Alan. I'll take care of him 'til you return."

I walked myself over to the Hospital, was quickly given a tetanus shot and told that I didn't need any stitches, and walked myself back to Annette's.

I found Alan in better shape. He had thrown up, and that seemed to have settled his stomach. His fever was gone, so we went off to Central Park to see the new zoo.

Three days later I couldn't bend the middle finger of my left hand. The morning of the fourth day, I awakened to throbbing pain. I soaked the swollen finger in hot epsom salts  while with the other hand skimming a medical plan directory for a doctor nearest my home. I suffered in his waiting room for two hours before being told to take penicillin for two or three days. He almost cost me my finger.

I went home and slept. Sleep and medication did not make me feel much better. By 10:00 p.m., the infection was spreading across my palm. It was red and swollen.

I called Merle and asked if it were possible to leave Alan with her while I took myself to the emergency room. "Alan can stay the night with us, if necessary," she reassured me.

I fully expected that after someone in the emergency room of Methodist Hospital had had a look at my hand, I would be sent home with proper medication. "You're not going home," they told me at midnight when my turn finally came. "We're giving you antibiotics through an I.V. all night long until the surgeon can take a look at you in the morning."

I slept on a stretcher in the supply station with a curtain drawn around me. I managed to sleep two hours before the nurses woke me. Whatever happened, I was being kept through the weekend.

A phone was brought to me, and I learned that Alan had slept through the night and was now home with our boarder, who had not gone to work because of this emergency. I called my parents in Connecticut. They were prepared to come to Brooklyn and take care of Alan for the duration of this crisis. I was wheeled into an alcove, where I spent the day attached to the IV but not being fed any solids in anticipation of possible surgery. My parents arrived at 5:00 p.m., as the surgeons came in to to examine me.

"We need to open up your hand. There may be pus. The tendon may have died. You got yourself here just in time."

Within moments I went from inertia to an assembly line. My belongings were bagged and numbered. I began to cry, terrified of facing surgery and anesthesia without Tony. The last time I had been in a hospital emergency room, the victim of a car accident, Tony had rushed to my side. I wept for him, for Alan, for myself. "Nothing must happen to me. My son mustn't lose me, too!" The surgeon already knew; my parents had told him.

"Is there anything we can do to make this easier for you?"

"Yes. I hate anesthesia. I hate suddenly losing consciousness. One minute awake, the next waking up in the recovery room. Can you warn me before you give me the needle or the gas or whatever?"

"Yes. And we can control it, so that you go out slowly."

He kept his word. They wheeled me into the O.R. while I was still awake. They explained everything to me again, and warned me just before anesthesia was administered. They told me what time it was, so when I woke a half hour later, I knew that nothing dangerous had been found. The tendon hadn't died, but a nasty infection from the kitchen knife would require a week in the hospital on antibiotics.

I was wheeled up to a ward with three other women: a fat girl in her twenties, a tiny Irish grandmother with a strangulated voice, arthritic hands and no legs, and a Caribbean woman. The fat girl was as connected to the TV above her bed as I was to the I.V. drip in my arm. The food was miserable, the room was hot. Friends came with their dear company and practical items, and my mother brought Alan to me that first night. We hadn't seen each other for twenty-four hours.

He was physically shy and kept his distance from me until just before he left, when he let me hug him.

"He said, 'Oh well, Helen's in the hospital, that's not so bad!' before he went to sleep last night," my mother told me, shaking her head. "Poor kid."

The day before I was to be released, a new, officious head nurse came on board. For three days, my parents had brought Alan with them when they came to visit me. I would leave the ward, and walk out to the elevator where we could have a private visit in an alcove. This new nurse denied them permission to leave the lobby and come up to my floor, and I, of course, was not allowed to leave. "Children must not be exposed to infections," was her flat explanation. "They might also be carriers of something our patients shouldn't come into contact with."

"My son is only six years old. He needs to see his mother. I need to see him. I am his only parent. I will see him at the elevator, away from the ward."

"He'll see you tomorrow when you go home. Sometimes we love our children in the wrong way."

I watched her march down the hall before I took the elevator to the lobby for a glimpse and hug of Alan before a guard separated us. I was discharged the next day, with physical therapy sessions set up once a week for several months.

We returned to Connecticut with my parents to spend Memorial Day Weekend with them. It was a pleasant and healing three days, shared with their friends. On Memorial Day, I saw a documentary about Arabs and

Jews that I could barely watch. Terrorists on both sides were interviewed, giving their cold-blooded reasons as to whether or not to toss a bomb at a particular time in a particular place, calculating who should die and when. Young people, together in a class, debated the morality of such politically motivated murder. Even though he had become close friends with a Jewish girl, it still took many excruciating minutes for an Arab youth to agree that it would be wrong to kill in retaliation if it meant his friend would be included among the victims.

I wept for a long time, lying in the darkness next to Alan.

## CHAPTER SEVEN

### June, 1973

People helped me cope with Clare. Friends and relatives invited us to dinner and gave parties. We took her to Long Pond, my parent's house in the country where the second ceremony and wedding party would be held. We took her to Washington for a weekend. Tony took her along on a two-day business trip to Pennsylvania. I took her to museums. Art was her passion, the human enterprise she honored above all others.

She had never remarried after Tony's father divorced her when their sons were grown. She supported herself by buying old houses, renovating them and then selling them for a profit. She was too old for that now, and so lived on Social Security and part-time sales jobs in department stores.

I took her to the Botanic Gardens her first day in Brooklyn and warned her not to contact her younger son Peter, as difficult as that might be for her. He was too hostile, too weird. We were sharing a quiet moment on a bench overlooking the cherry grove as a thunderstorm gathered over our heads.

"It's his birthday in five days," she said. "I have to try to see him. He's my son. I don't understand what he's doing. We sent Tony to Catholic school but we thought Peter was too sensitive. Now Tony doesn't believe and Peter has joined the Krishnas. You don't know what to do, do you?"

A week later, two days before the wedding, Peter arrived at our home to see his mother. It was a painful encounter. Clare tried to give him money. He refused. "My work is finding my path to God."

It was a relief to close the door behind his orange-robed back.

"You can see, now, why it's become impossible to invite him to the wedding, not that he'd come anyway. When we first told him in March that we were planning to be married in June, we asked him if he'd like to do the cooking for us, be the caterer. Tony says Peter is an excellent vegetarian cook. He said yes, then. Well. There's nothing we can do now."

The day before my wedding, I went to be with my voice teacher, Shirley. We sat quietly in front of her couch, she in her black swivel chair, I on the carpet. "This is a moment of such joy," she said. "This marriage means so much to the young women who are my students, who are in distress for one reason or another, unable to find suitable mates. You bring them hope, show them that they must not despair."

"I am very lucky, that's all."

When I had first raised the brass cat knocker on the door to her studio apartment eleven years earlier, I was one of the young women in distress. I was depressed, barely able to talk, let alone sing. Most of the first months with Shirley were spent talking. She became my mentor, a surrogate therapist, a spiritual mother. Her voice instruction was simultaneously guidance for rightful living. How could it not be when the stuff of singing is mind and breath, the voice an instrument one cannot put one's fingers on?

"You have to hear the tone first in your inner ear before you can produce it. Whatever you can imagine you can sing. With the proper support, you can produce any high tone as easily as a low tone. It is only fear that makes you anticipate failure. But each tone must be produced anew; supported anew; you cannot slide by on past successes. Measure the interval."

Midsummer morning, I woke first and placed my wedding gift on Tony's pillow, then kissed him awake.

"Morning, luv." He reached over for me and we held each other quietly. "What's this, then?" He opened the box and removed the lapis lazuli stone mounted on silver suspended from its silver chain. He read the words engraved on its back: "Tony 6/21/73 Helen."

"Meeting you and marrying you — pure magic."

The day was long and we moved through it in slow motion. The wedding was scheduled for early evening, but the sun was not planning to shine on us. Early morning clouds tipped over into drizzle, then showers, then a serious storm.

"Rain on your wedding day means good luck," he said, trying to sound as though he believed it.

"Says who? Probably recollections of ancient fertility rites. Anyway, we can't use the garden, that's for sure."

Mary, who had come up from Washington the night before to be my maid of honor, came to collect me and drive me over to the Brooklyn Society for Ethical Culture mansion on Prospect Park West. We had chosen to be married there because it graciously met all our needs. When we had emerged from our passionate preoccupation with ourselves and looked around for a place to celebrate our marriage, we had learned that we were merely part of a statistical trend that was threatening the Jewish American world: Interfaith marriages had reached 50 percent, and even Reform rabbis were reacting by refusing to sanction such marriages rather than welcoming the non-Jewish partner into the community. Did I really want to knock on doors and have Tony summarily rejected before I found a rabbi who would marry us?

"I'll do whatever pleases you, Helen," Tony told me, "but frankly, I would prefer a ceremony that is not religious. If that's possible."

When we met with the Leader of the Brooklyn Society, he told us, "We are often the place interfaith and interracial couples turn to, but very often we can not accommodate them because we do not offer a traditionally religious service."

Tony and I both sighed in relief. "That makes you completely perfect for us!"

Mary helped me dress in the upstairs bathroom. I had selected a dress appropriate enough for the occasion, and one I could conceivably wear again. I didn't want it preserved in plastic. It was from Mexico, white and blue-embroidered, long-sleeved and ankle-length. Shirley had given me a heavy silver bracelet as a gift. That was the "old." Mary handed me a handkerchief to complete the rhyme. "Now you have something borrowed."

I heard voices from below and went out to the landing to look down at the front door, right at the moment when our best man Steve, brought Tony into the hallway, still holding his umbrella above Tony's head. Tony, in his moss-green, velveteen suit, white shirt and yellow tie, the oblong blue lazuli necklace resting against the tie, dazzled me with his beauty. His face was relaxed, his expression alert, his hands extended towards one another, fingertips touching. I stepped back from the bannister, not wanting him to see me. I had the momentary illusion that this was the first time I was catching a glimpse of the groom, the husband chosen for me by a matchmaker.

We had planned to walk into the library together, preceded by our parents and Mary and Steve, followed by the two children, Adam and my niece Tamara. There wasn't an aisle and even if there had been, I did not want to walk down it on my father's arm to be symbolically handed over.

I wasn't prepared for the tunnel vision that enveloped me as soon as we walked through the library doors. I heard murmurings and rustlings and could sense that the room was filled with people, but I couldn't see anyone except my parents and Clare, who stood on either side of the Ethical Culture Leader waiting for us in front of the fireplace. I held onto Tony's right arm for support, praying I'd make it to the end of the long, narrowed path in front of me. I was terrified. I was walking by his side, we had been living together for months, and still I felt like I was walking off a cliff.

Adam handed the rings to Steve, who gave them to Tony. He put my ring on upside down and said the words I had written for us: "Helen, I choose you freely and in joy, to be partner, my wife, to journey with through all the seasons of our life together, to inspire you, encourage you, to nourish and sustain you, to honor and cherish you. May only death separate us. Amen."

Tamara refused to take the bouquet I handed her. It lightened the solemnity of the moment. By the time I figured out what to do with the flowers and was free to put Tony's ring on and say my vows, I kept smiling, even when I couldn't get his ring on past his knuckle.

As soon as the ceremony concluded people came over to congratulate and embrace us. The head of Tony's company introduced himself. "How did you ever manage to capture this fellow? He's broken a lot of hearts, you know."

I gave him a long, level look. "It wasn't difficult at all, was it, Tony? But I'll tell you something I've just decided — I'm never going through this again. This is my very last wedding!"

I kicked up my heels at the party. We danced, we sang, friends read their poetry and played their music, Tamara took over the microphone, hiked up her short dress and beamed us a song from nursery school. The photographer took a picture of me barefoot, enclosing Tony in a hug; he is smiling at the camera over my shoulder. We had done it!

Steve had booked a room for us in a motel on the Taconic Parkway a few miles north of the city. "He chose this for convenience," I said, "not for romantic atmosphere, obviously." We were both too exhausted to do anything except wish each other good night.

The next day, a Friday, Tony insisted on dropping by his office to check up on something. His office in Hicksville, Long Island, was not exactly on the way home. Stalled in traffic on the Kosciusko Bridge, I thought, this is not the best omen for married life.

"Surely no-one is expecting you to come in today, Tony! Can't this wait until Monday?"

"Yeah, I suppose, but here we are. It won't take long."

It didn't. After he astonished his co-workers and fiddled with his desk drawers, we left. It was just something Tony felt compelled to do, I guess, his equivalent "tunnel vision" attack. We drove home, picked up Clare and Steve, and took them with us to the movies. We held hands and laughed at the ten best sketches preserved on film from "Your Show of Shows."

Two days later, we did a lovely reprise at Long Pond. It was a steamy, hot afternoon. Our guests found shelter in the shady perimeter of the lawn facing the back deck, where we reenacted the exchange of vows. Tony put my ring on right side up, with the lazuli chip in the upper right corner. Friends sang songs and read poetry, my father made a speech, Tamara sang "Titwillow" with him.

We hired Ken Schneider, a filmmaker best known for the short, *Chicken Soup*, to film this party. His camera managed to be everywhere, even seeing things we couldn't see at the time: the moment when two beagle puppies took off into the woods, leaving their owners distraught for hours; my sister in shorts and halter hanging out laundry on the line behind my back while the formal entertainment was still going on.

At the very end of the program, at my request, a friend sang "Consummation," by Nina Simone:

"For thousands of years
my soul has roamed the earth in search of you . . ."

147

Our wedding day, June 21ˢᵗ, the summer solstice, now stands in awful symmetry with December 21ˢᵗ, the winter solstice, the day of his death.


## June, 1989

It was time for us to go to Lockerbie. Tony Stoppani called from his home in England to assure me that they could accommodate us in their home. "And I can introduce you to the police at Lockerbie, if you'd like."

The Brysons graciously offered to let us stay with them and to use their flat in Marble Arch as a base, but Alan was still fearful. "How would we get there? How do you know there won't be a bomb on our plane?"

"Because the airline companies are very careful now to prevent another bombing."

This wasn't completely true; six months after Pan Am permitted an unaccompanied suitcase containing the bomb that blew flight 103 out of the air to be loaded unto its plane without any inspection by hand — in flagrant violation of FAA and international security regulations — the FAA still found an utter lack of security in the Pan Am terminal in Frankfurt. I didn't know that until later. Even though Pan Am was still being utterly irresponsible with the lives of its passengers, the other airlines had begun to institute security procedures.

Pan Am had offered me a free flight to Lockerbie on December 21ˢᵗ. Was their offer still good six months later? Yes, Pan Am would fly us to London and then on to Scotland and back, and put us up in a hotel in Lockerbie for three days, at no charge.

"I dreamed I prevented the bomb from exploding by punching the terrorist in the head!" Alan rushed to tell me one morning. If only it were true! When I dreamt of Lockerbie, of preparing to go, I was anxious, protective, defensive. I identified the specific cause of my discomfort: It wasn't going to Lockerbie as such but flying Pan Am that was intolerable.

"I understand," said the Pan Am employee assisting me, "but I'm afraid I can't arrange a free flight for you and your son on another airline. What I can do, however, is set up a rail pass for each of you, so that you can travel around England and Scotland without charge." Though she knew that I was only going to be in Scotland for three days and in England for two weeks, she arranged for Alan and me to have passes for the entire three-week period so that even when we returned from France, we could still travel for free for the day or two that remained to us. And she arranged for us to stay at the most luxurious hotel in Lockerbie. She wasn't required to do this for us. I was very touched by her generosity.

She wasn't the last employee of Pan Am who went beyond official duties and guidelines to ease my way. Even the insurance company's representative never quibbled over my receipts. They paid for all long-distance phone calls and postage used to acknowledge sympathy cards, as well as assuming all costs of funeral, burial and headstone. Then, in June, my lawyer Lee Kreindler called to tell me that the insurers had agreed to release $25,000 of the Warsaw Convention's automatic settlement of an international airline loss of life, without challenging my right to sue them; it would simply be deducted against any settlement if and when we won in future. There seemed to be two Pan Ams: the men who had made the initial decisions to strip their airplanes and terminals of any meaningful security, concerned only about profits and reputation, and those individuals who treated us with unusual consideration, doing the best they could to help us in the aftermath of our losses.

The trip was planned for August. I intended to spend July at our cottage in Fourth Lake. Since our boarder Daniel was returning to Wisconsin, I placed an ad in the *Village Voice* looking for an *au pair* with driving skills. At the end of the summer, I hoped she would return to live with us in our home in Brooklyn. I decided to sell Tony's VW to Daniel. If I had a garage to park it, I would have kept it for Alan to play with. But I didn't have a garage or even a driveway, and the car itself was completely unsuitable for my needs. Not only was it a stick shift (I can only drive automatic gear), but it was too small to be useful as our summer transport. Selling it to Daniel, and buying a second-hand station wagon, seemed to be a good solution.

But Daniel drove off straight into an accident. We waved him good-bye at 9:30 a.m. on June 15th, and an hour later he called me from a garage on Flatbush Avenue. "The brakes stalled at the junction, and someone smashed into the right side." Could I please come and retrieve him and his luggage? It would take a day to repair the car. The right rear door was crumpled, a window was missing, the driving wheel was bent out of shape. I burst into tears. Tony loved that little car. But Daniel was not hurt, just shaken.

He left two days later, and Andy arrived in a taxi. She was the only person to respond to my ad, a theater-struck young woman from Detroit, Michigan. She had worked in summer stock in Connecticut and was eager and determined to get back to New York. She claimed to love kids and provided me with two references. "However," she added, I don't have any money for a train ticket to get to New York and my parents can't afford it." If I wanted her, I would have to pay her way.

Over the phone, Andy sounded enthusiastic and intense. Her references checked out. No one else competed for the position. I hired her sight unseen. My first view of her from my second floor study window was of an extremely thin, extremely pale girl with short orange red hair, removing her suitcase from the trunk of the taxi. It was hate at first sight. I ran upstairs to the bathroom and closed the door behind me and indulged a mini temper tantrum. "No, no, no!" I shouted, stamping the floor in frustration, "What have I done?" I knew that this girl was not as she pretended to be.

She barely said hello when I opened the door. She walked upstairs behind me, not saying a word, flung her suitcase on the floor of her new room, and announced that she was on her way into Manhattan. It was too late to find anyone else. I was stuck with her. As if reading my mind, but actually because she equally had no interest in living with us and helping me, Andy suggested that after she drive us upstate she return to Brooklyn and take care of the house, cats, and plants. I agreed immediately.

I purchased a second-hand Ford station wagon from the trusted mechanic of a family friend. The mechanic sold me the car at cost, and fixed the air-conditioning and the radiator hose.

A check for $25,000 arrived on the morning of June 21st, my 16th wedding anniversary. *Thank you, Tony. And thank you, Lee Kreindler.* The next day, I saw Rabbi Goldberg for the last session of his eight-week counseling program. He asked me how I was doing.

"Grief is exhausting. I have to go to sleep early every night. How long is this going to last?"

"The more deeply you allow yourself to experience your grief now, the more will you eventually experience joy." He reminded me to repeat his formula: "'I recognize my feelings.' Do not judge them. Do not deny them. Do not diminish them. You'll be all right. I'm here if you ever need me."

The next morning, Alan graduated from kindergarten. It was his second such graduation: When he had graduated from playschool and entered public school, we had decided to repeat his kindergarten year since, as a December baby, he would have been six months younger than his classmates in the first grade. The principal and kindergarten teacher both thought it best for him to be slightly older than his classmates. It was difficult enough making the transition from private school to public school.

Tony had been there for the first graduation, taking pictures of Alan and the other children in their miniature caps and capes. Alan seemed to enjoy this second ceremony more than I did. We didn't mention Tony's name out loud.

That afternoon, Alan and I took a train to Philadelphia for a weekend gathering of the Victims of Pan Am Flight 103. We were met by Stan Maslowski, a warm bear of man who drove us to his home in Haddonfield, New Jersey for dinner. The meeting was going to be held at the Haddonfield high school the next day.

"I would have given anything to have been on that plane instead of my daughter," he said. "To lose her would be like losing Alan. I'm not afraid of dying any more." Stan's 30-year-old daughter Diane had been living and working in London as the assistant vice-president of a major investment firm for the last three years.

Stan drove us to his home, where we joined his wife Norma, his daughter Susan, and two guests for a picnic dinner in their sunlit garden. The guests were a surprise. They came from Lockerbie and represented the town's council. Hugh Young and Moses Kungu had come to the U.S. to meet us and make amends for a rather unfortunate incident which had just occurred: Pan Am, at the suggestion of Ed, a junior high school student in New Jersey, hosted a barbecue on June 3rd for the children of Lockerbie, to compensate them for their lost Christmas. So many American families protested what they perceived to be an insensitive publicity stunt that many participating corporations withdrew from the proceedings. Disney's Mickey and Minnie Mouse declined to make an appearance; Coca Cola didn't provide the free drinks. The families of Lockerbie were surprised at the American anger and disapproval and had sent these two men to apologize. After dinner, Stan drove us to the Victorian bed and breakfast where his wife had reserved a room for us.

Childcare had been arranged by the Monettis, who also lived in Cherry Hill. They had lost their son Rick, who was one of the thirty-five Syracuse students killed on the plane. The next morning, a friend of Rick's drove Alan over to the Monetti's for the day. He was a blonde, athletic youth, as Rick had been, judging from the photos I had seen. He looked at me and asked, "What can I do for you? I feel so helpless! I don't know what to do to help, except be a chauffeur, amuse the kids this afternoon."

I didn't hesitate. I knew what he could do — what I needed, what we all needed. "Give me a hug!" He smiled and he opened his arms.

I walked to Haddonfield Memorial High School on a brick sidewalk under fragrant linden trees. I was surprised by the number of people pouring into the lobby, at least a hundred, drawn by the presence of two spokesmen from the Departments of Transportation and State.

Before the meeting began, I tried to speak to Susan Cohen. She was one of the people I read about in the *Times* coverage of the disaster, when I was finally able to read what the newspapers and magazines had to say. I had felt immediately drawn to her because she was a woman past childbearing age who had lost her only child. According to the article, she and her husband had learned of their daughter Theodora's death from their car radio en route to Kennedy Airport. She was also a writer. I thought we had a lot in common. But Susan was remote. She was on a mission. In a few minutes, I discovered what that mission was.

The first half of our meeting was devoted to our own business as an organization. We were going to hold our first election and choose our board of directors. Until this moment, the people who had gathered in The Crow's Nest in New Jersey in February had taken on responsibilities, volunteering to head up committees, and from the very first confrontation at the press conference in January, it was obvious that Paul Hudson and Bert Ammerman were natural leaders — and natural antagonists. Only one of them could be president; we were going to decide which one.

Before we got down to business, we welcomed our guests from Lockerbie. Hugh Young, a high school teacher, and Moses Kungu, the town pharmacist, offered their apologies and explanation for "Ed's Party." When approached by Pan Am, the town council had thought it would be a nice gesture for the children of the town, who had endured a traumatic Christmas and were still showing signs of distress. They really hadn't seen the event from our point of view, and were here, officially representing the town, to say they were sorry and hoped we would forgive them.

Suddenly, Susan and her husband Daniel stood up in the aisle and began hurling verbal accusations at Hugh and Moses. They accused the two astonished men of being "agents for Pan Am." " Did Pan Am pay for your flights?" they shouted. When the men admitted having been flown to the U.S. courtesy of Pan Am, Susan and Daniel stormed up the aisle and disappeared from the auditorium. They never returned to this or any other meeting. From then on, I only saw them on December 21st on our marches to the Pan Am building or to the UN, at occasional memorial services, and at the Pan Am trial when it finally took place in the spring of 1992. They became a team of two and carried on their own intensive lobbying.

We proceeded with our elections and chose Bert Ammerman to be our president. By September, Paul Hudson had resigned and formed his own organization, "The Families of Pan Am Flight 103." Several people followed him out of our group. There were political differences, tactical approaches which separated us, but essentially it was a personality issue: Did you want to work with Bert or with Paul? Given the fact that a traumatic loss had thrown us together, our schisms were predictable and appropriate. Eventually our endurance confounded both our critics and our admirers. But on that June afternoon, it wasn't so clear that we were going to make it, either as individuals or as an organization.

The press was there, both local and national, to report on what the two men from the Departments of Transportation and State might have to say to us. We had to listen to Kenneth Quinn of the U.S. Department of Transportation tell us that "we're committed to doing everything we can." Or rather, he had to listen to us.

"To my dismay, disgust and anger, I find airport security is no better than it was six months ago," Bert replied, and drew a standing ovation as he challenged the federal government "not to pass the buck to the airlines on the security issue."

Quinn tried to regain our respect by describing the new security procedures and new security technology for locating hidden explosives that were now being implemented in European and Middle Eastern airports. But all he got for his trouble was a man yelling at him, "Why wasn't that done before?"

"We have nothing to hide," Quinn insisted, but Kathy Daniels, who had lost her husband William, the father of her three children, disagreed. "I think they knew something was going on . . . certainly more than my husband did."

Frank Moss from the State Department then declared that the Helsinki Warning was merely a "coincidence." (On December 5th, 1988, an anonymous call placed to the American Embassy in Helsinki, Finland, had warned of an impending attack against a Pan Am flight leaving from Frankfurt, Germany during the weeks before Christmas. It was because of that warning that all State Department employees abroad were ordered not to fly Pan American on their flights back to the United States. If the State Department took the Helsinki Warning so seriously in December, we had no patience with the State Department telling us in June that their investigation hadn't led them to a verifiable terrorist plot.)

*"The intensity of their grief is frightening to an outsider,"* Peter Marks wrote in his *Newsday* article of November 12th, 1989. *"At a recent meeting of relatives in Haddonfield, NJ, to discus airport security and developments in the investigation of the bombing, a middle-aged woman who lost a child on the jet stood at the back of the auditorium and shrieked at a State Department official . . . 'HOW DARE YOU! . . . I AM GRIEVING THE LOSS OF MY 20-YEAR-OLD SON! DO YOU UNDERSTAND WHAT THAT MEANS? I DON'T HAVE A SON ANY MORE AND YOU STAND UP THERE AND SPEAK TO US IN THIS WAY? HOW DARE YOU!'*

*"At any other public gathering, someone in charge might have gently tugged the woman by the elbow and guided her outside to help her gain her composure. But not at this meeting or among these people. They sat quietly, not even turning to see who was letting go."*

I was among the "they" who sat quietly, but I did turn my head to see who was screaming, since I couldn't recognize her voice. So many mothers had lost sons. I felt numb. My anger stoppered my throat.

Moses Kungu offered to drive us back home to Brooklyn. He told us that on the night of the disaster he had been at work in his pharmacy in the center of Lockerbie, and had helped organize the emergency response. He was very paternal towards Alan and extended a personal invitation to visit with him and his family when we visited Lockerbie this summer. "I want our two families to be close."

# CHAPTER EIGHT

## July, 1973

The summer of 1973 was not the summer to take an extended honeymoon in Europe. The dollar was plunging every second. We lost $100 changing dollars into francs and back again. We were in trouble from the moment we landed in Paris and didn't find the car we had reserved waiting for us, and had to accept a yellow VW instead. A fellow on a motorcycle drew up alongside our car in Paris, glared at us and made an elaborate gesture, dragging his left hand under his nose, brushing both nostrils. Tony burst into laughter and promptly imitated him. The man roared away. I was frightened. "What did we do to offend him?"

"Maybe because we're driving this canary yellow VW. Maybe he hates Germans."

We drove from Paris to Prague, detouring in Germany to visit Heilbronn, home of the Beyer microphones Tony sold. At the German border, the Czechs demanded that we purchase a special visa for our rental car; they refused dollars or francs. They wanted only Deutsche Marks. They wouldn't even consider our Czech cronin, newly purchased in a minimal amount, so much per day of our intended visit. The whole point was to acquire hard currency; Czech money was valueless. Tony, in a pique of temper, grabbed the Czech bills off the table and flung them into the air shouting, "This money is no good. You don't want your own money!" So we used up the last of our Deutsche Marks crossing the border into Czechoslovakia.

Four days later, driving back across Germany, two gas stations refused to sell us gas for dollars. "Dollars are kaput!" They laughed at us and shrugged their shoulders and turned away.

"They've been waiting since the end of World War II to say that. But what are we going to do, Tony? The tank is empty!"

We were stalled in the Restplatz behind the station. Tony walked over to the car parked next to us and asked if we could buy some gas from them. The fellow said he'd gladly give us gas if we could figure out how to transfer it into our tank. Tony actually sucked on a hose to try to get the liquid moving, swallowed some and gagged. A young man gave us his emergency liter can and wouldn't accept any money. Thanks to these good people we didn't spend the rest of our honeymoon on the Restplatz waiting for the dollar to rise.

So eager were we to leave Germany that we drove all day, crossing the border into Strasbourg late in the evening of Friday the 13th of July — the eve of Bastille Day. The city was overflowing with tourists. Crowds lined the embankments to watch the gondolas jousting in the river with men dressed in medieval costumes, the entire scene floodlit. We wandered happily for a few hours, recording street sounds before searching for a restaurant where they refused to cash American Express checks. So we were forced to spend the last of our francs. The banks were closed until Monday and every hotel in Strasbourg was filled.

"Let's go to the police station," I suggested." If they can't find us lodgings, I suppose they would be obligated to put us up in their facilities, unless they're filled up too!"

"You mean, spend the night in a jail?" Tony was shocked.

"What's wrong with trying that? The cots are probably clean and certainly more comfortable than our tiny car. If I thought there were a sizeable Jewish community here, I'd seek out the synagogue and see if they could help us find a place to stay."

"Don't you have any self-respect? I'd rather sleep by the side of the road than give up like that."

I was astonished that Tony, for all his adventurousness and resourcefulness, wouldn't permit himself to cross a line of propriety someone else had established.

"What does this have to do with self-respect? It's the biggest night of the year, every place is taken, it's not our fault! And even if it were, self-respect isn't the bottom line, survival is. Maybe it's because I'm Jewish, I don't know. Asking for help isn't giving up, it's sensible. You asked for help getting gas, didn't you?"

"That was different. Any driver would try to help another driver."

We glared across the table, stuck with each other.

"Let's get out of here and drive towards Paris. Maybe we'll find something along the way," he said.

We drove in silence, down a dark, single-lane highway, past darkened gas stations and shuttered towns. It looked as though we'd be spending the night on the side of the road after all. And then out of the darkness emerged a beacon of light, a hand-painted sign, "Auberge Pour Les Jeunesse."

"Tony, that sounds like a youth hostel or something!"

It was a two-story house, visible from the road, some lights on upstairs and downstairs. It was close to 11:00 p.m.

We had stumbled into a Jesus Commune. There were young people from France, Belgium, and the Netherlands, on their way to England to see Billy Graham. They were filled up, too, but if we didn't mind sleeping on the floor or a table, blankets could be found. Or we could drive on a little further to the next town, Wassalone. There was an inn, L'Etoile, off the main square that might still have a room. They were open until midnight. Come back to us, the young people said, if they don't. Come back tomorrow night and share our campfire and food, *s'il vous plaît!*

There was a room in the ancient inn off the cobblestoned square. It was perfectly all right to pay them on Monday when the banks reopened. We were led up sloping stone steps, to a small square room with a washstand, bidet and enormous bed with clean sheets and soft blankets.

"Sanctuary at 'The Star' — who's writing this script, anyway?"

"I told you that you've got to trust yer 'awkins, luv."

We were awakened early the next morning by trumpets outside our window. Children in white blouses and dark shorts, with red sashes across their chests, were lined up in formations, readying to march into the town square.

"Tony, come see! We have ringside seats at Bastille Day! If we had gone to a travel agency, we couldn't have picked a better place to be today!"

We stayed the weekend, relaxed and restored ourselves, then drove flat out to Paris, where we were kept waiting three hours for the return of our deposit at the car rental. It was with considerable relief and a much lighter purse that we lifted off the ground and headed west towards England.

Clare welcomed us with a supper of cottage cheese and sausages and Coronation Street, the longest running TV soap opera in British history. Two days later, in our new rental car, with the Automobile Association's *Guide To England* open on my lap, I navigated Tony towards the West Country, where the needle of my imagination pointed, towards the village in north Devon where Tony's father and stepmother were waiting for us.

I was seized by desire the moment I first saw the return address on the blue air letter lying on Tony's kitchen table in Washington on Inauguration weekend —

*Hawkins*
*The Sages*
*Dolton*
*Winkleigh*
*Devon*
*England*

I longed to see The Sages for myself, to cross the threshold of its whitewashed walls and be welcomed by Tony's father under its thatched roof. I fell in love with his handwriting, his jovial humor, his name: Lacey.

"It's not his Christian name, actually. It's his middle name. He gave me the same middle name. He couldn't bear being called 'enry 'awkins, I guess. He's the only man I know who could carry off being called Lacey and not be thought of as a . . . well, you know."

"Well, so could you."

"Yeah, well, but I never wanted to be teased. I was in enough hot water as it was, for being Catholic. The boys would lie in wait for me every morning."

"What did you do?"

"You learn to run pretty fast when you're nine years old and small for your age."

The main road to The West (as Devon and Cornwall are referred to on road signs) was one lane in each direction, with cars backed up to the setting sun. Tony then proceeded to do a maneuver I wouldn't have thought possible: he began to pass each and every car in front of us, one by one, gearing up and down, tucking back into our lane before the car on the other side of the white line could collide with us. One by one. It took over an hour, but then there we were at the head of the line and free to go the speed limit and more.

"Does that qualify you for the *Guinness Book of Records?*"

"I should jolly well think so!"

We knew we had crossed over into Devonshire when the gently rolling road sank beneath the level of the fields and the hedgerows formed a continuous green wall over six feet high on either side. The trees arched over our heads in some places, enclosing us in long cool tunnels of dappled light. Tony was transported. "I had forgotten how beautiful England is! And you're here beside me!" Every time we passed a farm gate and got a glimpse of field and cows grazing on hills above our eyes, I expected to see the sea.

We reached Dolton at 10:00 p.m. It was a small, modern village. There were some picturesque cob cottages, but The Sages wasn't one of them. It was, in fact, the largest house in town, the only two-storied building. Tony's father and his wife rented a four-room apartment that had been carved out of the great house. We swung open the gate, drove around the back, parked the car near their doorway, and doused the lights. They had heard the engine and the crunch of tires on the gravel, and Pat hurried down the stairs to greet us.

"Welcome, you two! We were beginning to worry if you'd ever make it. Were you delayed by the traffic? We heard on the television that holiday makers are bumper to bumper on the main roads."

Pat was tall and slender, with very pale smooth skin, pure white hair brushed straight back over her unlined forehead, and a wispy voice. As delicate and silky as she was, Lacey was hearty and ruddy. He was standing in the living room, arms open for a hug. As soon as I saw him, I knew where Tony came from, his body and his spirit.

Lacey gave me a massive hug. "She's lovely, isn't she!" Then he hugged his son while chuckling with delight. "We've been beside ourselves waiting for you to get here, ever since we received the great news of your engagement. Such a pity we couldn't be there for your wedding, but you know my health didn't permit it." Lacey suffered from severe bronchitis and constricted arteries in his legs, the result of a lifetime of heavy smoking. We settled into the living room, sipping cups of Ovaltine and munching on Social Tea biscuits.

Tony made himself comfortable in the chair next to his father; I sat on the rug, my arms clasped round his legs, my head resting on his knees.

"Plenty of hugs at home these days!" He smiled at his father and stroked my hair.

"Yes, I have a lovely new daughter-in-law. Cuddly, isn't she! Now, tell us everything. We're starved for news. Pat and I are very happy living in this quiet little town, but Dolton isn't exactly teeming with excitement."

We chatted for an hour, then Pat intervened and urged everyone to bed.

"We have a long week of time together." She showed us to our bedroom, a cozy guest room which opened off their own. She had placed some books on the bedside table that she thought we might enjoy during our stay. I embraced her. "I'm so happy to be here, Pat. I feel as though I've come into a safe harbor at last on this honeymoon. This is going to be the best time ever, I can tell."

Close proximity to their bedroom required us to muffle our lovemaking, making it all the more exciting.

One afternoon, when the sun emerged after days of drizzle, we strolled down a lane and found a field without cows or sheep. Lying down in the tall grass we became invisible. There were slivers of rainbow around the sun and the clouds moved like sheep across the sky. I watched clouds nibble Tony's back and asked him, "How do you like grazing in this meadow?"

"There are only two buttercups in this entire field and they are right near your right shoulder!"

Days in Dolton settled into a routine of lovemaking nights and mornings, sightseeing afternoons, and evenings listening to Lacey's stories of his life in London as an art student and an advertising man during WW II.

The four of us relaxed around the dining table after another one of Pat's wholesome and well-cooked meals, lowered the lights, lit candles, and with the slightest encouragement, we were off and away to the most exciting days of their lives.

Lacey had worked for J. Walter Thompson as part of a team that, when it wasn't devising elaborate schemes to amuse themselves, was subtly helping the war effort.

Tony started him off with a leading question: "Didn't you make a paper airplane once?"

"J. Walter Thompson's was on the 7th floor in Bush House. Bush House is an enormous office block with a center quadrangle. Just as I got to Thompson's, the vogue for making paper airplanes by the art department was at its height. It started with ordinary little dart things, but each art director was competing to build bigger and better airplanes. Eventually, they were damned great things. You only had to launch 'em from out the quadrangle, they could circle round, they'd come down and you'd go and get 'em.

"But one day, the Russian art director, a chap called Obolensky, made a super one. And he launched it out, and it circled round, caught a thermal, went right over the top of Bush House and disappeared. About half an hour later, a police sergeant and another cop slowly come in, inquiring around. 'You make model airplanes?'

"Model airplanes? No, not here. This is an advertising agency."

"'Well, it's a funny thing,' he says. 'One of these things knocked down a little old lady in Fleet Street, and it's all made out of J. Walter Thompson's layouts!'"

Pat chimed in: "Dead give away!"

I could hardly speak for giggling. "Knocked her down?" I gasped.

"She was a frail old lady," Pat explained.

"Well, knock me down with a paper airplane!" I managed to say after I ceased laughing.

"Surely," I said at one point, "it couldn't have been a nonstop party for you, living in London through the war — no matter how determined you were not to give in and give up."

"Of course not. But there really was the most incredible spirit among us all, in spite of the fear — maybe because of it. And the most amazing things really did happen. Pat, do you remember when a piano in Bentall's — that's a well-known department store — stopped a bomb when it came crashing through the roof?"

"Yes. My sister-in-law slept under it, once, when she was caught in Bentall's during another bombing raid! She decided that she was probably safer there than going down into the shelter."

Undeterred by the rain, we set out every morning after breakfast with Lacey as our guide. He loved the little towns with names like Sheepwash, Chumleigh, and Zeal Monachorum, and locales like the sunken lanes and the rough coast.

Three days into our visit, we drove north and west to Crackington Harbour, where we watched families dressed in oilskins, clutching umbrellas over their heads, lined up on a pebbled beach, watching men in wetsuits surfing on waves not more than two feet high. "The English on holiday," said Tony with a smile, shaking his head.

Over Ploughman's Lunch in the pub — pickles and slabs of cheese in a roll — we caught the headline in the local paper: "Nixon Served With Subpoena." We had disconnected while on the Continent, and let ourselves remain out of touch driving towards Devon, but as soon as we reached

Lacey and Pat's living room, we plugged back in and watched a nightly roundup, with highlights from the day's proceedings.

During May, while Tony was still out in L.A., Nixon had denied knowing anything about the Watergate break in, but had admitted to limiting the scope of the investigation, "in the interests of national security." During the last week of June, John Dean had taken the stand and accused his President of having known about the White House cover-up since September 1972. It was his state's witness word against that of the President of the United States. Then, on July 13th, the day we crossed the German border into France, Alexander Butterfield, under close questioning by the Committee, gratuitously let slip an astonishing secret: Every conversation in the Oval Office had been recorded on a hidden voice activated Revox tape recorder!

Tony hooted. "Maybe I actually sold it to the White House! I did do business with them at one time."

The next morning the sun came out, and we packed a picnic lunch and took it to the North Boroughs, where I saw people sunning themselves in nests they had fashioned from egg-sized rocks on Pebble Beach. It was too windy and the water too cold to swim. Later in the day, we drove to Clovelly, a town without cars. After parking on the top of the cliff, we descended a long steep stairway of stone carved into the hillside to the town and its narrow, cobbled streets. The light was luminous, backlighting the trees draped in vines. If we had descended into Brigadoon, I wouldn't have been surprised.

The next day was our day to depart. Pat took out all her jewelry and displayed the pieces on her dresser, inviting me to choose a gift. "You are, after all, my favorite stepdaughter-in-law!"

I selected a three-piece set of small jet beads, necklace, bracelet and earrings, put them on, and hugged her. "I'll treasure these, Pat."

We all lingered by the car after loading it, not wanting to say our good-byes.

"Where's the "walking shambles?" That was my name for the landlord's huge English sheep dog who liked to sleep in the middle of the driveway, and slowly, disdainfully, agreed to leave the premises after the car horn had been blown in his ear several times.

"He's so happy you're leaving that he's making it easy for you," said Lacey. "And for us. Take it easy, son. Take good care of him, Helen. I know you will."

But Tony was not taking good care of himself. He had made me an unsolicited promise to cease smoking. He had offered it as a wedding gift. I did not ask him to do this, but once he promised me, it didn't occur to me that he wouldn't. For over twenty years, he had been a pack-a-day man, holding his Marlboroughs between thumb and forefinger straight down at his right side, concealing the cigarette in the curve of his hand as he blew smoke out of the lower left corner of his mouth. He never smoked in our bedroom, always kept a window open, disposed of the ashes, brushed his teeth before coming to bed. Still, his skin reeked of nicotine, and I was concerned about his health.

So when we sat opposite each other in a crowded café the very next afternoon in the town of Glastonbury, I nodded towards the cigarette curling smoke into the air between us and said, "What about your promise, Tony?"

He looked at me, then away. "I can't."

"What do you mean, you can't? You haven't even tried!"

"I know I can't do it now. I should never have said anything."

"You shouldn't say things you don't mean. I believed you."

Years later, I read an article about marriage that described what was happening in that moment. The writer asserted that during the honeymoon phase, the partners begin to become disillusioned with each other, that is, they begin to see each other as they actually are, no longer idealized. If one can be disillusioned without being disappointed, then real love is possible; an enduring marriage established.

We returned to Clare for our last week, although we both would have preferred to remain in Devon with Lacey and Pat. As it was, Clare had a difficult time understanding why Tony needed to take a week to be with them.

To make it easier to be with her, we went on jaunts. Tony drove us first to the suburban community his parents had moved to before the War and then to the Jesuit College (high school) he had attended. Later during that long afternoon, we drove to Farnham, in Surrey, where Tony's uncle Len lived with his new wife Vanessa. Len, the "baby," the youngest of the nine Stoppani children, was a distinguished artist and teacher who had recently been appointed to be head of Farnham Art School. He was a marvelous character, with lean, aquiline features and a forceful, original mind. His wife had prepared a generous lunch, but he concentrated on cigarettes, alcohol, and coffee. "I thrive on what's not good for me!"

Each day, we planned a full itinerary of visits all three of us might enjoy. The tension built, however, and Clare finally lashed out at me after she once again went on and on about her dress designing and I said, matter of factly, "I'm not interested in clothes, Clare."

"Then what do you do? Are you creative?" She was trembling with anger. "I write."

"Oh, anybody can write!" She dismissed me and returned to the TV set.

Tony comforted me, first with words and then with his hands. "I'm sorry, luv. She just does that to people. She finds a way to alienate them. You've treated her better than any other girlfriend I've ever introduced her to."

"It's a good thing the Atlantic Ocean separates us. We would inevitably come to blows."

Two days later, as we were packing to leave for the airport, Clare brought me her clothing patterns for my approval. I gave her the praise she needed.

During one of the afternoons we spent together in Brooklyn early in June, I had taken her to browse in our neighborhood bookstore. I pointed out the copy of *Our Bodies, Our Selves* in the center of the table, and the photograph of women of all ages and appearances walking together in a demonstration for their rights.

"I would never hold hands with anyone!" she said with a shudder, brushing one white gloved hand against the other.

Our flight was lovely, the icebergs blue jewels in the ocean, the copper sun molten on the Canadian rivers. The in-flight movie selected for our entertainment was the musical *1776* — a sly "welcome home" for an Englishman and his American bride.

Our homecoming was a shock. Landing in Kennedy Airport means driving through the unkempt highways of Queens and Brooklyn, the trash-littered streets, the potholes and the graffiti. I had found the reduced scale of houses and streets in England confining after a while, but now I longed for the green lawns and tended gardens, the cool cleanliness, the order. We landed in a heat wave, and were assaulted by the stench of garbage and throbbing asphalt.

And our house was a horror. The cats were fine and happy to see us, but the apartment was filthy and roach-ridden. Tony went back to work, and I slaughtered roaches. When Tony came home with a six-week assignment in

Los Angeles dangling like bait in front of us I leapt to be rescued from the oppressive heat and debilitating dirt. "Yes, yes! Take it!"

But we couldn't leave until the 16th of August. Tony would have to stay on in Los Angeles after I returned to work the first week in September. We were separated for thirty-six days, eventually. I looked at the pictures in the wedding album, the slides of our trip to Europe, and talked on the phone every night to my husband, who was a voice in my ear, a picture in a book, a memory in my mind.

## July, 1989

At the end of June, I loaded up the Ford stationwagon, and Andy — the thin, pale, surly young woman I had hired sight unseen to be my *au pair* — drove us up to the Adirondacks. She played a tape of *Les Miserables* during the entire drive. That was fine by me; that way we didn't have to try to make conversation. *At least she can drive. That much of what she claimed about herself is true.* Within a day, she'd be on her way back to Brooklyn by bus, to take care of the house and cats, and I wouldn't have to see her again until the fall. By that time, I'd find someone else to take her place.

The evening we arrived, Alan was invited to dinner by our neighbors across the road, so I suggested to Andy that she and I eat out together in a restaurant in town. Sitting in a dark wooden booth, she told me a unbelievable story about herself, confirming my intuitive distrust. "I need to tell you something. Andy is not my true name. I prefer it to the name the family I live with in Detroit gave me, when they adopted me as a baby — Marie — but my real name is Ashley Cavanaugh. I was 16 years old when I learned that I was adopted. I'm actually the daughter of an Irish Catholic mother and an English Protestant father, who is a Peer of the Realm. I was born out of wedlock, so she gave me away to be adopted. I have six half-brothers and sisters in England."

She opened her wallet and passed it across the table to show me snapshots of a blond haired young man with chiseled features. "This is my brother Reginald. I took the photo on my last visit to England."

How did she end up in Detroit as the only child of an Italian-American working class couple? How did she find out about her biological family in England? Why was she still living in Detroit and not in England? I don't remember her answers to these logical and puzzling questions, all I remember is that there was never a moment when she was at a loss for words to interrupt the flow of this fantastic narrative.

I listened quietly, a bit stunned by this development. That wasn't all. She leaned across the red and white checkered tablecloth and said very somberly, "I know exactly what you are going through because I was engaged to be married two years ago, and my fiancé was killed in an automobile accident last year."

"How terrible," I replied, trying to read her face. "How old was he?"

"He was ten years older than me. He was divorced and had a young child."

"Yes," I said carefully, "to lose someone you love is terrible, but an accident is not at all the same thing as murder, let alone an international conspiracy. It makes the loss infinitely worse."

Andy scowled. "It was terrible enough. I wanted to commit suicide."

"Yes. I can understand that. Do you have any pictures of him too? "

She shook her head. "No. It, it makes me too sad to look at him," she said feebly.

I indicated her plate. "Have you finished? Perhaps we should go back now." I motioned for the waitress. Andy had indeed told me the truth about herself, but it was more than she had intended.

I put her on the bus with money to be applied to the next two week's salary, as well as money for painting the kitchen. In spite of my dislike for her, and my suspicions that she was a pathological liar, I still gave her the money in advance.

Ten days later she called in a panic. "I can't live on what you gave me. I can't paint the kitchen without a hundred more dollars."

"Really? Where did the $350 go?"

I panicked. What was I going to do with her? She was 250 miles a way. In two weeks I was going to be leaving for a month, traveling with Alan to England, Scotland and France. How could I leave her in charge of my home when I was thousands of miles away? I didn't want to think about it.

Six day later she woke me, hysterical. "I was gardening in the back yard and I've just been bitten by a lyme tick. My arm is swelling up. I don't have any medical insurance!"

"How do you know it was a lyme tick? I've never heard of anyone being bitten by a tick in Brooklyn. The woman across the road was bitten by a tick in Connecticut this spring. I'll talk to her about it and call you back later."

The woman across the road laughed when she heard about Andy's phone call. "It takes five days for the symptoms to show. She probably was stung by a mosquito."

When I called her back with this information, Andy abruptly said, "Forget it, goodbye," and hung up.

I called my parents and consulted with them. We agreed that I had to get rid of her before I went to Europe, and that I should oversee her departure in person. To protect my property and make sure that she could not return in my absence, I would have to change the locks. Therefore, it would have to be a surprise visit. This required planning and other people assisting me.

I turned to the mother of Alan's friend up the hill. Would she be able to look after Alan for the few days I'd be gone? Of course. Moreover, she talked me through likely scenarios and helped me think about how to improve the possibilities for the future. After talking with her, I decided that I would look for a housekeeper rather than an *au pair*.

Then I called the friends who were going to be visiting the very next weekend and told them that I would like to return with them to Brooklyn on Sunday evening. The last piece fell into place when I learned that my cousin's husband was himself planning to go to Brooklyn that night to visit with his family. He agreed to come home with me and spend the night in my house as a protective presence in case Andy became nasty or destructive.

I called Andy and gave her notice to leave as soon as possible. I was giving her the maximum opportunity to find a place by the end of the month. It was now the 18th of July. She accepted my decision without protesting. She insisted that she was now hard at work painting the kitchen. "It will be all done before the end of the month, before I go," she promised. I took the chance that she might do some damage, but I thought it unlikely, as Jay was still renting a room at the top of the house and would call me if she did anything drastic.

That Sunday night, my friends dropped me at my front door and I opened the door to a house in disarray. The unpainted kitchen was dirty, dishes were piled in the sink. I hunted in vain for two cups in which to make my cousin and myself a cup of tea. I found all the cups later, in Andy's bedroom, each containing liquids encrusted by lush and colorful molds. There was a tiny kitten mewing in the corner and the parquet floor was strewn with discarded cans and bags of used kitty litter. I brought it fresh water and food. My own cats' litter pan in the toilet off the kitchen had probably never been changed for the entire three weeks. Andy walked in as I was changing their litter.

"You have forty-eight hours to get out. I'm not leaving here until you hand me the keys as you walk out the door. You've lied to me. You've taken my money and not done anything you were paid to do."

She didn't try to defend herself.

"Where does that kitten come from?"

"The neighbors found her and I've adopted her."

"I won't permit you to take her. She deserves better than you. I will take care of it until I can find her a new home." I walked away from her protests and went upstairs to settle my cousin in the guest bedroom. "See if you can manage to be out of here by tomorrow night."

The next day I found a neighbor to take the kitten. I cleaned the kitchen and weeded the garden while Andy worked the phones. I heard her screaming and stamping her feet, pleading with her parents to send her money so she could remain in New York. She found someone to move her out the next night. I sat in the high-backed chair by the front door as they carried her belongings out to the car, waiting until she flung my keys on the table. I locked the doors behind her and immediately called a locksmith to change the locks that night. I called someone who had worked for us before. He came immediately, although it was now after 11:00 pm. He remembered Tony fondly and was stunned to learn of his death. He refused to charge me.

"Is there anything else I can do to help you? Do you need someone to help you with the house, the child? You must, now that you had to get rid of this mistake! I know some young Russian women who need work. I'll talk to them. When are you coming back from the country?"

"July 30th. This is very kind of you."

"Tell me what time and I'll help you unload the car."

Sure enough, six days later, when I pulled up to the curb, there he was with a young woman eager to work for me in the fall. I could fly off to England free to focus on what I would find there.

# CHAPTER NINE

## August, 1989

*Memory work is my work now. I need to relive Tony's last days. That is why I am going to England now — not just to grieve with his relatives and friends, to comfort and be comforted by them — but to be with the people who saw him, touched him. I need to be in the rooms he ate in, talked in, slept in, walk the streets he walked, see the things he saw. And then I have to go to Lockerbie, to follow him to the place of his death. To see the place he never saw. The last place.*
— from my journal, August, 1989

I saw all the people he had seen, went where he had been, but not in the order he did. He had eight days; I had twenty-four. My first three days were essentially the same as his; I hung out in the London flat belonging to the Brysons, whose daughter Selsie had lived with us for a couple of years, helping us with Alan and becoming our friend.

Meeting her mother, I understood where Selsie had acquired her wide blue eyes and enveloping smile. Alan spontaneously greeted her father, "You look like a kid!" and then played with him as though he were. Selsie herself stopped by later in the afternoon, and we shared a raucous dinner of carrot and coriander soup, beans, fish and chips, all crowded into their tiny kitchen at the end of the corridor.

That night, I slept in Selsie's bedroom, where Tony had stayed. Looking up at the bookshelves above the bed, I was unable to sleep for many hours. I thought about the effect this trip might have on Alan. I wanted to help him strengthen his bonds with Tony's relatives, to learn about Tony's days here. Recollections were nourishing for Alan. But he probably shouldn't accompany me, I decided, to the warehouse in Lockerbie where all the unclaimed clothing and other items are displayed — although I did want him to be with me when we were taken to the place where Tony's body had been found.

Selsie's father took Alan on a shopping expedition to Henley's, London's equivalent of FAO Schwarz, while I went to Pan Am's office in Piccadilly Circus to pick up our special train tickets. They were there, just as I had been promised in June: First-class tickets good for three weeks, and reservations at the Dryfesdale Hotel in Lockerbie.

The train left on the dot of 9:00 a.m. the morning of August 5th, a warm sunny day, bright with summer color and promise. The first-class car was almost empty. It was painted a soft mauve, the color of Alan's lavender tee shirt, the same color of the masses of loosestrife growing alongside the tracks. Alan assembled his new Pirate World Lego set, while I closed my eyes and dozed.

Lockerbie was a stop like any other. A large white sign on the side of a grey stone wall announced our destination: ScotRail's bright red logo, which resembled two birds flying in opposite directions one above the other flew above three words in blue letters: Welcome to Lockerbie.

Welcome to Coventry, Welcome to Dresden, Welcome to Guernica, Welcome to the site of the largest mass murder on British soil, the worst terrorist atrocity in aviation history, the headquarters of the biggest murder investigation in British history.

Alan and I pulled our suitcases off the train, walked through the archway to the left of the sign, crossed the car park and found ourselves in the town's main square. We located the pharmacy, where Moses Kungu had told us to meet him, and went in. Seeing the black button on my coat — Pan Am 103/ Their Spirit Lives On — a woman grabbed my elbow. "Who are you? We're the Coyles, Matt and Jan. Our daughter Trish was on the plane." They were an attractive slender couple from Connecticut, staying at the same hotel as we were. There was a certain intensity in their eyes; *there must be the same in mine,* I thought. We didn't need buttons on our coats to identify our selves to each other. We arranged to meet for breakfast the next morning.

Moses welcomed us warmly and drove us to his home in Hightae, a hamlet a few miles outside of Lockerbie, where we had dinner with his family. He arranged to include Alan with his children on a trip to a local swimming club the following afternoon, so that his wife Liz and I could have the afternoon to ourselves. Alan and I were cocooned by kindness.

After dinner, he drove us to our hotel. The Dryfesdale was a renovated 18th-century mansion on a ridge overlooking the grey and white town and the green countryside. It was listed as a two-star hotel in the RAC registry at the front desk, way beyond my means ordinarily and far too formal for my taste. B&B's are more my style. I regarded the luxurious setting as another ironic consequence of Tony's death.

We joined the Coyles and their two daughters for breakfast the next morning in the elegant dining room. Matt played with Alan and his daughters fussed over him. They were on their way to Tundergarth, the village where their Trish's body had been found, four miles from Lockerbie. We arranged to meet again for dinner.

At 3 o'clock, Liz picked us up, brought Alan back to her house for the swimming party, then put herself at my disposal as a chauffeur and guide for the rest of the afternoon. "Where do you want to go today?"

"I don't really know. I didn't come to Lockerbie to see the sights, to spend the afternoon at the local castle or craft shops, doesn't feel right. I need to see the places in the town where the plane came down . . . and the cemetery, but later. I'd like to just be out of doors, walk a bit. Talk."

She thought a moment. "Yes, I know just the place. The Mare's Tail. It's a waterfall, steep climb, bit of rugged scenery. It's part of the National Trust, one of the places I had to check up on while I was working for them this past year."

"That sounds perfect. Liz, do you mind: I'd like to know where you were when the plane blew up?"

"No, of course I don't mind telling you. I was at home with our two younger children. Moses was in the pharmacy with our eldest, Katharine. I was in the kitchen preparing supper when Rachel came running in to tell me that the sky was all orange. First I thought, what a really super sunset. Then I realized that it was all lit up to the east of us, where Lockerbie is, and I thought, uh oh, there must be a terrific fire."

"You didn't hear the explosion?"

"No, for some reason, because of our location, the sound was muffled. Moses said it was like an earthquake, with the vibration and the shock waves. He was able to phone me, thank goodness, and tell me that he and Katharine were all right. There seemed to have been a serious airplane collision. You know, the first thought everyone had was that two of the American military planes that are always doing test runs above our heads had collided into each other.

"Our pharmacy immediately became a central control point, you know, for information, for supplies to help the injured. He was just going to be there to be of any assistance all night. As soon as the police and army took over, they set up the Incident Control Center in the school. They billeted the army there for weeks afterwards.

"A lot of Scotland has hill rescue dogs, and they were brought down to assist with the searching. But the soldiers did the majority of the searching for the corpses, and the material remains as well, and all the evidence, to try to piece together what had happened. Bits of the plane, luggage, personal possessions, were spread over such a huge area of the countryside. They've got some folk there still, concerned with the investigation and coordinating things for the relatives who are still coming over."

We drove quietly for a few minutes between the hedgerows, climbing higher into the mountains.

I said, "When I saw the television coverage on the 11 o'clock news that night, and I saw the houses burning, I immediately thought, 'It's a bomb.' Though it didn't have to be a bomb at all. The fire was from the burning fuel. Any plane would have burned like that, any plane coming down for any reason would have burned that way. But most planes, when they begin having trouble, don't fall in pieces. They fall intact. I think that may have been the rational clue for me. But I'm not even sure I was aware the plane had fallen in pieces. I just had this certainty: it's a bomb."

Liz brushed her dark hair away from her glasses. "That was my reaction too. A plane just doesn't fall out of the sky at 30,000 feet."

"Last night, I looked at the magazine they have for sale in the hotel, *Lockerbie Remembered* — have you seen it? It's really a history of the town, with lots of photos of Rotarian sports teams and things like that. But it does have three pages at the end devoted to the disaster, with a detailed map of the center point at Sherwood Crescent showing every house and indicating all the properties demolished or injured by the crash. It gave me some understanding of the magnitude of the physical damage the town sustained. I think I could make out that only two houses were destroyed outright in the crater, but about thirteen had to be demolished afterwards, and many others have had extensive repairs to their roofs. It seems to me that many more people lost houses than lost lives."

"Oh yes, that's very true, " said Liz. "Only eleven people were killed by the crash, whereas at least thirteen houses had to be demolished, as you've observed."

"I knew the numbers — eleven on the ground, two hundred and fifty-nine aboard the plane — from the headlines in the newspapers from day one, from the lists of victims that were published. But until I saw their names and their ages and their addresses in the back of this magazine, I couldn't visualize who they were. There seems to have been two elderly women living alone in adjoining houses, a married couple in their sixties, and then two young families, parents and children, who died."

"Yes, the Somervilles and the Flannigans. The Sommervilles were entirely killed. The Flannigans — young Steven was the only one who survived."

"Why was he spared?"

"A fluke, really. He happened to be in his next-door neighbor's garage mending his sister's bike. The house was totally obliterated, the neighbor's house was also totally destroyed, but the garage was spared. It burned down eventually, but he and his friend David were able to get out in time. You see, the two wings of the plane came down on the A-74, the main north-south road just meters away from Sherwood Crescent and the Somerville house. Because the plane was only thirty minutes out from Heathrow, the wings were full of aviation fuel. The Somerville house was where the crater is. It was totally obliterated. The huge fireball engulfed all the surrounding houses on both sides of the road, some of them so badly the people inside them were killed. In others, people managed to escape in time. As terrible as the damage was, it could have been a lot worse. The plane could have come down in the center of the town, for instance, instead of the edge. Or up in the housing scheme on the hill, where the housing density is so much greater. Or it could have come down on the rail line with a train coming through, or directly on top of cars on the A-47.

"The fuselage came down in the Rosebank area, further to the east, where there was a fair amount of destruction, but none of the people on the ground were killed. And the cockpit came down in Tundergarth, which is about 4 miles from Lockerbie. I can take you up there to show you where that was. And then there was the scatter of personal possessions for miles. The army covered the area pretty thoroughly, but there's bound to be bits of plane left."

"You've just reminded me of something," I interrupted. "Tony was English, and one of the years we went to visit his father and stepmother, we went to see one of their neighbors, a young man. This was in a small town in Devon. He had created a tiny museum located in his shed, which he proudly showed us. He had collected bits of German aircraft from World War II that he found scattered about, and catalogued and displayed them on the walls of this tiny shed. I can just imagine some boy in this town, doing the same thing with bits of Pan Am 103."

And then I thought of the two boys in their shed, fixing Steven Flannigan's bicycle when death dropped from the sky. "Steven Flannigan. What's happened to him?"

"He is being fostered by a family in Lockerbie. He was a student at the Lockerbie Academy and chose to stay on in the town. I think he will stay with the family until he finishes his education. He has an older brother who was no longer living at home and who hasn't returned to Lockerbie."

"Did you know the family well?"

"Steven's dad used to come into the paper shop every morning and collect his paper, the *Glasgow Herald,* and a pack of cigarettes, and the shop is right next to our pharmacy, and his wife used to run the playschool that my wee Esther went to. Not well enough to visit at home, but well enough to see in the street and talk to. My daughter actually knew both of the girls who were killed because they went to the same dancing class on the Wednesday. And of the class of six girls, two were killed and one was made homeless."

"Was your daughter seriously affected by all this loss?"

"She was not close friends with them. Strangely enough, all my children have been very matter of fact about it. Even Katharine, who was in our shop at the time and felt and saw everything. But I don't think what happened has really penetrated her."

"So, you didn't need to give your children sleeping pills, or therapy or . . ."

"No, no. The children who live in the town, who were closer to it, some of them have been badly affected by it. But then, I suppose, it was far more immediate to them."

"I would find that incomprehensible, except for what Tony used to tell me about what it was like for him as child, living through World War II in London. As long as his family and home were safe, the war was just a glorious adventure, he said. You heard the buzz bombs overhead, you counted the seconds, and if you weren't hit, you just got on with it."

"We've arrived." We turned off the main road. We were in a glaciated valley, surrounded by bare hills, a streak of silver gray marking a hill of dark rock in the distance. We parked the car and joined the other visitors climbing a narrow trail in the windy sunshine to the top of the thin wisp of a waterfall. It was a pilgrimage of sorts — to test one's legs, to pay respect to the site, to be elevated by the effort, the view. It was an ancient landscape, domesticated for our convenience, our needs. It was indifferent to my loss. I was ready to return to Lockerbie.

Liz drove straight to Sherwood Crescent, ground zero of the disaster. Lockerbie had first come to me on a flickering black-and-white screen, as a reporter with a microphone, flames and sirens in the background. Then it had been a horrific image in the newspapers: shattered houses and a crater where the wing had smashed into the town, leaving a scorched pit the shape of a ship's keel, two streets long. I wasn't prepared for the green of the grass covering the leveled earth, the calm.

"I'm astonished that the town has acted so swiftly. I assume that new houses are going to be erected to replace the ones that were demolished."

"Yes, for all the families that lost their homes. Most of the houses had to be knocked down later, or they suffered severe structural or roof damage. But many of the elderly couples who are entitled to financial compensation from the Lockerbie Fund, they say, well, it's all right. The house insurance will pay for most of it. It would help them to have more cash, but they haven't applied to the Trust Fund.

"I think the town has decided not to rebuild here, to never replace the Somerville and Flannigan houses. I'm not sure if they are going to mark this place in some official way. They're afraid of attracting the wrong kind of attention. They hated having the town crawling with journalists. And they do have the Garden of Remembrance in the Cemetery. for the families and the tourists they can't keep away. This is a cul de sac, in a housing estate. It can't bear too much traffic."

Sure enough, while we stood there, a car drew up, and a man got out and walked to the edge of the grass. "Are you a family member?" I asked him.

"No, I'm from Glasgow. I just wanted to pay my respects."

*And so would I have done, with Tony at my side, if he had come home to me. We would have returned to England this summer, as a family, to visit his relatives, and we would have gone to Lockerbie to see the place and the fate he had so narrowly escaped.*

"Shall we go on?" asked Liz, "Rosebank isn't too far from here. That's where the fuselage landed."

Rosebank Crescent was another housing estate, or scheme as Liz called them, similar to Sherwood Crescent, on a hill at the eastern edge of the town, all the two-story houses made of gray pebbled stone, with wide gardens behind low walls. Park Place was where fifty-nine bodies had descended, many of them students from Syracuse University.

"Just as my first thought was that the explosion was two military aircraft colliding, the people on Park Place thought it was the garage blowing up. Ruth Jamison who was working there that night, had a fairly close escape herself. She took to her feet and ran hell for leather up the road away from it. The gasoline did not go up for some reason, and that was a miracle because they have huge reservoirs of tanks underground where the petrol is stored. But it didn't explode."

We looked at houses, some with obvious damage, windows still empty and slates missing from the roofs. "That was from the fireball," Liz explained. "One woman survived a direct hit on her house. Ella Ramsden. Part of the fuselage landed in her garden. Her neighbors heard her crying and dug her out of the rubble. Her dog, too. Most of the bodies were found in the rubble. There's one place left to show you in the town."

DRYFESDALE CEMETERY AND GARDEN OF REMEMBRANCE

IN MEMORY OF THOSE WHO LOST THEIR LIVES
IN THE LOCKERBIE AIR DISASTER

A bronze plaque on a black iron gate in front of a sandstone cottage. We walked past all the modest tombstones of those who lived their lives in Lockerbie. Then we came to the area recently created to accommodate a different loss: two symmetrically perfect garden beds, planted in white gardenias and blue ageratums, bordered a rectangular grass plot. The focus of attention: three small tombstones. Beyond the rough-hewn granite stones, a circular plot of grass edged in round stepping stones, with benches placed at discrete intervals in a curving arc. The entire space was enclosed by a low wall.

As we approached the three tombstones, another tombstone, black with gold lettering, previously hidden behind the center stone, became visible. It was inscribed: STEVEN LEE BUTLER, 1952-1988. "Life Is Life — Enjoy It." The stone stood in the middle of the circular plot. The granite stone in the center of three said simply: In Remembrance of All Victims of Lockerbie Air Disaster Who Died on 21st December 1988. The stones to its left and right listed seventeen names in alphabetical order.

"Those are the people whose bodies were never found," Liz said quietly. "A memorial service was said here for them in January. Some were the folk living in Sherwood Crescent who disappeared into the fireball: Jean Aitkin Murray, Thomas Brown Flannigan, Kathleen Mary Flannigan, Dora and Maurice Henry, Lyndsey and Paul Somerville — but the others were passengers on the plane. . ."

I studied the names carefully. "I thought you said Steven Flannigan lost his sister. I only see two names — and the Somervilles — I thought that was a family of four. There are only two names here."

"Yes, for some strange reason, the Flannigan girl's body was recovered, and the Somerville parents. And one of the elderly single women who died, Mary Lancaster, was found, but the other was not. Her name is listed here — Jean Murray."

"At first I thought that all of the bodies had been burned," I said, "or broken beyond recognition, but once Tony had been located and returned to me for burial, I didn't consider that there might have been families who weren't given bodies to bury. How dreadful. But who was Steven Butler? Why does he have a special stone all to himself? His body was found, so?"

"I'm not sure. Either his family wanted to bury him here, or else there wasn't anyone in his family to retrieve his body and bury it in the U.S., so the town gave him a burial here. He was in the Peace Corps, I think. I don't think anyone else is permitted to be buried here now, though."

Someone had left a bouquet of yellow roses on the grass in front of the stones. Other people had left elaborate floral tributes, heart-shaped and cross-shaped arrangements under plastic, which were grouped several feet away. A family came down the walk and stood before the stones silently.

By the following summer, when Alan and I returned to participate in the dedication of the Remembrance Room at Tundergarth Chapel (in June, 1990), there were three black stones on the pavement directly in front of the three tombstones. The two surviving sons of the Flannigan family had placed them to honor their mother, sister and father. A wall of names listing all 270 victims in alphabetical order, inscribed in six columns on three granite blocks, had been erected in front of the back wall, becoming the ultimate focus of attention in the garden.

The names are a stark roll call of each person killed. By themselves, the names can tell us only how many males and how many females died. They yield ethnic origins but there is no way to tell in this anonymous alphabetization how old each person was or what family constellations they shattered as they fell through the sky. The wall was dedicated at the first anniversary memorial service on December 21, 1989. Later, during the winter, two families placed plaques personalizing their dead: on the left side, "THOMAS BRITTON SCHULTZ, A 20-year-old American Student," the white marble stone decorated with a cross, a thistle and a bouquet of shamrocks; on the right side, "CAPTAIN JOSEPH P. CURRY, U.S. Army Special Forces, Killed in the Line of Duty, December 21, 1988," in bronze.

By the time I stood in front of the wall in June of 1990, these two plaques were no longer alone. More than a dozen others softened the wall, each one unique in its particular size and shape, material and message. Two were most unusual; they did not use any words except name and birth and death dates to teach us who this person had been.

"NICHOLAS BRIGHT, 29 August 1959 - 21 December 1988" was given a landscape in subtle bas relief: distant mountains, a golden sky, two spruce trees on a peninsula in the left foreground, a greenish expanse of water. (His widow Eleanor told me that this was a picture of the island in Maine where her husband had grown up and where his family continues to spend their summers.)

"ALEXANDER LOWENSTEIN, February 25, 1967-December 21, 1988" encircled a dramatic sculpture in bronze: two dolphins leaping out of the sea, the setting sun, shells, rocks, and seaweed reaching beyond their frame. (Surfing was one of Alexander's joys; his family had a vacation home near the Atlantic Ocean and this sculpture was created by his mother, Suse, a professional artist.)

I felt most honored to have my bronze plaque for Tony placed directly below Suse's cavorting dolphins. Its simple rectangular shape seems to underscore the circle of life above it: "ANTHONY LACEY HAWKINS, 11/13/31-12/21/88, Cherished Husband, Father and Friend, You Are Still Trying to Come Home to Us."

It was time to retrieve Alan and return to Dryfesdale Inn. I thanked Liz for a healing afternoon.

We joined the Coyle family in the dining room and continued to exchange stories. Like Tony, their daughter Trish was originally scheduled to return home on a different flight. However, in Trish's case, it was Pan Am who had steered her onto Flight 103. Trish and her friend and flatmate Karen Noonan were expecting to take a direct flight from Vienna to New York on December 21st. On December 20th, Pan Am informed her that they were no longer running direct flights from Vienna to New York on a daily basis. Thursday the 22nd was the next time. If she needed to return home on the 21st, she still could, but she would have to fly via Frankfurt and London. Trish and Karen had already checked out of their flat; their bags were packed. They chose to take the three-legged trip home.

Jan first learned of her daughter's new plans from a message on her phone answering machine Wednesday morning. "I know you want me to take direct flights, but this is the only way I can still come home today." She learned of her daughter's death from the television screen in her office later that afternoon.

Matt gave me a copy of an article about his daughter from the *Record-Journal* in Meriden, Connecticut. *"The terrorists think they killed Trish Coyle along with the other 258 passengers on Flight 103, but they were much too late for that. For in the short span of twenty years, she had packed too much living for any group of madmen with some twisted cause to ever obliterate. (Trish's high school class presented a memorial granite bench to Sheehan High School listing her many accomplishments and awards: Vice President Class of 1986, Varsity Scholar, National Honor Society, Literacy Volunteer, German Club, Tennis Captain, Girls Football Captain, Class of 1983 Scholarship Award, Daniel Sullivan Scholarship and Boston College.)*

*"They silenced her heart, but they couldn't kill the love that it contained. They stilled her brain, but they couldn't cover the understanding that Trish so vividly exhibited. They drew the breath from her body, but they couldn't overcome the effects of her compassion. Tricia's love, understanding and compassion will live on in the heart of a young deaf woman from Yalesville and hundreds of others she touched long after terrorism has vanished from the face of this earth. For those are the very human qualities that will eventually bring such hatred to an end."*

I lay awake for hours that night, thinking about Tricia, thinking about Tony.

The next morning, Hugh Young came to the hotel to be our driver, guide and host for the day. Hugh was a high school teacher and a member of the town's council, and along with Moses Kungu the pharmacist, had come over to the United States in June to attend our group's meeting in Haddonfield, New Jersey. As soon as he learned that I was planning to visit Lockerbie, he also offered to help me. Today he was taking Alan and me to the Lockerbie Incident Center, the headquarters for the criminal investigation and the property store of unclaimed belongings. Everyone connected to the disaster went there. Assured that Alan would not have to see the property store itself, I agreed to take him along with us.

The policeman knew our names, and welcomed us warmly. "We have something for you," he said, and lifted Tony's soft gray shoulder bag, his carry-on luggage, up onto the table between us. Stored under his seat, it had survived the explosion and the fall through 30,000 feet. It wasn't even stained.

"Why don't you unzip it and see what's in there?"

I was stunned. No one had prepared me for its continued existence and normal condition. The bomb had been smuggled aboard in an unaccompanied suitcase and stored along with all the other luggage in the hold under the pilot's cabin in the front of the plane. Luggage in the hold was severely damaged. Things stored in overhead racks and under seats fared better.

It held a soccer ball — a Christmas gift for Alan — Tony's toiletry bag, a khaki long- sleeved shirt neatly folded, and a pair of black shoes stuffed with newspaper. (I didn't think to unroll the paper until I sat down to write this account and retrieved the bag from where it had been stored these ten years in my basement. The paper was a sheet from *The Mail* on Sunday, March 12th, 1989. Three months after Tony died, someone had carefully crumpled up newspaper in the toe of each shoe to help keep its shape.)

His documents were in a plastic bag labeled with his code number and name. These included snapshots of Alan that Tony had brought with him to show his family; a tape cassette (recording his visit with his cousin Tony Stoppani's family); snapshots that his cousin Tony had given him to show us (these were withheld from me pending further investigation; this was the evidence the police were currently examining); his passport; his billfold with about $100 in bills; a check addressed to AAA renewing membership (that's why they had never received it!); his business card file containing his Pan Am World Pass expiring December, '88, *The Independent Magazine* 17 December, 1988, and a black-and-white pocket address book I had given him for a birthday present on his last birthday. Its theme was Navajo rugs, and I had written on the red fly leaf page, *"For my darling Tony who is as warm and beautiful as any of these textiles, which, though created for practical purposes are imbued with classic beauty, simultaneously artifact and art; a state of grace to aspire to in our own lives."* The ink was smeared and the book warped from the wet, its red pages dusted with a fine yellow mold.

This bag, so soft, so vulnerable, had fallen just as far and just as fast as Tony, but its seams weren't split, its zippers weren't torn off their tracks. Tony loved this bag; he took it with him whenever he traveled. He had lifted it up and settled it on his right shoulder, raising his shoulder to meet its weight as he walked out the front doors of our home for the last time.

The soccer ball was the surprise gift within this gift. Soccer was the one sport Tony connected to. On our last visit to England in 1986, he had purchased a soccer ball to kick around with Alan in every park of every town we visited, until it was slightly the worse for being so vigorously used. This one was the replacement. Alan reached for it immediately and hugged it. (The ball lives now under a chair on the porch of our Adirondack cabin, long since deflated by overuse, too precious to discard.)

I looked through the shoulder bag one last time, hunting for the keys to the Brysons' flat that Tony had unintentionally taken with him, but they weren't there. The police eventually located and returned them to their London address. I wondered if the Brysons were ever able to use them again. Would pieces of metal still fit their locks after falling 30,000 feet into the mud of a Scottish field?

"Now, Mrs. Hawkins, we have a lot of unidentified property here you might want to look at to see what belonged to your husband — watches, cameras, tape recorders, that sort of thing, some clothing, of course," said the policeman.

"I don't wish to do so now, but I will return after lunch — in about an hour?" I glanced at Hugh and he nodded. Then I asked: "Did you, perhaps, find a large ceremonial dish? Very ornate. It belonged to his father. One of the things Tony was bringing back with him was this dish."

"That sounds familiar," said the policeman. "Wait here a minute and we'll have a look for it."

Hugh took Alan outside to kick around the new soccer ball. A few minutes later, the officer presented me with the ceremonial dish. This handsome platter, made from brass, about two feet in diameter, its surface entirely covered with intricate designs, had hung on the living room wall of Tony's father's flat in North Devon. It was something we had always admired whenever we visited him. It was one of the few large pieces Tony had been able to rescue from the flat when its contents had been summarily put up for auction after his stepmother died without a will two and half years earlier. Now it was distorted from the indignity of its trajectory. Unlike the shoulder bag, it had been in the hold unprotected from the fury of the bomb. I couldn't bear to look at it. It was far too large and awkward for me to carry. The policeman promised to have the American Consulate ship it to New York.

My mother happened to be visiting when the box arrived at my home in Brooklyn, at the end of the month. She forbade me to open it. "It can only distress Alan terribly. Why should you want to display something so damaged? Perhaps you could restore it."

"No, no. That would be wrong. I do not want to make believe nothing happened to it."

"Then put it in the basement."

That's where it sat for ten years before I hauled it upstairs from behind a stack of lumber, lifted it up onto the kitchen counter, and slit the carton open.

Its rim was buckled and torn, the entire surface undulating from the force of its fall, but not only could I  bear to look at it, I found it surprisingly beautiful. It looked like a piece of sculpture purposefully molded to express its fate.

When it was hanging on the wall of Lacey and Pat's living room, I had never examined it close up. Now I saw that what was hammered out in exquisite bas relief was not a pastoral idyll, but the war between the sexes: male and female warriors attacking each other with knives and daggers, clubs, swords, and axes, spears, bows and arrows, and taking no prisoners. This was a battle to the death. Their horses, too, were fighting for their lives, rearing up or writhing on the ground, mouths open, showing their teeth. In the center, on a raised circle, was a naked woman with her arms crossed behind her back, surrounded by the tools of war. Perhaps this was Antiope, Queen of the

Amazons, carried off by Theseus to the city of Athens, and perhaps the men and women fighting so fiercely in a daisy chain of death were the Amazons battling Theseus and his army in the very midst of the city, a battle the Amazons ultimately lost. There is no way to know. The ceremonial shield is unsigned and undated. It holds its own terrible history mutely in its contorted shape.

It was loved and admired, grievously wounded, rescued and returned, buried in a box in a basement, and now, finally, restored to sight where we can see it every day. I brought it up to the top floor of my home, where it hangs from the ridge of the roof beam, suspended beneath cloud-patterned wall paper and catching the changing light of the sky through a skylight.

Hugh drove us to his home in Sherwood Crescent, where his wife gave us lunch. Hugh and Linda and their two children lived in the housing estate where the fuel laden wing had fallen. By sheer luck, their area didn't suffer any damages at all. However, when Alan went outside to play with their children after lunch, he occupied himself with collecting pieces of the plane. Even after eight months and a scrupulous police search, they were still to be found scattered throughout in the town (just as Liz Kungu had said they would be).

While I had been sorting through boxes of damaged watches and tape recorders in the property store, trying to identify Tony's (I wasn't able to), Alan had been finding jagged fragments of steel — some charred and crumpled from the force of the explosion, others tinted green and pitted by lichens, others carrying the curve of their purpose with perfectly round holes where rivets had once held the plane together. The largest demonstrated this with utter authority: a row of four shiny heads, smooth as buttons on a polished bar. No human force could have ripped this asunder, and yet it had been torn away from its backing, leaving a gaping hole instead of the fifth shank.

When Alan presented me with his afternoon's findings, I carefully protected them in a plastic bag, placed it in Tony's gray shoulder bag, and brought it back home with us. We put the bag in the basement and didn't look at it again for ten years. Handling these bits and pieces of the plane helped Alan understand what had happened to his father; it helped me, too. It was more tangible than being taken to the site where his body had fallen.

Hugh drove us into the countryside near the town. Although ninety-four bodies had fallen on to the streets of Lockerbie, primarily on Sherwood Crescent and Park Place, others, due to the trajectory of the plane's path as it blew apart, were scattered to the outlying farmer's fields. The death certificate placed Tony's body on Halldyke's Farm, several miles from Lockerbie, retrieved at 14:00 hours on December 22nd.

Hugh parked the car, consulted his map, and directed us up a rutted road. Two women were walking towards us down the hill, having just returned from visiting their site. One of them extended her right arm towards me, displaying a dainty wristwatch.

"My daughter was wearing this when . . . It's still ticking." She held it against my ear. I listened to the soft insistent tick. We looked at each other wordlessly and continued walking in our opposite directions.

"This is it, " Hugh proclaimed. We were standing on rough, shrubby ground fenced off from an expanse of green and golden fields. I expected to see the impact hole Tony's body made when it hit the earth, but there was nothing to see here except thigh-high grasses and brambles and bushes. Was his outline hidden beneath the careless spring growth? Or had the prickly surface cushioned his fall and then recovered itself as soon as his body's weight was removed? This plot of earth was keeping its secrets.

One of the secrets was an inaccurate reading of the police grid map. Tony's body hadn't been found on the shrubby side of the fence, but on the other side of the gate, in the wheat field. I didn't learn this until a few years later, and didn't have the opportunity to revisit the site until the summer of 2000, when, on our way home from the Scottish trial in the Netherlands, we returned to Lockerbie and once again walked up the hill. This time, Alan and I opened the gate and walked into the field. We stood quietly, shoulders touching. I thought about the golden field Tony and I had wandered into during our honeymoon summer in Devon, where we made love, hidden by the tall grasses. Alan bent over and bowed close to the earth, his dark clothes black against the bleached stalks.

I didn't feel closer to Tony. I didn't feel his presence at all.

"Tony was dead when he was here, wasn't he?" Alan asked as he thwacked the grass on the other side of the fence.

I looked out across the neatly mown hay waiting in green rows to be gathered, at the miniature sheep grazing in the mid-distance and the bare plateau beyond a grove of dark fir trees, and replied, "Only his body was here. He wasn't."

His body. His body had been returned to me in a sealed metal coffin three weeks after he died. No one who knew him identified his body before it was placed in that coffin; the police used dental records, perhaps, or a wallet in his pocket, or the description of his wedding ring. I could have asked permission of the mortician to be by his side when he opened the coffin, to confirm that it was really him. I didn't.

I didn't because I have never wanted my last memory of someone I've loved to be their corpse. I didn't out of respect for Tony's modesty. Though he was very comfortable being naked with an intimate, he had a horror of being seen unclothed by strangers, so much so that he wouldn't get out of bed until I had closed the drapes or repositioned the blinds. The most telling memory that guided my choice was the time that I found him sitting in the bedroom of my parent's country cottage, unable to emerge because it meant opening the door into the dining room where the entire family was waiting for him to join them, and having everyone see him with his hair mussed from his nap, his shirt wrinkled. It was a few weeks before our wedding. He wasn't being vain, as such, he was just mortified at displaying himself below a personally acceptable standard of appearance. In the end, I had to bring him a hair brush before he would set foot outside the door. I knew that he would be ashamed to have me see him at his worst, utterly defenseless.

The mortician said, "His skin was white. He wasn't burned. But it was good that you didn't look." I appreciated his understatement and didn't ask any questions.

Under normal circumstances, one sees the dead body either because one is present at the time or shortly thereafter. If that is impossible, one sees the body to identify it before burial. More than anything else, this experience is fundamental for the newly bereaved to accept the reality of the death. Pat Simpson flew to Lockerbie within days of the disaster. She told me that there was an angry confrontation between the families and the social workers on the one side, and the police on the other, over the issue of viewing the bodies, let alone claiming them and bringing them home for burial. The police included the corpses as part of the criminal evidence of mass murder and denied access to the families.

Under normal circumstances, one is handed an autopsy report within hours of its completion. We were not given ours until two and a half years later. The Lockerbie police had their reasons for holding on to them for so long — to prevent their exploitation by the media — but it came as a terrible shock to have to confront the issue so many years later. We had to choose whether or not we wanted to receive this information at all, and if we did, whether or not we wanted the photographs to be included. We had to make up our minds quickly and definitively because the police were going to destroy any records not claimed.

I chose to receive only the report, not the photograph. And when the 6" x 8" glossy, tan, sealed envelope, "On Her Majesty's Service," arrived in mid-June, 1991, I filed it away immediately. This may be the only time in my life I have been able to leave a container closed. Pandora is my middle name.

It remained unopened and unread for several years. Then one evening, after a long conversation with another widow who had practically memorized her husband's autopsy, I walked over to the file cabinet, located the envelope, broke the seal, read the five-page report, then returned it to its file folder. I re-read it recently for this chapter.

The mortician had said, "It was good that you didn't look," and he was right. Reading the dry, precise listing of Tony's "Multiple Injuries" — the phrase used on his death certificate — is all I can bear. It is as close as I have ever come to seeing his body, and it is closer than I could ever come with my eyes alone; it takes me beneath his unburned skin. When I finally learned that his body had been identified, I began to grieve; when I finally learned the extent of his injuries, I began to really believe he died.

The autopsy had been conducted over a four-day period, concluding on the day I held my memorial service for him. I had held a service as soon as possible, fearing that his body might never be found, and all the time, A. Busuttil was carefully taking meticulous notes on what remained of my husband.

The strangest thing A. Busuttil wrote was that body #094, subsequently identified as that of Anthony Lacey Hawkins, had brown eyes. Tony had blue eyes, pure blue, not mixed with grey the way mine are. His eyes were a color that matched his personality: candid and sunny. I later learned that eyes darken after death due to something that happens to the blood.

The autopsy told me how they identified Tony while his cousin was sitting in my dining room in Brooklyn, New York, drawing a picture of my wedding ring to give to the Lockerbie police. Tony's wallet in his trousers contained multiple ID documents.

The multiple injuries were listed in order from skull to feet. His body had been broken and torn in so many places that it was impossible to determine which assault had silenced his heart. It was also impossible for me to tell which injuries had occurred within the plane at the time of the explosion, and which when he was flung against the ground.

One of the widows, examining the autopsy of her husband, did not know why he had died. "Nothing was broken. He was intact. He fell into mud. Maybe if they had found him in time . . ."

I was not plagued with such haunting questions. Tony was killed a dozen times over even before the autopsy began and the knife opened his chest wall to uncover the extent of the injuries hidden from sight. The only organs found to be intact were his intestines, appendix, gall bladder, ureter, bladder, and penis. Though he had smoked a pack a day for thirty years, he would never have died of lung cancer or emphysema as his father had done: "the pleura appeared normal, some traumatic emphysema and scanty fat but no bone marrow emboli were seen. The trachea appeared healthy, with no signs of inflammation or of inhaled carbon particles." His liver "appeared healthy with no excess fat present, and no evidence of significant inflammation or fibrosis." What a way to learn that his body had healed itself in the six years he had ceased smoking.

Tony died of multiple injuries, multiple times. He died when the bomb exploded, tearing open the skin of the airplane and the air pressure and oxygen plummeted collapsing his lungs, starving his blood. He died when his body smashed to earth after falling 30,000 feet, fracturing his skull, lacerating his brain, breaking his ribs, snapping his spine at the T6 disc. He died when the autopsy carved open his chest. He died when his broken body was placed in a blue metal coffin and the lid sealed and he was shipped home. He died when we buried him in Green-Wood Cemetery.

"His body was here. He wasn't. Let's go."

"I think it's wicked of you to take a little boy like that to Lockerbie. Positively wicked. You've upset his mind. It's done now. There's nothing for it." Selsie's grandmother scolded me self-righteously as soon as she walked into the living room of her son's flat and saw Alan asleep on the couch. We had just returned from Lockerbie to London, and were alone in the room. The family was out for the evening.

I sighed. "It would have upset him more to be left behind."

"Why's he asleep then? You've tired him out. Poor thing. I met your husband. He was a lovely gentleman." She glared at me: the bad mother, the inadequate wife who failed to protect her husband and was now mistreating his child.

I stared at this tiny angry stranger and refused to respond to her cruel attacks. I was constrained by etiquette — she was after all, the grandmother of my friend — and my own emotional exhaustion. She was the worst person who could have walked in on us at the moment, and even though I disagreed with everything she said, her barbs stung. I turned away from her and telephoned Tony's favorite aunt, Laura, whose own husband had died in an auto accident, leaving her with four children to raise.

"I've been with you through all of this, believe me, even though you haven't heard from me as much as I would have liked. I know exactly what you are going through. It was thirty years ago this month my husband died. That's a long time. You just have to keep going.

"Tony saw me as much as he was able to," Laura continued. "He'd pop in for a short visit returning from somewhere else. He never wanted to spend the night. So busy rushing around, trying to do too much. He was tired. He was only looking forward to going back to you and Alan. Doing his Christmas shopping. He worshipped you. Don't forget it. You did more for him than anyone else.

"I knew as soon as the plane went down, it was his plane. It shattered me. I don't think I've been the same since."

I held the phone to my ear and wept while the rain fell on the other side of the window.

Four days later I went to visit Laura on my own. I left Alan in the care of Tony Stoppani's family in Chatham, where we were now staying, and took the train back to London. Laura lived in Wimbledon, not far from where Tony had attended a Jesuit high school. When we used to visit her, Tony and I always came by car, and we always arrived at night, or so it seemed to me. It was odd getting off at a train station in daylight and negotiating the narrow sidewalks on foot by myself.

Laura lived in a small two story row house on the second floor. There was a low gate and a tiny front yard. I had always thought that her flat was tiny, too, but actually she had, in addition to the front parlor, eat-in kitchen and bedroom, a good-sized room right off the bathroom at the end of the corridor. She made her flat seem small because she filled it with things. Not a surface was clear: laundry piled high in the back room, clothes displayed on hangers outside of the open closets, magazines and newspapers neatly stacked everywhere. But the entire effect was cozy, not cluttered, and warm as she was.

We settled down to tea and cookies in front of the gas fire with her miniature white poodle in her lap. When I had first met Laura during my honeymoon summer sixteen years earlier, she was still living in a dark, nasty flat in an unappealing section of London, where her husband's company had placed her, rent-free, after her husband died. She was still stunned by his death, still struggling to raise her four children, still overwhelmed by the change in her circumstances. They had been living in a gracious suburban house. He had left her without life insurance. Within a few years, her middle son Peter, named for his father, was also killed in an automobile accident at age 16, and just as his father, he died because he wasn't protected by a seat belt.

Somehow she managed not only to keep living, but to keep caring for her other three children and, by now, her grandchildren, as well as her innumerable friends and relatives, all without a touch a self-pity. When Tony's mother had died four years earlier, she came down to stay with me in Brighton for the week after Tony had to fly back to work, keeping me company, helping me clear out Clare's flat, helping me with Alan. Whereas Tony's mother had been consumed with bitterness, Laura had only kind things to say about people and dealt with her difficulties, which included chronic ill health, with equanimity. She had never spoken of her losses to me before.

"Tony is with you. He is giving you strength. He'll never leave you. It's been true for me."

"Do you mean, you've felt Peter's presence? Not just your thoughts of him?"

"Yes. And though I'm an atheist like you, I believe I will see Peter my husband and my son again and my mother and father somehow. I don't believe in reincarnation, either. I don't advocate living alone, though that is what has happened to me. I hope it doesn't happen to you."

I cried again, listening to her, but she did not. Not that she was beyond tears. "I still cry myself to sleep sometimes. The pain gets better, but it never goes away completely. Every time I look at the doorway, I see Tony putting his hand there, as he turned to go, his last visit. I loved him. He urged me to take care of myself, get myself together so I could come over and visit you in New York."

"When did he come to see you that last time?"

"His last night in England. He had just returned from New Milton, visiting his father's sister, and it was so late. I urged him to sleep here but he refused."

"Do you know exactly where he went after he left you?"

"No. I assumed he was going back to Farnham."

"But I just visited with Vanessa two days ago and she still insists that he didn't come back there his last night, so where on earth could he have gone? Among other things, he was taking back some of his father's things stored in their attic, so if he didn't sleep there, he must have already packed and loaded them in the car. Why would he have chosen to go to a hotel? He would have wanted to spend as much time with Len, that was the reason for his trip in the first place! It makes me very uncomfortable not to know where he spent his last night in London."

It didn't bother Laura the way it did me. "It doesn't really matter now, does it?"

And it didn't bother Selsie's father. He smiled and declared, "Everyone is entitled to take one secret with them to their graves," when I told him that I hadn't solved the mystery of Tony's whereabouts on his last night. Tony was entitled to take as many secrets as he wanted to his unwanted grave, but not where he spent his last night alive. I couldn't explain my agitation at the time, but I think that it had to do with needing to be able to follow his footsteps until the very moment the airplane doors closed behind him. Not to know where Tony slept his last night was to lose the trail, lose my connection with him.

It didn't make sense that he hadn't returned to his uncle's home. Of course, that is exactly where he had gone! Vanessa's memory was simply wrong. Len had been too ill to question during the seven months before he died, but fortunately his sister Marie recalled his telling her that he had seen

Tony for the last time on the morning of the day he was killed. They had breakfasted together before Tony drove his rental car back to the airport. Marie shared this critical piece of the puzzle when she came to visit me in Brooklyn a month after I returned from Lockerbie, unraveling that small but painful knot.

I was successful in finding out when Tony had exchanged his return ticket. Both Mr. Jones at the London Pan Am office and Tony's cousin confirmed that he had changed his flight the day after he called me for permission to do so. His cousin added a disturbing detail: Tony had tried to book the earliest flight leaving on the 21st, but the only one with seats still available was the evening flight, the 103. Until that moment, I had assumed Tony had selected Flight 103 to give himself as much time as possible during his extra day. But all he was interested in was another night in England so that he didn't have to choose between visiting his Aunt Violet or our friend Mavis. If he had only arranged to see either one of these two women on his third or fourth days, he wouldn't have called me on the morning of his fifth day feeling pressed for time and seeking to stay "one more day."

Though I reassured Tony's Aunt Violet again and again during the three days we visited her that she was in no way responsible for Tony's death and she shouldn't add feelings of guilt to her considerable anguish at his death, I did secretly resent that it was because of arranging to visit her on the night he should have been flying home safely that Tony had been torn from us.

Before we left London, I took Alan along with me to meet David Leppard, the reporter who had phoned me in March inquiring about unreturned property. He invited us to visit him at work. We took a taxi to the edge of the Thames, beyond architecture, beyond history, beyond the city of people's homes and lives. The building that loomed before us was a neon fortress. IDs and phone calls and passes were required in order to penetrate this heavily guarded realm of *The Sunday Express*.

David himself was a pleasant young man with glasses and rumpled hair. He showed us the vast humming presses from the height of a catwalk. Then he took us to the morgue, where dead articles are reverently stored, and let me sift through the Lockerbie file, pulling out any that I wished to take home with me, and he promptly arranged to have them copied. I noted that many more articles focussed on the individuals who had been killed and the reactions of the people of Lockerbie than in American newspapers and magazines.

He gave me a copy of David Johnson's book, *Lockerbie, The Real Story*. Johnson, a journalist with Radio Forth in Edinburgh, had rushed to publish his sensational version of the terrorist conspiracy first, and by May, 1989 it was on the stands. Without any proof, he named two individuals who were among many of the early leads the police were following about who might have brought the bomb onto the plane. This was privileged information. Johnson's careless disregard for journalistic ethics caused irreparable harm and excruciating anguish to the families of the two "suspects" who were later proved to be innocent beyond doubt.

I already knew that about Johnson's disagreeable book. I didn't know he had caught me in his net as well. "You're in the book," Leppard warned me. "He's given you two pages."

"What? He never interviewed me!"

"He didn't have to. He's obviously used someone else's interview without attribution."

He had taken Douglas Martin's feature story on me in the *New York Times* and, without giving him any credit, made subtle but significant changes in what I said, probably to cover up his theft. "This can't be legal!" I said.

"It's not, but it happens all the time. Martin's article is in the public domain. All he had to do was to quote it accurately with footnotes, but that would have spoiled the effect he's trying to create — close ups interspersed with narrative, as though he put the entire thing together himself."

I felt violated, and ashamed that my vanity was wounded. The very first time I see my name in a book — and my words are twisted out of context or altered without my knowledge or approval. It was much worse than what Douglas had originally done, which was to include statements I hadn't realized he would quote, about my financial problems. Douglas had actually interviewed me with my consent.

The other thing that bothered me was that I didn't even come by this attention through my own efforts. The explosion had thrown me onto a stage where journalists and hacks sought me out.

I swore that I would send a blistering letter to Mr. Johnson c/o his publishers. Tony had a name for people like him: "gannets." That's what he called the tow trucks rushing by us on the road, following reports on their short wave radios from police cars and ambulances, hoping to beat them to the accident. But I never did send the letter. Compared to what he had done to the two families, this was too minor to complain about.

On our last night in London, I took Alan to see "Danny, Champion of the World," a film starring Jeremy Irons and his son Sam, based on the novel by the same name by Roald Dahl. In every one of Dahl's books for children, the children are orphans or living with people not their parents. (Matilda is the exception, but her parents are so monstrous she has to be rescued from them and adopted by her teacher.) In this story, Danny lives with his dad, his mother having died when he was born. They live in a gypsy wagon parked at the garage where Danny's father repairs engines. The relationship between father and son was so sweet, so compelling, I felt Alan basking in its warmth. Danny was even given the opportunity to rescue his dad from a difficult and dangerous situation.

"The best movie I've ever seen!" Alan declared.

He spotted the book in the airport shop a few minutes before we had to board and brought it to me triumphantly. "Now you can read it to me all the way home."

And so I did, enclosing us in a shawl of serenity. We left our private world for an unexpected adventure when Alan saw the captain of our plane strolling the aisles, greeting the passengers, and ran over to him to find out how he could be walking around while the plane was flying!

"Come and see what's going on," said the captain, inviting us to follow him up the stairs of the 747 to the upper level, then even further, up the private staircase to the cabin.

There was nobody at the controls. The plane was flying on automatic pilot. The two co-pilots were glancing every now and then at the flickering lights, but that is all they were doing.

"I preferred not knowing this," I told the captain.

"Oh, it's perfectly safe, even safer than hands on," he reassured me.

"This is cool!" Alan said, walking closer to the control panel.

"You can sit in my seat, and to make it look official, take this," said the Captain removing his hat and putting it onto Alan's head.

"Alan's head ought to be big enough by now to fill it out. The Chief of Scotland Yard gave him the hat off his head to keep, when our cousin took him there for a visit," I explained.

"Yeah, and the bobbies wanted to know why I got to wear it when they can't," Alan boasted.

"Well I'm afraid I need mine back, but you can wear it while you sit in my chair," the captain said with a smile.

"Thank you very much for doing this. This is more important than you realize. Alan used to love planes. His father would take him out to the airport sometimes, just so they could watch the planes taking off and landing. But he became one of the passengers on Pan Am Flight 103. Alan's been terrified of flying ever since. He slept through our flight here three weeks ago. To see him now, so at ease, even making believe he's making this plane fly — just wonderful. Thank you."

"I'm so terribly sorry, " the Captain said quietly. "Please accept my deepest condolences."

"We could have flown Pan Am. They offered us a flight at their expense, but I just couldn't do it. The thought of sitting in a plane with their logo painted on it . . . it was difficult enough walking through an airport."

I couldn't tell the Captain that in the hour before our departure, I had walked over to stare at the Pan Am desk, located next to Iranian Airlines, and imagined Tony checking his luggage, walking through that gray doorway, and disappearing. Walking through our own airline's corridor had given me mild vertigo; walking the gauntlet of five security checks had made me angrier and angrier. *Now they're taking special precautions. Now. This is all for show, anyway. The bomb wasn't in anybody's carry-on luggage. Are they opening unaccompanied suitcases?* But I thanked everyone at each checkpoint, and showed them my black-and-white button: Pan Am Flight 103 — Their Spirit Lives On.

The first day home, I was told that a recent TV documentary exposed how lax Pan Am's security still was, eight months later. The FAA had just fined them for disregarding airport security rules at Frankfurt.

Back home, we set up the wading pool under the apple tree and invited Alan's friends over. I overheard the following conversation with one little girl who had been Alan's friend since playschool:

Ania: "I love my mommy more than my daddy."

Alan: "I love my dad more than my mom."

Ania:"I think I want to say something. It will make you sad. I don't know how to say it. It's about Tony. He was a good man. He used to pick his nose and make us laugh!"

## August, 1988

For forty-five days the temperature never dipped below 90°. Tony and I were suffering from more than the heat wave; we were skewered by our own debts. Buying a house in the Adirondacks on impulse was draining us of money. We hadn't had sufficient savings to buy the cabin outright, and Tony was self-employed as a free-lance salesman of microphones, tape recorders and his own product, The Runaround, an editing trolley. His income was modest, unpredictable. My full-time salary as a lab assistant in a high school was sufficient to maintain us and handle the mortgage of the house we had bought in Brooklyn, but it couldn't stretch any further. Yet a bank had been willing to give us a home equity loan using our house as collateral as soon as Tony could show sufficient reliable income.

He looked for and found a job in Manhattan. He began working in December, 1986, but lost his job the following summer, the day before Independence Day. He asked me to reconsider buying the cabin, fearing that we couldn't cope with this additional financial burden, but I was filled with confidence that he would make a go of it free-lancing, and was loath to stop the process that was bringing us the house and land we both wanted. Things would work out.

So we'd gone ahead and bought the cabin and spent our first summer there. Or rather, I spent the summer with Alan, and Tony came to visit on extended weekends. It was everything I wanted it to be for us, but Tony had been right. Although he managed to make an occasional sale of a microphone, continued to sell The Runaround, and even secured a major commission from the New York University's School of Journalism, it wasn't enough. Then, at the beginning of the new year of 1988, the interest rate on the home equity loan was uncapped and burst the boundaries of our budget. We were hemorrhaging money.

We decided to use the cabin only for July and rent it to family friends in August. At least that would pay the taxes. In the Adirondacks, August is usually cool. The lake becomes too cold to swim in and the electric heating boards get turned on to take the chill out of the air in the mornings and evenings. Who knew that this August would be part of a record- breaking heat wave?

Tony drove us up at the end of June and stayed through the 4th of July before returning to work. He dropped to his knees on the living room rug to give Alan a hug and a kiss. "Good-bye boy. See you soon." He stood and gave me a massive hug, then lifted his bag to his shoulder and walked out the door. I walked him to the car and waved him down the driveway. When I came back into the living room, I found Alan sitting in a chair, withdrawn and sad.

"I feel as though I've come from a funeral," he said in a very small voice.

"Oh sweetie, Tony'll be back in two weeks. A lot of the daddies have to go to the city to work. Most of them can't come back and forth here as often as Tony can. Max and Jacob's daddy lives too far away to visit them again this summer. They won't see him until they're ready to leave here at the end of this month."

"I know. But it's how I feel."

Two weeks later, Tony returned on a Friday night, bringing Alan's best friend with him. Alan had fallen asleep on the living room floor waiting for them to arrive and woke to see not only his daddy, but Leah as well, standing in the doorway.

The next afternoon, all four of us went on a canoe ride across the lake through the marsh harbor and up the channel as far as the beaver dam. Thunder threatened our return home. We were still in the middle of the lake when we saw lightning flashing in the distance. Alan became very agitated and began to cry, "We have to go home now!" He had been caught in a powerful local storm while at the beach with his cousins the week before and was now terrified of electric storms. We made it to our front door before the clouds burst.

He ran into the living room sobbing. Tony held him in his arms. The lights flickered and went out. "I can't stand this! I can't stand this!" Alan whimpered. Leah remained calm. I scrounged candles and flashlights and set low lights around the room. Alan and Tony lay down in the middle of the living room rug side by side and within minutes fell asleep together, leaving Leah and me to listen to the storm. I read to her to keep her calm. She was wonderful until bedtime, and then she lost it. "I'm scared! I want to go home!" The only thing I could do was be matter-of-fact.

"I wish I could take you home but that's impossible. Your family isn't even home tonight, they told me they were going to a party. You can call them in the morning."

She fell asleep while I was reading to her in bed. Tony and Alan were still sleeping on the living room floor when I turned in. By the time Tony left with Leah Monday morning, we all agreed that though the children had enjoyed being with one another, they were still too young for this kind of extended weekend so far away from home.

"I want to be quiet with you," Alan said after they drove off. We spent a lot of time together that week. One night we took a canoe ride across the lake in the moon's light, but his pleasure in the adventure ceased as soon as heat lightning flickered over the distant hills.

"We have to go back now!" he cried.

"But there isn't any thunder, Alan. Listen. There isn't any thunder. That means that the storm is very very far away. It may not even be a true storm. It's probably what they call, 'heat lightning.'"

My son turned around and looked at me while he slowly and carefully tried to get through to me. "You're not afraid of lightning because you are a grownup. But can't you understand that I'm still afraid of lightning even though it's far away?"

"Doesn't it help that I'm here with you?"

"No. Just a tiny bit."

We beached the canoe and I held his hand as we hurried homeward.

"You would never remarry, would you," he asked me another night, "if something happened to Tony?"

I didn't know where these new anxieties were coming from. "Don't worry about things like that, Alan. I don't."

Five days before Tony was to come and bring us home to Brooklyn, he called to tell me he had only managed to earn $40 that day. "I'm very depressed." And I was very worried. He found us on the beach the day he arrived, his face lighting up as he spotted Alan absorbed in building a sand fortress with his friends. He crept up on him carrying his camera, but Alan looked up and saw him before he could be surprised.

We were supposed to greet our renters on August 1st, show them around the kitchen, and take off, but because the weather had been so stormy over the weekend, Tony hadn't had much of an opportunity to be at the lake. They were very accommodating about letting us enjoy a late afternoon and early evening, now that the sun had appeared, and stay the night sleeping on the convertible couch in the living room before leaving the next morning.

They weren't as pleasant with each other, however. They had long ago settled into a routine of constant bickering.

"If we end up like that Tony, we separate!"

"No danger of that happening, luv."

Alan fell asleep in the back seat as we talked quietly. We both felt peaceful. Tony was glad his family was coming home with him; I was glad he wasn't going to feel so isolated any more. But when we began talking about his work situation and our financial obligations, the air became fierce.

"I bet you wish you were alone right now," I said as we turned east toward the Taconic. I certainly did.

He answered me very quietly, never letting his gaze leave the road. "No. Whatever happens between us, I never think that. Never."

It was the significant difference between us. It was what made it possible for us to continue.

The three of us traveling together in our little car through the sea of hot, heavy air — Alan asleep in the back seat, his parents squabbling about money in the front seat — was a perfect symbol for our situation. There was no escaping the heat or the financial mess in which we were stuck. We had to ride it out until the heat wave broke and restored us to the cool, and we had to persevere until we found our solutions that would bring us financial relief.

The heat blanketed desire and thrust us apart. Under the roof of our large, un-air-conditioned house, we sought distance. Tony disappeared down into the basement seeking relief from the heat, my disapproval, his own anxieties, by constructing another Runaround for sale. At night, he fell asleep on the couch watching TV or on the floor in Alan's room or by my side — and then his snoring would wake and drive me from our bed to lie down beside Alan who, more often than not, would wet the bed before waking.

I registered Alan in a day camp, which he was reluctant to attend. Even when I gave in and let him stay home, he complained about being bored and lonely. I immediately began looking for part-time work and found it at the Curriculum Division at the Board of Education. I was given a delicious assignment to rewrite lessons on pre-human fossils in Africa. It meant I could sit at a desk in front of a typewriter in a blessedly air-conditioned room for hours each day, reading stuff that fascinated me, all the while accumulating extra dollars to see us through the summer. And Alan agreed to go to day camp.

I escaped the city, taking Alan with me, to the country house where my brother lived. The air was as hot and steamy as the city, until midnight, when I woke up shivering and groped for the string to silence the ceiling fan. The heat wave had ended! In the morning, the skies were blue again for the first time in weeks. We gorged ourselves on hot buttered corn from the farmer's market and returned home to Tony.

Alan chattered happily to me, "We have our special bath in the lake and our special shower in the rain. Wouldn't it be wonderful to swim in the air?" And, slyly, "I'd like to marry Leah. You should marry your friends since you can't marry your parents!"

Even after the heat wave broke, we still had to resolve the question of cabin we could no longer afford. A friend suggested that we put it up for sale, but try to retain rental rights for ourselves. Tony reluctantly agreed that this was the sensible thing to do, for it offered us a way out of our escalating debts without losing the place altogether.

I turned my attention to Alan's school status. He was entering kindergarten in the fall, and two obstacles remained before he could make the transition. First was the matter of the zoning game. We lived on the wrong side of the eastern boundary of the good school district by one block. The school in our district was inferior to the one across the dividing avenue. I had to acquire an appropriate address. Merle, who lived on the right side of the boundary, agreed to sign a lease indicating I was her tenant. We had it notarized and I brought the lease along with a phone bill to give to the school secretary. I had invested in a phone with call forwarding service to be installed in Merle's house. The school personnel knew what I was doing and didn't really care, but needed the proper paperwork in my file.

During the month, I had a peculiar dream, which I noted down in my diary. "An airplane journey to England ending in a crash we could all walk away from." This was my first foreshadowing of the tragedy that was stirring on the horizon.

When Alan and I returned to Brooklyn from one of our last weekend trips out of town, I called Tony from the local subway station so he could meet us halfway as we walked home. I saw him before Alan did, approaching an apartment house on Glenwood Road. I saw his delighted smile, his tiptoe walk, holding his finger to his lips warning me not to call him to Alan's attention, to give Tony time to hide behind a pillar at the apartment house entrance, the better to surprise Alan. I can never pass that building without recalling that moment of reunion, how we hugged each other, so pleased to be together again, Tony taking my hand in one hand, the luggage cart with his other, Alan dancing between us.

Tony had been having a difficult time scrounging for work and had finally found some. Feeling better about himself, he was able to relax and enjoy us.

We made love, delighting one another as the old month slipped out of sight and the new one came into view.

## CHAPTER TEN

**September, 1989**

We are all here;
We all are here!
By night we are hurled
by dreams, each one, into a several world.
—Robert Herrick

Back to school, back to work, back to living with each other in a house without Tony. The work went smoothly, both full- and part-time jobs. It was a relief, actually, to get back into a routine that took me out of the house each morning. School for Alan was a reprieve from the feelings which he was able to leave behind him at our front door.

I was successful in finding an excellent person to be our new, non-live-in housekeeper. Over thirty people responded to the ad I placed in the *Irish Echo*, and I chose the last one who left a message on the answering machine. I liked her soft, polite voice. Vicky was a young woman from the Caribbean, enrolled in a journalism program at a local college. Her duties included shopping, cooking the dinner meals during my working week, and general housecleaning. Most importantly, she was to be available to pick Alan up from school if our neighbor wasn't able to bring him home, and to be at home to keep him company until I returned. But on her own initiative, she included making our beds each day, a luxurious touch which more than anything else contributed to my tentative feelings of well-being. Coming home from work to a warm supper on the stove and an immaculately made bed lifted my spirits, and helped me to deal with Alan's temper, which seemed to be increasing. I never knew when he would explode.

One morning, two weeks after we returned from England, Alan woke in a peaceful mood, which quickly turned contentious. First he fought me verbally over the issue over which pair of shorts to wear or not wear; then he threatened me with the police truncheon he had been given as a gift from the police chief of Scotland Yard. He surrendered it and left it on my desk after I commanded him to do so. He ran upstairs and pounded the door of his bedroom into the wall behind it, until he made a hole in the plaster. He burst into tears.

"I didn't know I was so strong! It's over now." He hugged me and later played cooperatively with his friend Ania and me when she joined us in the wading pool under the apple tree.

But the very next afternoon he slapped me in front of a fellow who had come to meet us to decide whether or not he wanted to rent a room in our house.

"You have to order these Legos NOW!" he shouted, and threw a slinky at me.

"You're seeing us at our worst," I told the young man.

"Give me a week to think about it," he said, and I never heard from him again.

My brother slept over one night, leaving early the next morning to attend a conference for environmental educators at the Brooklyn Botanic Gardens. I joined him for lunch at the outdoor café.

"Alan really needs to see you more often," I told him. "He was so disappointed to find you gone this morning. I found him sitting on the stairs outside your room, typing 'Tony' again and again on Tony's portable typewriter."

"I'll see what I can do," said my brother.

Alan played air controller wearing Tony's glasses. He found the tiny rubber tire under the couch that they used in their game "Splat," and rolled it around the living room floor. He looked at a pair of tongs in the kitchen drawer and recalled how Tony used to hold the cookie bag with them, pretending the bag was in jail.

"Tony used to say, "dead smack in the middle" and "fucking roll on" and "cor" and "bloody hell."

Our new "family" — The Victims of Pan Am Flight 103 — was also struggling to contain temper tantrums. The editor of our monthly newsletter, Georgia Nucci, put it very tersely: "Paul Hudson Resigns from Organization. *Citing philosophical differences with the goals and methods of the organization, Paul Hudson has resigned from The Victims of Pan Am 103, effective immediately, and has decided to work alone on his personal agenda in regard to the bombing of Pan Am 103. We thank Paul for his tireless initiative and energy and wish him well in his solo endeavor.*"

*The Times Union* of Albany had a harsher version of what had occurred: "Adversarial Tactics Split Lockerbie Jet Crash Group. *Internal differences simmering since April have split the family organization formed after the December 21 explosion of Pan Am Flight 103 over Lockerbie, Scotland. . . . Paul Hudson of Albany, an early force in the formation of the 400-member organization, has decided to form a new group along with several other leaders of Victims of Pan Am Flight 103.*

"'There are major philosophical differences,' said Eleanor Hudson, whose daughter Melina died aboard the jumbo jet. 'When you have differences, you don't sink the ship. You take another boat out if you can.' . . . Eleanor Hudson said that the new group . . . has the support of at least 42 victims' families, including several members of the original group's board of directors.*

"'It was a difference between a hard-core take no prisoners approach, to one that is adversarial but where you can talk to your enemies,' said Bert Ammerman of River Vale, N.J., President of Victims of Flight 103. . . . He said that the split also stemmed from the growing role the organization played in providing survivors with emotional support. . . . While substantive issues divide the membership, Georgia Nucci of Claverack said personality conflicts also contributed to the separation.*

"'In the first few months, the group succeeded in capturing the national spotlight but has seen the disaster slowly fade from national consciousness. . . . 'We are a bunch of people operating under tremendous stress,' said Nucci, who plans to* *stay with the original group. 'There is a lot of frustration and anger involved with these issues. We haven't been able to get all the results we want, so members of the group have focused their anger on one another.'"*

I, too, chose to remain with the original group. Even though politically I was more inclined in Paul Hudson's direction, friendship was more important, as was the unapologetic inclusion of an emotional support group following every political meeting. The voluntary exodus of the dissidents did not end dissension nor prevent ineradicable, irrational differences between us. Our losses were not equal; they were inherently distinct. Losing a child was not the same thing as losing a parent or losing a spouse; and those of us who lost our husbands could not help but compare the longevity of our married lives or where we were in relation to our children, if we were lucky enough to have any.

At the September meeting, for example, which was held in a hotel in northern New Jersey, I had lunch with two other widows both significantly younger than I. One had only been married seven months; the other, ten years. One was childless; the other's child was less than two years old when his father was killed.

"I have been robbed of his child and well as his love," said the first.

"My son has been cheated of knowing his father, deprived of the brothers and sisters we planned to give him," said the other.

I blurted out, "Alan and I talk about Tony every day," and could have kicked myself into a corner. I felt inordinately blessed that my only child had had six years with his father, and ashamed of what I had been given by indifferent chance.

I was amazed to find myself envying the couples who sat in the chairs in front of me when the meeting resumed after lunch, arms on each other's shoulders, whispering into each other's ears. I didn't know then what I was to learn later, that their loss could be a barrier between them. Now I stared at them through resentful eyes. A week later on the eve of Rosh Hashanah, Rabbi Goldberg called to wish me a less painful new year. "May you continue to grow towards peace. Honor your honest feelings."

I went to synagogue for the services and listened to the story of Hannah who had given up her miracle child to serve God. I felt deprived of grace and the possibility of accepting any.

## September 1988

The day after Labor Day, I returned to my job as a lab assistant in a high school. I had been in the school system since the late 1960s. In 1986, when I transferred from the school where I had worked since 1971 to a better situation in another school, I realized that my job had more continuity than any other aspect of my life. I had not lived in an apartment or been involved with anyone for as many years as I had been connected to this same department in this same building. In 1986, I had been married thirteen years and lived in four different places with my husband. In the fall of 1988, I returned reluctantly to a job that I had long since outgrown, but which had become a financial necessity.

No matter how dreary the chores, the job always had one stunning advantage: it was over by 3 o'clock in the afternoon and I could walk out the door without carrying it with me. No lesson plans to modify, no homework to evaluate, no tests to design or score. It had therefore been possible to seek employment in a local college as an adjunct instructor teaching an afternoon or evening course.

I aimed my missives at institutions reeling from years of fiscal cutbacks. The City Colleges had just ordered a freeze on new hiring, and everyone else responded to my queries by apologizing for their empty purses. They were just barely able to offer their own adjuncts work for this year. But then the phone rang on a Thursday morning. It was Pratt calling with an offer of a job. Their instructor had switched his ecology course from Wednesdays to Tuesdays and then remembered he could not teach it due to a professional commitment. The course was due to begin in six days with a registration of over twenty students. Could I step in on this moment's notice and take it over? I had to report to them tomorrow afternoon, meet with the chairman be given a course outline, etc. I could and would.

Tony was pleased for me naturally, but concerned what this would mean in terms of our routines, the way we divided up household and Alan care responsibilities. I could not know what impact teaching one three-credit course meeting one afternoon a week for fifteen weeks would have on our lives, but I had to accept this opportunity.

The interview was gracious. The chairman apologized for hiring me in this hasty last-minute manner, "but at least we're able to give you a job this term after all." He gave me materials and some advice. "You have the weekend to select a textbook and to rough out an outline of lectures, reading assignments and test schedules, and to prepare your first presentation. Do you have slides? You can sign up for a projector in the library. Just be straight with the students. You're a brand new teacher who's been handed a brand new course. By the way, because of your previous experience teaching an elective mini-course at City College, we are pleased to welcome you as a visiting assistant professor."

I floated home to an empty house. Tony and Alan returned from their errands after school. "Tony took me to a garage, Mom. I learned so much about cars!" I told them my good news.

"May I kiss the assistant professor?" Tony was so proud.

"Only if she's visiting."

My new job did have an enormous impact on our lives, rather like an earthquake which, though low on the Richter scale, continues to generate aftershocks for a long time and causes, if not a shift, at least a crack in the ground.

I had never undertaken such a responsibility before. Not only did it require me to allocate endless hours immediately to initial preparation, but once the course was off the ground, I had to set aside hours each week for grading homework, generating quizzes, and insuring that each week's lecture, a minimum of two hours, could hold the attention of my students. This time was carved out of time that used to belong to my husband and child. Tony, although supportive, resented it. He was fighting for his professional life and never the most highly disciplined of men, found it difficult to create and then adhere to a schedule. Being a house husband suited him temperamentally and would have pleased him if he were still not gripped by the dream of being self-supporting, of making a fortune out of his own ideas and hard work. Tony and I found ourselves locked in a conflict impossible to resolve. Each of us wanted the other to take over the household whenever we were overwhelmed by our work responsibilities.

Alan was going through a difficult transition himself. The night before he was to begin his first day in kindergarten, I came downstairs after typing my course outline, and found him in the living room on the couch, sitting in his father's lap, with red swollen eyes and nose and trembling lips. He began weeping again as soon as he saw me. He put his head down onto

Tony's chest and sobbed.

"It's the film we've just seen, about a boy and his dog. It's the first time I've ever seen him so grief-stricken," said Tony tenderly, stroking his son's back and kissing his head. The film was about love and loss and transcendent loyalty, and Alan was shaken.

Though his first day at school went well, Alan began throwing ugly temper tantrums at dinner time. We had our worst head-on collision in the middle of the second week on Yom Kippur, a day the public schools were closed. When told that he had to cease playing with Leah in order to get ready to leave for a children's service at her synagogue, he hurled abusive insults at me through a closed and locked bathroom door. Finally, he calmed down and emerged, eager to go with me. We exchanged meaningful looks during the rabbi's sermon on angry words being like feathers shaken out of a pillow; once let loose into the air they cannot be retrieved. One can only apologize. "That's what Yom Kippur is for," the rabbi said. "It's our opportunity to apologize to anyone we've wronged and to try to be more self understanding so that it may not happen as often again."

"I miss you when you're out," Tony said, looking up from the television, as I walked in the door  after 10:30 p.m one evening. Alan was already asleep, having given up waiting for me to come home.

"I'm sorry, Tony, I am trying to do right by you and Alan as well as myself. Let's go out together, just the two of us this Friday. I can't remember the last time we took ourselves to the movies."

But Friday was a bust. There was a scene with Alan at the dinner table before Tony and I left him with our boarder and drove a few blocks to the neighborhood theater. Tony could not tolerate the sound system at the theater and demanded his money back, and then we got lost trying to find the other movie house in Brooklyn showing the same film. I thought he was behaving like a prima donna; he was angry with me because I didn't acknowledge that it was important to stand up for quality, not to tolerate the shoddy, the second-rate. We returned home in a crackling silence.

# CHAPTER ELEVEN

## October 1989

I attended my first bereavement counseling session in early October. There were five couples and two widows, Wendy and I. Wendy was significantly more withdrawn than she had been when we sat near each other at the press conference in January. When the therapist paired us off to perform a "healing" exercise, Wendy refused to look in my eyes as directed. She said to the group, "Jay and I used to look at each other wordlessly and he'd say, 'God I love you so much!' I don't belong anywhere any more! All my friends are either married or engaged and they don't know what to do with me. I make them uncomfortable. And I'm too young to go to a widow support group. They're all women in their seventies and eighties. This is the only place where people at least know who I am, what happened to me. God I miss him so much!" She held my hands while continuing to avoid my eyes. I felt awful, personally rejected by her even though I knew that she wasn't rejecting me, she was grieving the death of her husband and the loss of her social place in the world.

The husbands and wives spoke of how their grief isolated them from other people and created a barrier between them. The men found their loss excruciating, yet couldn't talk easily to their wives about their feelings. Nor could they find relief in tears. Shame compounded their grief: How had they failed to protect their children?

"I should have been on that plane instead of my son," one man said quietly.

The counselor tried to lead us in an exercise in "forgiveness." She had us close our eyes, think about any people we might be angry with, and explore the possibility of forgiving them. Then we were to try to do the same towards the specific people responsible for the horrific death of our child/our partner. The purpose of this exercise was to try to restore ourselves to an inner equilibrium, to reduce the intensity of the corrosive anger within us. Forgiving didn't mean forgetting or extinguishing the passion for justice, she assured us.

I found it possible to consider forgiving the people against whom I carried longstanding hurts and resentments, but it was impossible even to contemplate forgiving the terrorists who had built the bomb, or the Pan Am executive who had ignored international warnings from the Finnish and German police, or even President Bush, who had tried to ignore us. I held onto my anger; in fact I fanned its flames. By the end of the session, I left the room feeling, in fact, worse than when I had entered.

A week later, taking over Tony's traditional job of cutting the Hallowe'en pumpkin, I began to weep uncontrollably. Alan began shouting at me, "You're not roasting the seeds right! You're not doing it the way Tony did!"

He began hitting me. I had to physically restrain him. After he calmed down and I got him to bed, I called another widow, a mother of two young children. I had hoped that our sons could become friends, and that we could, too, but now she made it clear that it really wasn't going to happen. She was moving from Queens to suburban New Jersey to be near her relatives, and she was completely preoccupied with them and her job. We would continue to see each other at the monthly meetings, but that's all she could handle.

"I wake up sobbing in the middle of the night, calling my husband's name," she said. "I ache from my toes to my eyes."

Hearing her express pain as all-consuming as my own made me feel better, in spite of the fact that I was as alone with my grief as ever and that Alan's lashing out made me feel that I was failing him.

I told Alan's therapist about Alan's temper explosion about the pumpkin seeds and that his first-grade teacher had reported he was afraid not to be perfect. Peter said that this was all normal, all to be expected.

After Alan's session, I brought him to the Grand Army Plaza library to register for his first library card. He chose a book about the Titanic to bring home. He asked me to read it to him at bedtime.

"These people went onto the ship the way people went onto 103," he said. "They didn't know they were going to be killed."

I told him that our people on the plane were conscious and happy one minute, thinking about going home to their families, and the next minute they were unconscious. "They didn't suffer any pain." I was fairly certain this was true. I needed Alan to believe it.

"If it had gone off on the ground, Tony would still be alive," he said matter-of-factly.

## October, 1988

On October 1ˢᵗ, Tony's Aunt Marie wrote us a very upsetting letter. Tony's Uncle Len was seriously ill with terminal cancer. Marie had traveled from Vancouver to Farnham, England to visit him. But that wasn't the chief reason she had written to us. She and Len had gone to see Tony's mother's grave in Brighton's Cemetery and had discovered that it was lacking a headstone. "To find Clara without a marker on her grave after being dead for four and a half years is very distressing and sad, especially when you are living each day with many of her possessions," she said.

It's not that we had intended to neglect Clare, it's that we had chosen to invest whatever funds we did have to help Tony launch his own company. He had decided to leave his position as national sales manager of a microphone company the year his mother died. He had taken the job to support us after Alan was born, but the position had required him to travel two weeks out of every four. He had endured it for two and a half years, before resigning. He couldn't bear being away from Alan so frequently.

The information about Len was devastating. He was Tony's favorite uncle. Marie believed he hadn't long to live. He was currently in remission. Tony thought he would see him in the new year. "I think you better plan to go sooner than that," I said.

"Maybe I'll go in November. I'll see how my work goes."

His work wasn't going well. He decided to devote his time to working with a fellow inventor. It was in a somber mood that we went upstate to see to our cottage during the Columbus Day weekend. When we arrived early Saturday evening, the real estate agent told us that she was going to show our house all weekend. The next morning we were awakened by the agent and a couple walking on our patio. I was hot with possessiveness and resented their casual invasion of our property. This was not going to be as civilized a transaction as I thought. By mid-afternoon, the real estate office called with a firm offer of $45,000. The woman wanted to live here all year and had secured a mortgage based on her promise to dig her own well. Real money in our pocket, but we would lose our second home: There was no negotiating a guaranteed summer rental from this prospective new owner. Should we accept this offer and liquidate our debts or hold out until we found the ideal person to sell to? It could be years before we found such a person.

In the end, after careful consideration, we turned down the offer. It had taken us over a year to buy the place. Why should we be in such a desperate hurry to sell under any circumstances? Our idea to find someone who wants us as guaranteed summer tenants was a good one. We just had to be patient until we found that person.

We saw this difficult month out with a quiet stroll through our neighborhood streets on Hallowe'en. Ordinarily, we would have driven over to Park Slope to march in the local parade there. Tony and I were both Hallowe'en enthusiasts. When we discovered the artist's parade in the West Village in the early '70s, we loyally followed them as they moved up into national prominence and their parade became a spectacle requiring police barriers. But after Alan joined us, we shifted to the family-paced parade in Park Slope and donned modest costumes ourselves. A mask and a cape transformed Tony into an 18$^{th}$-century gentleman, myself into a gypsy, Alan into a cat. This year, we accepted the invitations of new friends, the Brennans, parents of Alan's best friend in kindergarten, to remain in Midwood and walk with our children as they rang doorbells.

It was a mild, moist evening. We held hands and scuffed our shoes through the damp leaves, walking up and down the dead-end streets between the subway tracks and Ocean Avenue, behind the children who ran in front of us swinging their orange lanterns through the twilight.

## CHAPTER TWELVE

### November, 1989

The season of anniversaries was upon us, a minefield of private birth- and death-days culminating in Christmas, which was now forever the anniversary of our loss. There was no escaping what lay in wait. The only question was how were we going to survive it? Tony's birthday was the first to negotiate; he would have been 58 years old. Alan had the same idea as I did, to have a little party with ice cream and a cake with candles and invite his friend Leah to join us. "Let's celebrate Tony's birthday every year from now on for as many birthdays as he would have lived, okay?" he asked.

"That's a splendid idea," I replied.

"Wouldn't it be strange to have a robot in the house just like Tony? He could do all the things Tony used to do with me like play Legos and make me sandwiches. But he wouldn't know how to talk like Tony."

"And he wouldn't know how to hug like Tony. You know, even though we can't feel his hugs any more, we can hear his voice. Would you like to listen to him telling stories?"

Alan surprised me by saying yes. I didn't ask him very often because the first time he had listened with me to a recording of Tony's voice, he had complained that it upset him too much. I went to find the tape letter to Lacey and Pat in which Tony describes one of the four surprise birthday parties I had given for him during the sixteen years we lived together.

Tony: *"Helen suggested why don't we get a bit better dressed, so I thought, Well, I'll humor her, you know . . . so I put on a pair of 'smarty pants' and a blazer with a white thing. I looked quite dashing, really! And, uh, we had this dinner and talked about things . . . At the end of the dinner, it was very nicely timed, there was a ring at the door and Helen said, 'Are you expecting anybody?' And I said no, so I went down to the door and in came a whole stream of people, because Helen had secretly invited everybody to a party. And I don't know if I'm particularly surprisable."*

Helen: *"OH, YES YOU ARE!!! YOU ARE THE EASIEST! THIS IS THE THIRD TIME I'VE DONE THIS!"* (Dissolving into giggles.)

Tony: *"See, if I didn't know before, I know now! This has been Gullible's Travels. Actually, call this tape Gullible's Troubles!"*

Helen: *"There's a kind of a tradition of having a surprise party for Tony's birthday."*

Tony: *"And all our friends who came before to the previous ones are surprised that it's a surprise! That's the funny thing! 'Doesn't he ever learn?' Anyway, it was very beautiful."*

Helen: *". . . I must say, in case you think your son is feebleminded, the reason I can pull this off successfully is that I don't do it every year, you see. When a year goes by and I don't do it, he forgets that I have this potential and it can very easily happen again."*

Tony: *"And who the hell can assemble a specific close-knit group of friends, who can assemble people for a Monday night party? It's unbelievable! It's quite unthinkable that anybody would want to go to party on a Monday night, let alone practically everybody you invite."*

Helen: *"There were about six people who couldn't come because it was so last-minute."*

Tony: *"Yeah but I didn't know about them!"*

Alan said quietly, "That makes me miss Tony too much."

We had to celebrate Tony's 58th birthday a day late, because on the day itself, Alan was staying over at my parent's home in Connecticut, and I was at a hotel in Springfield, Massachusetts at a Victims of Pan Am Flight 103 meeting. I walked into the lobby late on the Friday evening of that weekend and saw everyone standing in front of a huge TV monitor displaying images of people streaming through the Berlin Wall. It had just fallen. Hope was exploding in the world, and I couldn't share it with Tony. He had served in the British Army in Germany in the 1950s as an intelligence officer. He would have been moved to tears to see that wall come tumbling down.

I wasn't the only one reacting to this historic event within the context of my own. One of the mothers confided, "I feel guilty whenever I feel good. I know it's all right not to feel terrible all the time. Nevertheless, whenever I catch myself feeling happy or excited about something, I feel disloyal to our dead daughter."

That night I dreamt of being held by a friend's husband, skin touching skin. Though my body had begun to betray me, my daytime consciousness was not yet ready to fulfill Alan's persistent request, "You are allowed to get married again, aren't you, Mom?" Nevertheless, I felt obligated to do so. I began to see the wisdom in the medieval social practices of my ancestors who decreed that widows be permitted to remarry within three months.

I envied the bereaved parents who were able to adopt children through legal and socially accepted means. There were hundreds of thousands of children in the world — millions, probably — in need of loving homes. All one had to do was go to an agency and register one's desire to adopt. But as far as I knew, there wasn't any service that matched appropriate men interested in becoming stepfathers with the women and children in need of them.

One of the books I read to Alan at bedtime contained, as a plot device, pills that restored one instantaneously to a younger age.

"If I took one of these, I'd be 30 years old again, before I met Tony."

Alan said, "We would have Tony back again, and this time, we wouldn't let him go to England."

When Alan was asked by a family friend what he wanted for his birthday this year, he replied, "What I want, I can't have."

The nightly battles over homework worsened. They became physical. I was desperate. I tried a technique described in a book about how to comfort disturbed children.

I held him firmly and told him, "You can always let your anger out on me, but you can't hit me." That did help somewhat.

My main support at this time, and Alan's surrogate paternal presence, was the therapist he continued to see for one hour every week, and whom I consulted through these distressing outbursts. He continued to tell me that all this was normal, all this would pass. Actually, it didn't: the intensity and frequency of his outbursts did, but not Alan's difficulties with authority, with rules and limitations. Eventually I sought guidance from a behavior-modification therapist; it wasn't only Alan's behavior that needed to be modified!

A few days after Thanksgiving, the doorbell rang. It was a man with a special-delivery package from Lockerbie. He handed me a large padded envelope. "I've never delivered something like this. I'm very sorry for your loss."

"I've never received anything like this. I don't know what it is. Thank you."

It was a TDK 60-minute cassette tape, slightly smudged and stained, marked "12/88 vi. 1" in Tony's handwriting on both sides. "Vi" turned out to stand for "Violet," Tony's aunt, whom he had visited the night before he died. As they had sat in her living room, looking at the snapshots of Alan he had brought to show her, he had recorded their conversation. Tony used tape recorders the way most people use cameras, to document their lives. Our friends became used to seeing the little Sony at the edge of the table as we sat around telling stories, and, of course, Alan became his favorite subject. The police had already returned a tape he had recorded at his cousin's home when they handed me the contents of his shoulder bag in August at the Incident Center in Lockerbie. I thought that tape, which wasn't particularly interesting, was the only one he had made during his eight days in England. It wasn't. The police had retrieved this tape somewhere in their inch-by-inch search of more than eight hundred square miles of Scottish countryside, listened to it, identified the family, and returned it to me when they were done examining it for potential clues. Months in the mud hadn't damaged it. When I put on the headphones that night and turned on the cassette recorder, I entered Violet's living room in New Milton and sat down at the table.

Tony: *"That was the day he left his school. It's called graduation. They actually wear caps and gowns."*

Violet: *"That's a good one. I like that one!"*

Tony: *"Yeah, he's at the dining room table with his Legos — or is it the floor, let me see . . . he's on the floor . . . getting tired on a nice oak floor."*

Violet: *"How long have you been there in that house?"*

Tony: *"Since November '80. So we've been there eight years."* (Clears his throat.)

Violet: *"I like these close-ups of him."*

Tony: *"I've taken some really beautiful close-ups of this boy. . . . I've never got them printed, but I'll do it, I'll do it!"* (Stirs his spoon emphatically in his tea cup.)

Violet: *"Is he looking forward to Christmas? I expect he is. Great excitement . . ."*

Tony: *"Alan wrote you a Christmas card . . . He likes airplanes."*

Violet: *"'To Aunt Violet' . . . I'll treasure that, Tony. He's grown into an interesting little boy, I expect."*

Tony: *"Yes. Very much so. What can I say? Adults are very pleased to have conversations with him, he'll approach anybody, he's never afraid to talk to anybody. Never has been. And he doesn't get the kind of brush-off that you see adults give small boys, you know. It's beneath a lot of people to talk to kids either because they have nothing to say or they think the kid is going to be childish. But you find in a minute or two that people are responding and real conversations develop every time. It's fantastic. I was never like that! I was quiet."*

Violet: *"You went to Wimbledon College for awhile, didn't you?"*

Tony: *"From 11 to 18."*

Violet: *"The family had to pay for you there, I s'pose."*

Tony: *"No, I was on a scholarship."*

That's how the tape began. Towards the end of the first side, Violet asked what flying was like; she'd never been in an airplane.

Tony: *"I finally woke up on Wednesday because I had this terrible flight — when was it, Monday night? I got there on Tuesday, and I just had to sleep, Tuesday was lost."*

Violet: *"What's it like, crossing the Atlantic?"*

Tony: *"Well, you're sitting in a nice armchair, which is a little bit cramped, and you can lean it back sometimes. You're eight hours in the plane, seven and a half hours flying. But we were nearly twelve hours in it because it didn't take off for a long time. It had trouble. They couldn't ignite the engines. It's like igniting a gas flame so they had to change the igniters."*

Violet: *"What's that airline called?"*

Tony: *"Pan American. And so we arrived hours late . . . although the plane was so nearly empty that everybody had three seats to sleep in. Every passenger had three seats. They were two thirds empty."*

Violet: *"When you think of the millions of people that fly . . ."*

Tony: *"Four hundred people, thirty-five thousand feet high, thirty-six, thirty-seven thousand feet high — all having dinners! (Laughing.) It's really rather funny."*

Almost all of the remaining tape was devoted to Violet's reminiscences. Tony had let the tape roll, forgetting that we had already interviewed Violet on tape, covering essentially these same stories. Then Violet asked him a leading question: When did you decide to go to America?

Tony: *"I was managing a sound equipment shop in Shaftesbury Avenue . . . among the customers were . . . famous rock groups, so I would talk to the BeeGees and The Who and all those people. The guy who called himself Donovan would come in and just hang out with us, he liked us. I heard a song of his the other day and I can't get it out of my mind. 'Hurdy Gurdy Man.' He was great.*

Violet: *"Who was that ugly one?"*

Tony: *"The Stones? Mick Jagger? I had a small conversation with Mick Jagger. He wanted to buy the tiniest part of a gramophone you can imagine, and I said, Well, look, here's this thing and it's only fifteen shillings and it's got it in it, and he wouldn't. He was very footsore. He'd been walking all over London looking for this sort of tuppony screw. Sixpence maybe. He wouldn't buy the fifteen-shilling thing. He was already a millionaire. That's my only contact with him. . . . The Who and Pete Townsend. And Pete Townsend, it'd be about . . ."*

Dead stop. The tape had run out. I'd never hear the rest of the story which somehow connected Pete Townsend and how and why Tony first came to America.

When I was a child, there was one story I never tired of hearing my father retell. It resembled Rip Van Winkle in that someone goes to sleep and wakes to find that years have passed. But it takes this theme and explores something else entirely. A young boy, granted the wish of becoming a man overnight, finds that his mother has long since left their village to go in search of him. Along his journey to find her, he acquires three gifts: a shell in which he can hear her voice, a mirror in which he can see her knocking on doors in foreign towns, and finally, a horn through which he can speak to her. As soon as he cries out to her, she collapses and dies from shock.

This tape, plucked from the wounded earth of Lockerbie, was like that shell in the story. More than any other in my collection that I used to keep Tony close to me, this one rescued him from memory's gloss and notoriety's glare. Here was the living, breathing man — stirring his tea, talking, laughing, clearing his throat, recollecting, explaining, inquiring, listening — a few hours before his life was taken from him. Before he was turned into a number, a name listed in newspapers and books, a name carved in walls, a name recited in memoriam, a photograph, a statistic, before he would be reduced to victim and distorted by eulogies, his voice was captured and preserved. By the time this gift was given to me, I had already begun to think of him as fated to be on that flight.

But he was not. He was fully confident that he would be reunited with me and with his child in twenty-four hours. If the people whose responsibility it was to prevent the bomb from getting onto that plane had done their job, he would have come home to us.

The next morning I placed a call to Lockerbie and asked to speak to the officer in charge. I wanted to thank him for this unexpected gift, and, like the mother in the classic joke of ingratitude, asked if he might have found another one. Because this tape had been labeled #1, there was, presumably, a #2. I could hear him explain how Pete Townsend was connected to his coming to America. The officer was so very sorry to inform me that this was the only tape they had found in the field. They had held onto it such a long time because it had to be examined as evidence first, before it could be returned to me. Someone then had to listen to it and match the names mentioned — the wife, the child, the man himself — with each victim's profile.

(A mother and her child are playing by the edge of the ocean. A wave sweeps the child away. The mother bargains with God. "If you return my child to me, I will obey all your commandments." The next wave brings the child back to her. The distraught mother grabs her baby, hugs her and after checking her carefully for injuries, looks up and says, "Where's the other shoe?")

But the tape was not really the shell in my father's story. Tony could not say anything new. The tape went round and round in its sealed container. I could not interrupt what he was saying and he could not hear my voice calling his name in the darkness.

## November, 1988

*"'These are the happiest days of my life,' I told Tony this morning after we made love. Ardor and warmth, playful pleasure, has returned to us. I'm able to be utterly uninhibited with him, and he's so patient and eager to please me. I feel in harmony with my life; everything is in balance."*

I wrote these words on November 5th, in the one-inch slot allotted for that day in the engagement calendar for 1988. Almost every page in that calendar is crowded with my writing, in different colored inks, spilling into the margins, sometimes squeezed underneath the photograph on the opposite page. It was my habit to write at night, in bed, to try to capture the essence of the day that had just ended before turning out the light. To open this beautiful book — whose cover photograph is of white roses climbing a gray stone wall between two moss green doors — is to walk down the pebbled path under an arcade of roses as they recede towards a flower-draped wall. The doors remain closed. The wall hasn't any gate through which to see what lies beyond. I can walk page by page through the days of that year, savoring each one, and whether I walk slowly or quickly, each day brings me closer to the last day of my husband's life.

*"These are the happiest days of my life."* I defied the gods. I said it out loud; I wrote it down. I was happy and fully aware of my happiness; there is no higher form of bliss.

On the other hand, I was also plagued by fatigue and distressing dreams, succumbed to a severe cold by Thanksgiving, and had to bring Alan to his doctor to be treated for a throat infection by the end of the month. My $5^1/_2$-year-old philosophized as we waited, "God does not believe in us. Why do people come to believe in God anyway? Sometimes I believe in God. Where does the earth come from anyway? Just some iron that bent around itself, and some jelly?"

November 13th, Tony's fifty-seventh birthday, fell on a Sunday, the day of the family art class we were attending at the Brooklyn Museum. Tony came with us occasionally, when his work permitted him to. Alan and I painted scenes for a story the class had collectively created in preparation for acting it out the following week. That evening, after dinner, we watched another episode of "A Perfect Spy," a dramatization of John Le Carre's novel. While Tony was still sitting on the couch with Alan, I brought in a piece of carrot cake with a single lit candle, and Alan joined me in singing the song, as Tony blew it out in one puff. I gave him his gift, a Navajo rug pocket address book, and a card that pictured a car and said, "When you're over the hill, you pick up speed." Inside I had added: *"November 13, 1988/ Dearest Tony/ My pleasure and my joy to celebrate another birthday with you. This one feels like one of the best in its modest way — returning in the midst of a time of much mutual satisfaction and renewed love. Your abiding wife, Helen."* He was very touched.

The next day, I worked on my Pratt lecture, which was going to focus on the topic of coal. Tony offered some personal experiences from the years of his childhood growing up in the London of the 1930's and '40s. "Those were the years of the killer smogs, you know, luv. I remember going out with a handkerchief wrapped around my nose in order to breathe, carrying a torch (that's a flashlight to you) in order to help guide motorists who couldn't see to drive home! But we felt very macho about the whole thing, you know. That's just the way it was in London. It wasn't until later, in the '50s, that it got so bad that the government finally passed legislation to force a change in what came out of the chimneys."

On a luminous day after a week of rain, Tony awakened me. I was roused as much by the idea of making love before leaving for work as much as by the sly things he was doing with his hands. We met a few hours later, in Alan's classroom. It was Open School Day and parents were invited to sit in on their child's kindergarten class.

"We have to stop meeting like this!" I whispered, as he covered my hand with his.

"Why? You're cute. May I have your phone number?

On November 22nd, the eve of the twenty-fifth anniversary of his assassination, we watched, "Remembering JFK." I saw film footage I had never seen before: Jacqueline Kennedy wiping away the tears from her face as the coffin was carried down the steps. The entire texture of that time returned to me. We stayed up late, talking quietly on the couch together before we went to bed. That night I dreamed . . .

*I'm desperately fighting to keep my head above water, calling out into the darkness.*

*"Tony, where are you? Are you all right?"*

*He's more than thirty feet from me slipping below the surface into clear green water. I won't be able to reach him in time. TONY!!!!*

I woke myself and shook Tony awake.

"Wha, what is it, luv?" He took me into his arms.

"I've had a bad dream…"

But he was asleep again, snoring softly.

# CHAPTER THIRTEEN

## December, 1989

December opened with my fiftieth birthday and closed with a memorial service on the first anniversary of Pan Am Flight 103. In between, we unveiled Tony's headstone, appeared on Phil Donahue's television program, and celebrated Alan's seventh birthday.

My friend Carol had insisted that my fiftieth not pass without public acknowledgement. I didn't think I could handle more than a quiet dinner party. Carol offered to hold it in her large, comfortable row house in Park Slope and to prepare the food. I invited my parents and four friends to join us. As I stepped into the living room, someone emerged from the shadows to embrace me.

"Lia! What a special surprise. You are my birthday gift!"

"I had to be here. I flew in last night and am leaving tomorrow." Lia was a friend from Brooklyn College days who now lived with her family in the Midwest.

Annette asked me about the program she had seen on television the night before, a news forum hosted by Sam Donaldson and Diane Sawyer on the topic of Pan Am 103. Everyone in the studio audience on stage had been from our family group. The polite discussion had changed tone when a representative from the State Department casually referred to the controversial warning posted on the cafeteria walls of the Department's Moscow Embassy as "a mistake that wouldn't happen again." That posted warning had ordered employees not to fly Pan Am out of Frankfurt Airport during December, but to fly another American airline home for the holidays. The order was based on the so-called Helsinki Warning of December 5th, 1988, when the U.S. Embassy in Finland received bomb threats against a Pan Am flight originating in Frankfurt before Christmas. The fact that a careful investigation later insisted that the warning was a hoax was irrelevant. The State Department had taken it seriously and notified every embassy in Europe to take protective action. Their mistake was in displaying such privileged information where the world could see that our government had protected its own and not everyone. Hope Asrelsky, whose daughter Rachel, along with every ordinary passenger and even pilots and crew, hadn't been given such prior warning, had stood up without permission and confronted the State Department lackey: "Our children were the best and the brightest, and you didn't protect them!"

"I looked for you on the show, but you weren't there," Annette said.

"I was invited," I explained. "Everyone in the New York area was, but I chose not to go. I didn't need to be there."

"You all represent each other, I know," she said.

We shared a poignant, low-key evening, emotionally equivalent to gathering around a campfire in the winter darkness. I was grateful not to be alone.

The next afternoon, I went to the Donahue Show and took Alan along with me. Phil Donahue had invited the Victims of Pan Am 103 to be the focus of his forthcoming program on December 12th. Alan immediately befriended the techie guys. One of the audio engineers took him around behind the scenes in their studios in the RCA building and let him handle some of the equipment.

The staff welcomed us into the auditorium. Enough of us had turned up to fill the seats on the right side of the aisle. The other seats were vacant, waiting for the people who were lining up on the sidewalk. Four members of our executive board took seats on the stage. Donahue joined us to prepare us for the format of his program.

"Every program is built around a theme. Tonight, the theme is your group, and your issues regarding Pan Am Flight 103. After talking with the people on stage, I will walk through the audience with a cordless microphone, letting people speak to the topic. Think of what you might want to say, because you have to keep your points brief. The show is on tape and will be aired at different times around the country. It will be broadcast in two days in New York City."

I found him intelligent and sympathetic, and was not disappointed in the way he orchestrated the program. The show was powerful. Many people in the audience on the other side of the aisle were hearing some of the facts about Pan Am 103 for the first time and were stunned to learn about the total disregard of security procedures before the bombing, and the cavalier way we had subsequently been treated by the government and the airline. I asked my question, which concerned the way Pan Am had encouraged students and businessmen to purchase tickets for the flight at the very last minute in spite of all the warnings they had received from the State Department and the German police.

On the day the show was to air, December 12th, I was very anxious all day while at work, without understanding why. Then, while walking in the early twilight along Eastern Parkway, I put it together: This was the day Tony had left for London, the anniversary of the last time I had been with him. Memory resides in the body more deeply and surely than it does in the mind.

As we watched the show, Alan really listened to what our executive board members said about Pan Am's criminal neglect of passenger safety. He hadn't understood it before. He sat there with his mouth open, shaking his head in disbelief and anger.

A few days later, after enjoying a Danny Kaye film on TV just before bedtime, his mood suddenly turned ugly, sarcastic. "You can't make me take a shower!"

"Okay. There won't be a story tonight. Good night."

He was furious, then began to sob. "I'm upset. I'm upset about Tony."

I opened my arms to hold him. "It's good to let your feelings out."

We celebrated his birthday on the very day of his birth, December 14th — the first ever without Tony. All of Alan's school friends came to our home. There was lots of laughter and we didn't talk about Tony's absence except the moment one of my friends murmured, "Alan was Tony's life."

The first anniversary memorial service was held on December 21st at St. George's Episcopal Church near Second Avenue and 16th Street. It was Hope Asrelsky's parish, and both a priest and a rabbi were going to officiate. A few of us organized a program. I planned to read my poem, "Incident at Altitude." My parents ordinarily would have left for Florida early in December, but they wanted to be there with me and so endured the unusually bitter cold that gripped the city. Alan asked to be excused. Tony's memorial service had been the last one he was able to go to for many years. I let him stay at Liam's house.

It was a long day. Before the service, we conducted a procession and vigil through the streets of Manhattan. At 11:00 a.m. we gathered in front of the New York Public Library on 42nd Street, and walked slowly up Fifth Avenue. We paused in front of Pan Am's ticket office at 48th Street and stood quietly for a few minutes before proceeding to the Pan Am Building at 45<sup>th</sup> Street and Park Avenue, where we read out all 270 names. In spite of the severe cold, the sidewalks were filled with people doing their Christmas shopping, and we attracted their respectful attention.

We headed downtown to St. George's after a cup of warming soup. Two hundred seventy carnations with name labels were waiting in the vestibule to be picked up by the family members for use in a concluding flower-and-wreath ceremony. The service began at 1:30 in the afternoon, so that we would all be in our seats when the church bells began ringing at 2:03 p.m., commemorating the moment of the explosion.

"So great a grief cannot be borne without being shared," Governor Mario Cuomo said at the memorial service held at Syracuse University immediately after the disaster, and repeated again in a letter written to one of the Syracuse parents for this occasion. His words expressed the significance of this day and the feeling in the church that afternoon. We had gathered together not only to mark the first anniversary of so much death and anguish and loss, but to reaffirm what we had achieved in this most difficult year. We shared our grief in a program that alternated music and poetry with personal statements by family members.

John Zwynenburg, father of Mark: "Their legacy lives on through us. We have helped each other to cope by comforting each other through this terrible crisis in our lives. We have worked hard to bring about changes, in our hope that other families will not have to endure similar grief. I feel sure our loved ones would be happy we have been able to find solace with each other . . ."

Joanne Hartunian, mother of Lynn: "Your loved ones have become my loved ones, your children, my children, as I know my child has become your child. I don't need the anniversary of our tragedy to remember the victims of Pan Am 103, but I need to be here with all of you, my new family. Last year I cried alone. Today, I share my tears with all of you."

I read "Incident at Altitude." In the dark vastness of the church, crowded with grieving relatives and friends, the words floated slowly through the air to follow each person as he or she fell to earth.

As each name was called out, a white carnation was placed in the large fir wreath by a family member or friend or someone who stepped forward to take their place. Since twenty-two nationalities were represented in the roll call of the dead, and over forty states among the Americans, there were many families unable to be with us that afternoon. At the conclusion of the ceremony, the wreath was entirely white.

Two days later as we were preparing to leave for Boston, the UPS man brought us two packages. Alan couldn't wait to open his. Fred Zeller, the audio engineer for the Donahue show had given him a pair of sophisticated two-way radio walkie talkies. I called to thank him.

"It was a joy meeting you," Fred said. "I hope this Christmas will be better for you than last year. And I hope my son grows to be as fine a boy as Alan is."

I opened my gift when I returned from Boston. It was a photograph of Alan and me as we appeared during the Donahue show, at the moment when I asked my question. Fred had painstakingly screened the video, found the frame he wanted, and enlarged, printed and framed it — and then had made sure that it arrived in our home before Christmas Day. This tragedy had enabled us to meet the most extraordinary people. The photograph is prominently displayed in my living room. It reminds me not only of the experience of being on that program, but of receiving Fred Zeller's gift that first difficult Christmas.

The journey to Boston was frantic. Everything was behind schedule and every place swarmed with crowds of people. We were the last two to squeeze into the Amtrak train and had to sit on our luggage on the platform of the car until New London, Connecticut. People were standing in the aisles as though on the subway. Alan befriended a young man and played Legos with him, sitting on his lap. I envied Alan's ability to get what he needed.

Fran met us at the station. We bought Chinese take-out food, ate a late supper in her kitchen, and went to sleep. I was glad to be there, away from my home where my kitchen walls would be asking me, *Where's Tony? He's supposed to be making the trifle, carving the turkey, setting out the champagne glasses . . .*

The next day I went out to the local supermarket to help with the shopping and to try to think about other troubles in the world. I picked up the *New York Times* to read about the latest upheaval in Eastern Europe. The front page had a photograph of a handsome, clean-shaven young man with untroubled dark eyes: Abu Talb, the first official suspect in the Lockerbie inquiry. "Portrait of Pan Am Suspect: Affable Exile, Fiery Avenger." The probable killer of my husband was staring back at me.

I turned the page and saw the wall of names at the back of Dryfesdale Cemetery in Lockerbie. Two blonde women stood close to wall, blocking some of the 270 names, but I could just make out, by holding the paper close to my eyes and squinting, "Anthony Lacey Hawkins" above the shoulder of the woman on the left. Tony and I had stood side by side before a wall of names two years ago on an Indian summer afternoon in Washington, DC. Those names weren't carved in alphabetical order but by date of death, the date they had died in Vietnam. Now Tony's name was carved in a wall in another country to honor his death in an act of war against the United States.

There was no escape. There was no place I could go to hide from the consequences of that moment. It would follow me anywhere I went.

## December, 1988

In my calendar diary for 1988, November — covered with writing resembling the stylized script Paul Klee used in his paintings of alphabet enchantment — pours into December. A photograph of "The circle garden at the Rashtrapati Bhavan Bagh in New Delhi . . . planted in concentric rings of color," glows on the other page. My recollections trace and retrace those days, each reading of the record yielding another gesture, another word, another insight. At the center, always at the center that I can only approach but never enter, is the man himself who both recedes into — and is rescued by memory from — oblivion.

The month began with my forty-ninth birthday, clouded by illness and anger. Alan was too sick to go to school, so Tony stayed home with him while I went to work. When I relieved him at 4:00 p.m., Tony was seething from frustration and a parking feud with our next-door neighbors. I tried to rescue what remained of the day by arranging for a baby-sitter and making reservations for dinner at one of Park Slope's more charming restaurants, followed by a film at the Plaza Cinema. While dressing for dinner, I unexpectedly came across the garnet ring Tony had given me in England on our first wedding anniversary. I thought it had been stolen in a burglary six years earlier. I took it to be a good omen and slipped it onto the fourth finger of my right hand, to keep symmetrical company with the wedding band on my left.

We were able to alter the bad vibes of the afternoon and make a special occasion for ourselves. It had been too long a time since we had been each other's date. After a cozy dinner at the Park Café, we strolled across Flatbush Avenue to see "Crossing Delancey," a cautionary tale: You should always listen to your *bobe* (grandmother), especially when she insists on playing *shadkhn* (matchmaker); true love can come in the form of a poetry-loving pickle-vendor. As contrived as it was, I cried.

At home, Tony presented me with a simple, handmade card. Inside a folded translucent piece of manuscript paper, he had written in brown ink in his best calligraphic hand: *"Love is an undulating curve which comes to a peak on birthdays."* At the bottom of the page, he had drawn a cheerful schematic flower in orange and yellow.

"Thank you, dear," I said. "I think that you've outdone yourself with this one."

We had to decide when he should plan to visit his Uncle Len. He hadn't been able to go in November after all because of two commissions to design, build and install editing consoles. I remembered that he had flown so often during the years he was the national sales rep. for Beyer Dynamic, he was entitled to a free round trip to Europe on Pan Am. I was the one who checked out the dates and discovered that this Frequent Flyer perk would expire on December 31st, 1988. I urged him to take advantage of his hard-earned, unused privilege. If it had already expired, or if it were going to expire in 1989, Tony would have waited until the cheerful frenzy of December had passed, and visited his uncle in early January. This free flight with Pan Am tempted him to travel in December, so he planned to leave after Alan's birthday party and get back in time for Christmas. He booked his flight through a friend at a travel agency to leave on the evening of December 12th and return on the evening of December 20th.

That's how he swam into the net.

The emotional highlight of December, the event around which Tony planned his departure, was Alan's sixth birthday party. As the actual day, the 14th, was a Wednesday, we arranged to celebrate it on the preceding Saturday. This year, in consultation with Alan, the theme of his party was chefs in the kitchen. Alan and his friends were going to prepare their own pizza. Tony drove into Manhattan and bought paper chef hats and linen aprons at a supply house and I shopped for the ingredients and Alan's birthday gift in Brooklyn. I returned to find the house filled with Selsie's whooping laughter. Pan Am's afternoon flight, 103, had brought her in earlier than expected and Alan was very excited to see her. She was his special birthday treat.

We hadn't seen her in over a year. She was on holiday, visiting friends and family coast to coast. By coincidence, she and Tony were flying out from Kennedy on Monday the 12th — she to California, he to London. She had already arranged with her family to let Tony stay in her bedroom during the first days of his visit to England.

It was as though she had never been away. She and Alan settled in on the couch, two kids together, one 25 and the other 6, while Tony read them *Noisy Nora*, one of Alan's new books. They laughed themselves silly.

The party was our last day together as a family. The last images I have of Tony are in my mother's informal snapshot style: Tony in the kitchen in a chef's hat; Tony at the dining room table, mouth open like a bird's waiting to taste the cake, eyes closed against the camera's flash. Tony was the chief chef with the kids in the kitchen and I entertained the adults in the dining room. We moved to the living room for the gift opening ritual. Tony's gift for Alan was a radio-controlled car. He set up the car in the front parlor behind partially closed pocket doors and handed the controls over to Alan. As Alan moved the knobs, the car whirred across the parquet floor to him. It was a beautiful touch.

The day before Tony's departure, we all went our separate ways. He needed to be in his basement workshop putting the finishing touches on the 181st Runaround. The name was characteristic of his wit; it was an elegant pun, describing as it did, the feature which distinguished this tape-editing trolley from all the others on the market, namely its ability to roll around a studio, to travel wherever needed. When Tony brought Alan into the office to show him off a few months after he was born, one of his colleagues quipped, "Here's the latest Hawkins' Runaround!"

Even though it was bitterly cold, I took Alan with me to a faculty Christmas party on the lower West Side the following evening. We had to walk directly into the fierce wind blowing across the Hudson River before we reached the shelter of the little house where the party was being held.

Alan was the only child in the room. He managed to engage the attention of several men to play with his new Lego set, which he had cleverly brought along with him. After the usual pleasantries with my colleagues, I unexpectedly found myself in a serious conversation with a couple who had known the journalist Paul Cowan and his gifted family. Though I had only known him through his long autobiographical articles, his recent death from cancer, in October, still affected me. He had taken me on so many vicarious journeys. I missed his active presence in the world. Surrounded by laughter and holiday music, garlands of Christmas lights in the potted trees, people helping themselves to the generous spreads of cheeses and fruits and warm breads, the three of us sat and talked about losing people you love to accident, to disease, about trying to make sense of it, or accepting death without imposing a meaning.

The husband said, "You know, Paul had become religious several years ago and he kept questioning what was happening to him as though there were a purpose, as though he might in some way be responsible. He couldn't accept that his illness was just bad luck."

I came home to find Tony upset with me. "You're never home or I don't see you when you are!"

His attack seemed to come out of nowhere. I couldn't understand him. We had recently spent so much time together. I thought he was being irrational; I became angry and defensive. I went to bed alone, he slept on the couch. The truth is, I had spent plenty of time with him, but not private time, not time for the two of us alone. Our night out together for my birthday at the very beginning of December had been the notable exception to the pattern. And I had been going to bed and to sleep before him, night after night.

The next day, I came home directly from school. I found him in the basement, panicked, trying to finish the Runaround he'd been working on all day Sunday. "It has to be shipped out to Philadelphia tomorrow!"

I tried to talk about the quarrel — "You know, Tony, both of us are right . . ." — but that just made him angrier.

He leaned against a pillar and jammed his hands in the pockets of his blue workcoat. "Why do I always have to defend myself?"

I turned away and walked over the washing machine and began hanging up the damp clothes. *We can't part like this!* "Tony, what can I do to help you?"

"You can get my clothes together and do the supper, stuff like that. Thanks, luv." He was back at the polishing wheel, fussing with the control knob.

I had seen him in this panic state before, under deadline pressure, but not so extreme. I did what he asked me to as quickly and competently as I could.

As soon as he finished eating, he went into the living room, got down on the floor and played a game of "splat" with Alan. This was a game they had created together, rolling tiny rubber tires from Lego trucks from one side of the room to the other, Tony trying to catch and flatten them under his large right hand. When Tony sat on the floor, he either sat on his folded knees, Japanese style, or he lay on his side. This evening, he lay on his right side not fully relaxed, dressed in his travel clothes of blue jeans and suit jacket.

He met me in the hallway with his suitcase. There were tears in his eyes. "I don't want to leave you! I hate going away!"

I almost said, "Then don't go, cancel your trip," but Tony was back in his office in the front parlor.

"Let me show you the invoice for the Runaround, okay? Please call UPS tomorrow and get them to pick it up. I promised them I'd send it out this week. Can you call car service for me, please, while I run up to the bathroom?"

We embraced in the hallway in front of the bench by the stairs. I kissed him on the lips and touched his left cheek with my right hand. He was wearing his Burberry khaki trench coat. He picked up his two suitcases, settled his gray overnight bag on his right shoulder, called, "Good-bye, boy!" and walked out through the double set of front doors. On impulse I ran after him, and stood on the porch watching him load his luggage into the back of the car.

"Safe journey, " I called.

He couldn't hear me for the roar of the engine, and stepped around the back of the car, cupping his right ear.

I called again, "Safe journey!"

This time he nodded and smiled, opened the rear left door of the car and got in.

Two days later, on the evening of Alan's actual birthday, Tony called. He asked me to put Alan on the phone, but Alan was engrossed in his game so he called out his greetings through the air. It was something he would openly regret for many years. "If only I had spoken with Tony when he called! I didn't know I'd never get another chance."

That night, I wrote in my journal: *"I've had a waking nightmare, frightful fantasies of Tony dying in an auto/airplane crash, never seeing him again. What will happen to Alan, to myself?"* These fantasies returned repeatedly throughout the week. They occurred while I was awake as daydreams, as complete images that flashed across the screen of my mind. I had never had such fantasies before — nor have I since. They were vivid, urgent, obsessive. Even during the first two and a half years of Alan's life, when Tony traveled two weeks out of every four, I didn't suffer from these "visions." I hadn't even been anxious that with all his frequent flying, statistical probabilities were increasing in favor of an accident. At the time, I interpreted them as further evidence of my chronic anxieties about our financial situation. I would not let myself dwell on them, be affected by them.

He called the next night, a bit embarrassed, having misplaced the list of addresses and telephone numbers I had given him. I gave him the information again, saving him the time and trouble of pouring through phone books or bothering 'Inquiries.' Now he could contact all of the relatives he wanted to see.

The next morning he called from his uncle's house. "Listen, luv, I'm running behind in my schedule. I'm feeling rushed. I've just not been able to do everything and see everybody. Would it be all right if I stayed one more day?"

I was at my desk, surrounded by my own clutter of unfulfilled responsibilities. "Have you been over to St. Catharine House yet?" I asked, referring to the registry of birth, death and wedding records for England, a resource we had begun to use as we slowly pieced together his paternal family tree.

"No. That's one of the things I could do if I stayed another day."

"Well, who knows when you'll get back to England? I guess we can manage without you one more day!" I smiled. We made small talk. We said goodbye and I went back to my preoccupations.

It was done as simply as that. His life was shunted onto the short track that led directly to a seat in a plane which would explode on December 21st at 7:03 p.m., 35,000 feet over Lockerbie, Scotland. How did I feel at that moment, when he placed his fate in my hands? Disappointed that he wanted to delay his return by a day, but feeling that twenty-four hours was nothing. If it would make the difference between his feeling rushed and feeling relaxed, why, of course, that was the sensible thing to do. Honestly, I didn't give it much emotional attention. I didn't even recall the peculiar visions disturbing me all week, the crashing cars and airplanes. They didn't come into my mind at all. If they had, would I have mentioned them to Tony? He still had to get on a plane to come home to us. I don't know. I was even feeling slightly annoyed that his call interrupted whatever it was that I was doing at the time.

In the years to come, Alan would focus on this moment as the time I could have saved Tony's life. "Why didn't you tell him to come home?" It didn't really do much good to explain again and again that if I had suspected anything, I wouldn't have agreed to let him stay one more day. It helped a little to reiterate to myself as well as to Alan that I hadn't been the one to suggest returning on the 21st, that it had been Tony's own decision. I had merely given him permission. I don't have to live with the knowledge that certain women whom I later met have to live with. They were the ones who insisted when their children announced new plans that they keep to their original arrangements. "I want you home for Christmas." "No you can't go to Paris." "No you can't stay a few days more." "No I don't want to fly to England for the holidays." "I want you to come home on Wednesday."

A young woman whose non-stop from Vienna to New York was canceled months earlier by Pan Am was informed of this only on Monday, December 12th. But "not to worry, we can still get you home by Wednesday night the 21st. We can fly you from Vienna to Frankfurt to London and then home to New York." And so this girl, whose parents had always told her never to take connecting flights if she could avoid doing so, let Pan Am put her on 103, risking their disapproval to the greater good of family reunion on the expected evening. There was a young man returning from a year in Israel, who disobeyed his aunt's advice and changed his flight from El Al to Pan Am because it suited his desire to come home a few days earlier. There was another young man who couldn't bear not being home for Christmas and called at the last minute to find out if any tickets were available. "Hey Ma, I'll be home Wednesday night!" "How were you able to get an empty seat four days before Christmas?" "I don't know. I got lucky."

It hadn't even occurred to me to ask Tony how he thought he could find a seat on another flight at this time of year. Flight 103, which had been completely booked by Thanksgiving — there are young people alive today who tried and failed to secure seats next to their friends on that flight — began opening up in early December. When it took off from Heathrow on December 21ˢᵗ, one third of its seats were unoccupied.

None of this matters. None of us is responsible. Unlike the terrorists or the men and women who worked for security at Pan Am in Frankfurt and Heathrow, or the people who worked for the British Transport Authority, or the F.A.A. or the C.I.A. or, for that matter, the German police, we were doing our jobs. We were not evil or incompetent or careless. We didn't put the bomb on the plane; it wasn't our responsibility to find and remove it. We didn't kill the people we love. And yet, if I had said something different, Tony would not have been killed. If I had said, "No, you can't stay one more day. Come home as planned Tuesday night," he would have come home to us. I will live with that knowledge until I die.

And what can I learn from such an experience? I will never be given a second chance to save someone's life by saying the right words under conditions whose contours I recognize and whose consequences I can predict. One of the continuing effects that moment has had on me is to find myself temporarily paralyzed whenever I am forced to make a decision, or worse, to chew obsessively over any decision made when it proves unfortunate. I am plagued by the "if-onlys." I see, as though with x-ray vision, the way choices conspire to create catastrophes.

A few years after Tony's death, a friend and I took a bike ride together on a paved trail that leads to a park near a lake. She put her bike down near the edge of the trail before preparing to go in to town for something to drink. I thought to tell her to pull her bike back and then didn't. Less than five minutes later, we watched in horror as a young woman came down the hill on that path, swerved to avoid hitting my friend's bike, lost her balance, and fell forward over her handlebars onto the pavement. She wasn't wearing a protective helmet. We heard the thud of her skull as her head hit the ground. I blamed myself and scolded my friend. The woman did not lose consciousness, she never suffered more than a headache. She was lucky. So were we.

Eventually, after the initial moments of paralysis pass, I am able to make decisions, to confront anyone, to say anything that needs to be said, or listen to whatever someone needs to tell me; to cut my losses if necessary and move on. If I am struggling with a relationship, all I have to do is imagine that this is my last, my only opportunity. After this person walks out my door he will be struck by a truck. What, then, will I feel if I fail to act now? I live as much as possible without regrets, without accumulating any more "if onlys." I can not bear their weight.

The day after Tony called, I decided I would take Alan with me to the March for the Homeless. Tony and I had taken him with us the year before. I thought it important to continue this tradition. We caught up with the March at the very beginning, as people jostled for a glimpse of Jesse Jackson before setting out from the Coliseum down Broadway to Times Square. We walked as far as Carnegie Hall. "This will get bigger every year," a Korean Vet assured me. He was currently sleeping on "terra firma" — the sidewalk — in his army jacket. "It really isn't painfully cold yet. It's okay."

"This movement needs some music of its own," I said. "We've got to do better than another round of 'We Shall Overcome!'"

That night, Alan, rosy-clean and towel-dry from his bath, said shyly, "I don't remember what Tony looks like any more."

"Do you want me to show you a picture?"

"No, I'll remember when I see him tonight!"

The day of my last class at Pratt before the Christmas break was unseasonably mild and I was fatigued from insufficient sleep. I monitored the final, which every student but one completed within an hour. I went home directly and tumbled into bed by 10:00 p.m. I wrote in my journal:

*"During these days of being alone with Alan without Tony, haven't really centered my attention on Tony. His absence has been neutral for Alan as well as myself. I know that it flows from certainty of continuity. Alan would be devastated if Tony never returned to him and the only way that would ever happen would be by a fatal accident or mortal disease. In this situation — a ghastly plane or car crash. The impact on me? I can't begin to imagine . . ."*

When I opened the journal thirty hours later, to write and talk myself through that endless night after Tony's death, these words were there waiting for me.

When death is sudden, unexpected, violent, when the bereaved has been deprived of the right to see the deceased, it is especially necessary to learn as thoroughly as possible what happened and when. Every detail helps to make the death real.

Before the phone rings, and Tony Stoppani tells me that "We've had a rather serious crash in Scotland of a Pan Am plane, flight 103. What plane was Tony supposed to be on?" I want to let Tony relive the last week of his life.

Even before I actively solicited any scraps of information about how he spent his last days, people began writing and sharing such recollections with me. Two days after he died, my friend Mavis wrote me a letter:

*"I have only just read the list of passengers on the Pan Am flight and I can't express my shock and grief at finding Tony's name there. Words are so inadequate, but I weep for you and Alan and only wish there was some way to comfort you.*

*"Tony paid us a visit on Monday evening and we had such a lovely evening with him . . . Tony showed us a new and ingenious product produced by a friend which he was going to try to sell to the USA. It was an oil filter and he was very confident about it. He spoke with pride about you and Alan and brought me the cuttings and photos you sent. He also showed us recent photos of Alan."*

A month later, in response to my written request, she wrote me a very long letter with as full a description as she could put down of her evening's visit with him. Mavis is the sort of person who can recall not only what she talked about with someone, but what they actually said. Reading her letter was almost like listening to a tape recording.

*"Tony arrived at about ten minutes to 8:00 and, after welcoming him in, I left him to Richard (her son) and returned to the kitchen to complete the dinner. I had also invited a friend of mine, but he was to arrive rather late.*

*"I joined Tony and Richard with the salad course and asked after you and Alan. As often happens, the conversation turned to a number of topics not related to each other, and, on recollection, I cannot remember how we got from one subject to the next. Nor can I recall how each subject cropped up.*

*"Tony was very much amused at the arguments between me and Richard and, although his contribution tended to support my argument, he expressed himself very gently and without vehemence. Looking back, I can see that his very carefully worded arguments served to temper and diffuse what could have been a more heated argument between me and Richard. Anyway, it all remained friendly and Richard enjoyed the exchange even though he got the worst of it . . .*

*"I started to tell Tony about my venture into selling American 501 Levis, a venture which had not been successful . . . and Tony was very sympathetic . . . he made observations very much to the point on the problem of selling, finding the right market, matching the product to the market. He said with a*

*wry smile that he himself was not a very successful salesman and that he didn't make very much money at selling. The remark reflected Tony's honest sincerity but I suspected that he might be too modest and perhaps was a little harsh in his self-judgment . . .*

*"Oh, I remembered something just now. I said to Tony at one point, 'Did you at any time consider having more children?' He misheard the question and thought I meant now. He said that you were now 49, not an appropriate age for having children. 'No,' I said, 'earlier. Were you and Helen not tempted to have another child soon after having Alan?' He gave me a sort of half-amused smile and said, 'We've done our bit.'"*

In mid-January, I received a loving note from Tony's Aunt Violet, his father's older sister and only surviving relative on his father's side:

*"Of all the thousands of flights across the Atlantic, this terrible tragedy should take Tony, who had only just told me that though he had flown thousands of miles over the States he still did not like flying . . .*

*"As soon as I suspected . . . I phoned Uncle Len at Farnham. He told me, 'Alas, it is so.' I then phoned you immediately. I wanted to tell you how much Tony was looking forward to getting home and Christmas with you. I had recommended a local bookshop to him and he was delighted with their large selection. He bought a bound annual of Alan's favorite comic and two other suitable books for him.*

*"Helen dear, I thank you for giving Tony such a happy and fulfilled married life! When you are sad, always remember that!"*

She wrote again at the beginning of February.

*"You ask me to fill in for you Tony's last Tuesday. He called me about 12:30 midday on the Monday, the 19th, to tell me that he postponed his flight to Wednesday. That's when he said he's flown thousands of miles all over the States and still doesn't like flying . . .*

*"He arrived about 12:30 midday. After a very pleased and warm greeting (I thought he looked very well and also very attractive in a light cream suit (he had put on a bit of weight), he told me that he does the cooking for the Christmas dinner, that he was planning to cook a twenty-pound turkey. Just before he was to leave me, I suddenly had this impulse to get Len's phone and address which I didn't have. I wasn't well the next day, the Wednesday. And then Thursday came the news about the plane. Was it Tony's plane? I didn't know. I called Farnham and Len put me right over to his wife, Vanessa and she talked with me a long*

*time. I was just shattered.*

*"Tony was so nice to me, Helen! He put his hand on my shoulder when leaving and said, 'I think you're wonderful,' and I replied, 'I think I'm wonderful, too, Tony, after a few bad years!' Helen, I weep for him."*

I called her on February 3rd, the day I received her letter; it was her eighty-ninth birthday. Her deteriorating health made her a prisoner of her three-room flat in a small town on the southern coast of England. After her brothers and sisters-in-law died, Tony and I had become her closest family. She felt responsible for having been the cause of Tony's postponing his original flight from Tuesday the 20th to Wednesday the 21st, and therefore, for his death. I told her that I believed he had postponed his departure day in order to have dinner with Mavis on the Monday, that when he called me on the Saturday morning, he was already feeling pressured and wanting to stay one more day . . . but most importantly, that she, Violet wasn't responsible for Tony's death. The men who placed the bomb on the plane and the men and women who failed to remove it were responsible.

But until Selsie sent me a very neat outline of Tony's activities from the day he arrived at her parent's flat in the Marble Arch area of London on December 13th until he departed three days later, I didn't understand why he had decided to stay one more day.

*"Arrived 13th December — slept all day — had tea with the family in the evening.*

*"Wednesday 14th — exchanged money at Barclays. Very chuffed it only cost him a pound. Lunchtime had a good meal with Dad at Vechhio Milano (he ate pizzicata). Visited a friend that evening? Dad bought Alan slippers with bees on them.*

*"Thursday 15th — spent all day with Dad.*

*1. Went to Ealing and met the "ultrasonic" man (was concerned that ultrasonic sound would affect human hearing. The other man said no, because it's beyond human hearing range but not beyond that of birds and mammals.*

*2. Enjoyed themselves at a transport café — bacon and eggs.*

*3. Went to Dad's launderette in South London. Dad showed him the heater coil system. He said he'd put one in the house in Brooklyn (conserve energy — cheaper bills).*

*4. Went to Stockwell/Brixton Road where he showed Dad his grandparent's first home (his Italian grandparents who had nine kids). Saw little yard behind the Georgian house which is now converted into a mews house and was previously their garden. When his grandfather became maitre d' at the Dorchester, they moved into a richer area; showed Dad the house in Albert Square where they lived.*

*5. M&S late-night shopping (Marks and Spenser). Bought 4 steam puddings (single portions) which I'm sorry to say my dad ate one by one until by Tuesday there was only 1 left for Tony to take to NYC!*

*16ᵗʰ Friday — Went away the whole day. Came back in the evening and then went away again. Did not return to Cumberland Ct. but rang and said he's organized to stay an extra day.*

*"He said he hadn't been so happy in a long time! Dad gave him a sketch for a wooden chair for handicapped people from an inventor friend of my father's which he took with him. He was going to make a wooden prototype. Dad gave him an oil filter to show his friend."*

I loved the details and the English slang, that Tony had been "chuffed" (pleased? Pleasantly surprised?) exchanging money at a low fee at Barclays; that he ate a pizzicata at Vecchio Milano's; that he ate bacon and eggs at a transport café; that he had taken Selsie's father to see the two houses where his grandparents had lived. Now I knew that along with the special books for Alan he had purchased while visiting Violet, a steam pudding, a pair of slippers decorated with bees, an oil filter and a drawing of a wooden chair for handicapped people had also gone down with the plane.

And I at last knew why Tony had been feeling "rushed," why he felt he needed one more day. He had lost a day by sleeping off jet-lag all day Tuesday and then spending Wednesday and Thursday enjoying himself with Selsie's father; it wasn't until Friday that he was first able to attend to his uncle. I knew that he also hoped to do some business while he was in England. Selsie's careful calendar also told me that Tony had "organized to stay an extra day" — before calling me. My okay merely supported a decision he had already made the day before. It comforted me to learn this.

So now I had the first three days of Tony's week, and the last two, but the middle was vague. I knew where he had been, with his Uncle and Aunt at Farnham, but I hungered for more details. Len's wife Vanessa was not able to write me her letter until early March and by that time, her memory of Tony's visit was somewhat confused. Instead of a neat day by day accounting I received random recollections:

*"Please forgive our lack of communication. This is because Len is very unwell at the moment. Your dearest and beloved Tony saw Len at his best after his first treatment; but since then there has been regression; the pain in hips and back returned . . .*

*"To answer your first letter re: Tony's movements . . . To our knowledge he spent the first two nights and days with a friend in Marble Arch . . . He then came to Farnham for three nights only . . . he went up to our attic and packed a tray and some books. He also put a lot of books out for waste collection. He told Len 'They are out of date and of no use now.*

*"The next day Tony said he had to go to London. He came back for dinner at 8:30 . . . Later he and Len talked about his childhood and the past. Both were tired by 11:00 p.m. and went to bed. The next day we had to be out for the evening — we left Tony a prepared dinner and came home rather late. He said he had seen his aunt again and been to St. Catharine's House . . .*

*"On his last day here he said, 'How much I love being here with all its birds and squirrels.' They really played to the gallery for Tony with all their charm and antics on the garden table in front of the kitchen window. Tony watched them and many different birds for a long time."*

Len fought for his life for another three and a half months, then died before the worst deformations of the disease afflicted him.

When the police returned Tony's shoulder bag to me, I found notes in his own hand listing people he wished to visit and the towns where they lived. On another sheet of paper he had sketched out a daily log:

*"12/13 Nalgo. Mavis sick today.*
*Laura out in by 6 o.k.*
*Len 5 o.k.*
*call after 12 tomorrow*
*Wed. eve Laura*
*Th*
*Fr*
*Sat*
*Sun*
*Mon*
*Tues Day"*

Since Tuesday was "Day" that meant he hadn't yet decided to return on Wednesday, which meant that he had written it before Friday. And perhaps if Mavis hadn't been sick, he would have been able to arrange to visit her earlier in the week and would not have felt pressed for time. Another "if."

There was something else in the bag — an unmarked 60-minute TDK audio tape cassette. It was a record of the Sunday afternoon visit with his cousin Tony. He had set up the recorder in their living room while they looked over family photographs. Most of the 60 minutes is taken up with their casual comments. Apparently he forgot it was on and let it run through a TV program while everyone stopped talking. Then he asked his cousin about his responsibilities investigating the triple train wreck and finally just before the tape ran out, with TV soundtrack and family conversation obscuring his voice, he says,

*"I ought to go soon. . . . I had a nice dinner . . ."*

*"It was nice to see you again,"* says Mavis, Tony's wife. *"Perhaps we'll see Alan next year."*

*"I hope so. I hope we can make it . . . I'm using this gray bag as a briefcase. It's the largest thing that can fit under an aircraft seat!"*

*"Have a good journey home. Hope the fog doesn't hold you up."*

*"Pan Am's pretty good. I'm on the flight free because that job I had flying around. I was a frequent flier on many airlines but on Pan Am I racked up enough to have a free trip to Europe. And this is both the first opportunity to take it plus the last chance because it disappears at the end of this year. It was 1,983 miles you see, and it's only good for five years. So with Len being ill and one thing and another and being between jobs, it was time to take it."*

There's some more discussion inaudible under the TV blare, then Tony's voice very close to the microphone as he says, *"Well, he's . . ."* before he abruptly clicks himself off. This is especially frustrating, because there is at least ten more minutes of recording time remaining on the tape. The exchange about his carry on luggage and his free flight status was almost impossible to make out through my portable recorder's limited volume control. I had to put the tape into a more powerful machine and press my ear to the grid to make it out clearly enough to transcribe accurately.

He was jaunty. He was confident. *"Pan Am's pretty good."* He lifted the gray soft suitcase to his shoulder and walked out the door.

## There Was So Much To Love

> *"Goodbye, goodbye!*
> *There was so much to love, I could not love it all . . ."*
> — *Louise Bogan, "After the Persian V"*

So I loved you and love you still all in all.
When you are still, my love is there for you, a staff
on which to lean that will not break nor fail
to guide you as you climb or leap or stand quite still,
a comforter to hold against the chilling wind.

I live inside you now I can no longer live
beside you. I will never leave you utterly
alone. I chose you freely and in joy to be
my partner, wife, companion. My vow remains in place
though I am gone; this gift is more then memory allows.

Helen Engelhardt

# AFTER WORDS

### Present Imperfect, Future Unknown

On May 20th of this year, I had just settled down in my study to resume proofreading this manuscript when the phone rang. It was a reporter from the *Daily News* calling to tell me that "he's died." It took me a moment to realize whom he must mean, the only man convicted for the Lockerbie Disaster — Megrahi.

"Oh. It's about time. It's been a long three months, hasn't it?"

Twenty-four years had passed, and I was still learning about significant developments in the Pan Am case from reporters calling me on the phone, or by hearing it on the radio or seeing it on the front page of a newspaper.

I had first seen Megrahi behind a glass wall at the Scottish Court in the Netherlands, during the summer of 2000 when I attended the Lockerbie trial at Kamp Zeist. The three judges and the lawyers and their clerks had already entered and taken their places, but Abdel Basset Ali al-Megrahi and Lamen Khalifa Fhimah — the two Libyan men indicted for the conspiracy of assembling and concealing the bomb (inside a Toshiba tape recorder brought aboard with the luggage in a Samsonite suitcase) that blew up over Lockerbie, Scotland — had not yet appeared. I never saw them enter. I turned my gaze to my son, perhaps, and then when I looked back, there they were, in their robes and skull caps, sitting attentively with their guards behind them. Directly in front of them, separated by the glass wall, were their families.

I didn't feel a thing. I didn't know what I expected to feel, but something, not this neutral nothingness. These were the two men responsible for blowing up Tony and 269 other people. Some of their families were sitting here, bearing witness for them. I stared at the young woman who was probably Megrahi's daughter. *You have the privilege to see your father, to offer him comfort. My son can't do that.*

They looked like ordinary men, not mass murderers. Megrahi wore glasses and was slender. He looked like the functionary he was, a member of the Libyan Intelligence Service, a connection he denied. Fhimah was even more unremarkable. He had been tasked, as the man in charge of Libyan Airlines at the Malta airport, with securing Air Malta tags and slipping the unaccompanied Samsonite suitcase into the stream of luggage on an Air Malta plane bound from Malta to Frankfurt, where it would be transferred on to a Pan Am plane to London and then onto Pan Am Flight 103, destination JFK, on December 21st, 1988. Megrahi was responsible for acquiring the Semtex and the electronic triggering device — a long-delay timer manufactured by a firm in Switzerland — and making and putting the bomb inside the tape recorder, and buying the clothing to fill up the rest of the suitcase.

Before the trial began, based on what I had already learned from evidence my lawyer Lee Kriendler had discovered and various investigative journalists had uncovered or described in articles and books, I believed that both Megrahi and Fhimah had carried out orders from Libyan officials (unnamed in the indictments but going up the chain of command at least as far as Sanoussi, Gaddafi's brother-in-law who was the head of Libyan security, and probably Gaddafi himself). Listening to the evidence presented by the Crown convinced me that Megrahi was not only following orders but had been selected because he was the intelligence agent who could most successfully accomplish the complicated task entrusted to him.

The last time I saw him was on January 31st, 2001 when the judges declared him guilty as charged. While we were still reverberating from that word, we heard the judges declare Fhimah "not guilty." Scottish criminal law differs from American jurisprudence in several vital regards: the death penalty does not exist, and three separate pieces of evidence must be accepted in order for a "guilty" verdict to be applied. However, a third category of judgment exists: "not proven." Fhimah was declared "not guilty" because one of the three separate pieces of evidence was rejected by the judges. To my mind, he should have been declared "not proven."

Fhimah barely had time to say goodbye to Megrahi before he was led out of the courtroom. We learned later he had been almost immediately driven to the airport and flown back to a hero's welcome in Tripoli.

Lord Advocate Colin Boyd addressed the judges and Megrahi with a list of the numbers of people who were Megrahi's victims, analyzed by categories (widows, orphans, entire families). Later, when he joined us in our private lounge, he told us that entering such a document into the court record was unprecedented.

On December 21st, 1988, 400 parents lost children — 46 of them their only child; 65 women were widowed; 11 men became widowers; 140 children lost a parent; 7 children lost both parents.

We left the courtroom and took refuge in the lounge created for us when the former NATO base was converted into a courtroom and prison especially constructed for the Lockerbie trial. Alan had not been able to accompany me; it was the middle of finals week in his high school and we were given only twenty-four hours' notice that the judges had arrived at their decisions. I made the mistake of sitting next to a woman I respected and enjoyed arguing with, but who was utterly convinced that all evidence to the contrary, Libya was not responsible. There was no one with whom to share my relief, satisfaction and, yes, feelings of triumph. It was worse in the lounge, where families coalesced into private gatherings. I sat alone with my grief. The drama of the trial and the process of justice were over, but Tony had still been murdered, had still been deprived of his life, had still been torn from us. One man sitting in a prison cell in Scotland was not going to return him to us. The wife of the American ambassador to the Netherlands saw me sitting alone and came over to comfort me. I am forever grateful to her kindness.

We live in a world within the world, with the molten pain of the unending loss of the people we love at our core. In the early days, we walked on tears towards them. Then the tears began to dry up, because they must, and the pain began to recede, but it never ceases to exist. It can be unleashed when provoked, especially by developments in the criminal case, which remains, as we are periodically reminded by our Department of Justice, open to further investigation.

When Secretary of State Madeline Albright convened a special meeting in Washington, DC during the summer of 2000 to explain to the families how the trial would be conducted, she invited us to ask questions of herself and the Scottish Lord Advocate and Scottish lawyers. I took my turn on line and asked if we would be allowed to face the two indicted men and personally address them. Unfortunately, no. Ultimate justice for me would have been for Megrahi and Fhimah to be required to listen to each one of us describe the person or people taken from us; to be shown family films and snapshots; to read aloud from *On Eagle's Wings,* edited by Georgia Nucci (whose son had died on 103), describing each one of the 270 people who were killed. I thought naively, then, that ultimately their hearts would have broken open and they would have felt remorse and asked for our forgiveness.

Seeking an answer that could help him understand what had been done to him, my six-year-old son asked me within days after his daddy had been killed, "Didn't they know they were killing people we love?" I couldn't bear to tell him the truth: that it was precisely because they knew we loved them that they murdered them.

I told him that the men who had done this were seeking revenge against our country, that they had aimed their bomb at the United States flag displayed on the tail of the plane, that they hadn't considered the passengers, their families and friends.

When Gaddafi was killed in his home town of Sirte on October 20th, 2011 after nine months of civil war, the young men who captured him documented his bloody death on cell phone cameras. After being dragged into the light from his hiding place and beaten, he pleaded with them, "Don't you know right from wrong?" and "What did I ever do to you?" I was sorry they didn't keep him alive to stand trial for his 40 years of tyrannical rule, but I understood why they couldn't resist shutting his cruel mouth forever. Perhaps it was those very words — revealing an utter and incomprehensible lack of understanding of the crimes he had committed against them — that triggered someone's gun pressed against his skull.

We flew home from the Netherlands to special meetings with Secretary of State Colin Powell, Robert Mueller of the F.B.I., and the congressional representatives who had been our stalwart supporters — especially Senators Kennedy and Lautenberg — where we were congratulated and reassured that our Justice Department would continue to follow the evidence, wherever it led, and that our government would pressure Libya to fulfill the remaining requirements of the United Nations Security Council, namely, to accept responsibility for the actions of its officials, to pay appropriate compensation to the families, and to cooperate with the Justice Department in its work to learn all the facts in the conspiracy to bomb Pan Am Flight 103. Then we got on with our lives. Megrahi remained in prison at Kamp Zeist and appealed his guilty verdict. A year later, his appeal was unanimously denied and he was flown to a prison cell in Scotland to begin serving a minimum 20-year sentence.

In November, 2008, Scottish judges rejected his appeal for early release because of his prostate cancer. In May 2009, Megrahi dropped his second appeal to the Scottish Criminal Cases Review Commission, letting the guilty verdict stand unopposed in order for him to qualify for "compassionate release." On August 20th, 2009 — a day of personal infamy for many of us — Scottish Minister of Justice Kenny MacAskill, in spite of official protests by the United States government and the U.S. Department of Justice, and in spite of personal appeals and testimony from numerous family members, while upholding Megrahi's "guilty" verdict, nevertheless released him on grounds of "compassion" because the prisoner was expected to die within three months. The one government we thought we could trust implicitly throughout these twenty-four years had betrayed us.

Almost immediately, the British press was filled with articles exposing the business negotiations between BP and the Libyan government (no oil without Megrahi's release). It was reported that a Prisoner Transfer Agreement had been altered to permit the transfer of Megrahi, and that all the other doctors consulted on Megrahi's health declared that he probably wouldn't die within three months. Indeed, he lived nearly three more years.

In spite of having achieved more than we thought we ever could — two public trials, two guilty verdicts — we are still battling conspiracy theories and still need to insist on the basic facts. Personally, I am not invested in any legal decision. From the beginning of its formation, The Victims of Pan Am Flight 103 has had two fundamental missions, expressed in the two buttons we wore to our meetings and demonstrations: Their Spirit Lives On, and the Truth Must Be Known.

***Their Spirit Lives On*** This was our first obligation. The night he died, I vowed to Tony that I would do everything in my power to find out who and what were responsible for his death, but especially to keep him a vital part of our lives. I included him in daily conversations with my son, began writing this memoir, and eventually established an award in his name at New York University to promote and encourage audio drama, an art form he cherished.

Indeed, I have done more than that: I have taken a significant portion of my Libyan settlement — my misfortune — and established a fund from which I support organizations and individuals who are actively promoting peace and justice in the Middle East, social justice in the United States, environmental causes, and artistic ventures. I am especially gratified when I can enable a creative young person to follow his or her dreams. Tony enjoyed mentoring the young and was passionately devoted to all these concerns. He co-signs every check I write.

***The Truth Must Be Known***     From our very first press conference in February, 1989, when I disregarded my lawyer's advice and chose to make a statement to the international press, I have continued to make myself available to the media for interviews. Among the media outlets that have used me as a source are *Newsday,* the *New York Time, USA Today,* Al Jazeera, Germany's *Stern* magazine and *Berliner Zeitung,* and numerous other outlets across the U.S. and around the world. I have also authored my own op-ed pieces in the *New York Times* ("When Grieving Really Begins," August 10, 1991) and other periodicals.

In the fall of 1995, I became the fourth editor of *Truth Quest,* the newsletter of the Victims of Pan Am Flight 103. By the time I turned it over to someone else six years later, I had edited twenty-one issues. There were approximately six hundred people on our mailing list, including in Congress, the State Department, the FAA, the Office of Victims of Crime, the library at Syracuse University, and the Newspapers and Periodicals Library at the State Historical Society of Wisconsin. We also had subscribers in England, Scotland, Canada and Germany.

Our organization and individual family members have been dedicated to having all the facts revealed about this complicated conspiracy and the circumstances that made it possible for it to succeed. We were responsible for President Bush signing an executive order in August, 1989 creating the President's Commission on Aviation Security and Terrorism, which issued a report on May 15th, 1990 describing systematic lapses in security by Pan Am and the FAA, with sixty specific recommendations that formed the basis for the Aviation Security Improvement Act of 1990.

Caught in the crosshairs of our nation's foreign policy and the political interests of England, Scotland, Germany, France and Italy — and ultimately the UN Security Council and General Assembly — we walked the halls of Congress, lobbying and inspiring legislation and indictments. The timeline that I have provided (see page 251) lists the major accomplishments and setbacks of the past twenty-four years.

The most astonishing, unforeseen development in 2011 took place in that part of the globe responsible for altering our lives: the so-called Arab Spring, which ignited in Tunisia, grew into a flame in Egypt, and then burst Libya wide open.

I found myself advocating for active U.S. intervention to protect the Libyan people from Gaddafi's rage.

The man I saw pleading for his life on YouTube in October, 2011 did not resemble the egotist tossing his robe over his right shoulder and swaggering up the aisle of the U.N. General Assembly in September, 2009, barely a month after Megrahi had been released and returned to him. Forty Pan Am 103 family members stood alongside at least three times as many members of the American Libyan Freedom Alliance on the plaza across the street from the UN, united in protest against his tyrannical regime. Reading their signs and especially their two-page handout — "Gaddafi in 40 Bloody Years. This is the harvest of Gaddafi's years, a chronology of chaos, mayhem and the destruction of life and property the world over" — I realized how understandably overwhelmed I had been by my personal tragedy and consumed by the political and legal battles that preoccupied us. Now The Victims of Pan Am Flight 103 were able to acknowledge the suffering of the Libyan people.

"There are Gaddafi victims all over the world. He killed his own people by the hand of mercenaries." This is what Libyan Ambassador Adjouli said to us on December 21st, 2011 when we gathered at the Cairn in Arlington Cemetery for our annual memorial service.

"We do remember exactly how much suffer the families; behind each one of you there is a story. Children suffered, husbands suffered, wives suffered, parents suffered, friends. All of you suffered.

"Gaddafi is responsible for that. And there is no such action like this can be taken without his blessing, there is no way, there is no way.

"We work very hard and we will work very hard with you and with the State Department to find the facts, to find the truth, which everybody want to know. This madman who has been ruling the country for more than decades, nobody was safe from him.

"I never believe, I never believe in my lifetime that Libya will enjoy one day freedom. I never."

(And I never believed I would ever hear the Libyan ambassador to our country tell us that Gaddafi was ultimately responsible for the conspiracy which blew up Pan Am Flight 103.)

As of this moment, no further developments have taken place in Libya regarding the people who were involved and know the details of the conspiracy, and relevant documents have not yet been released. The Truth still has to be sought and publicized. It is the least we can do for those whom we love and represent.

Tony's spirit endures in how his son and I continue to live our lives. The Ethical Culture Leader who conducted Tony's memorial service put it beautifully:

"Every day that they think about him, and every time Alan ever does anything that makes for more justice in the world, or for good storytelling in the world . . .

"The deepest kind of immortality for Tony rests in each of you, in the way in which you live out, in your own life, the best of what he wanted his life to be. You keep him alive as much as you want to have him in your life. In that sense, none of us ever die. We live in the radiations of those around us . . ."

# Time Line

## for the Pan Am 103 Criminal and Legal Cases

**December 21, 1988**  Thirty eight minutes after take-off from Heathrow Airport, London, Pan Am Flight 103, en route to New York City, explodes over Lockerbie, Scotland, killing all 259 aboard and 11 on the ground.

**December 23, 1988**
Reports surface that on December 5th the U.S. Embassy in Finland received bomb threats against a Pan Am flight originating in Frankfurt some time before Christmas. Also reported are warnings shared with government and airline officials abroad

**December 28, 1988**
British investigators report that a bomb in the luggage compartment caused the explosion.

**February 19, 1999**
Victims of Pan Am Flight 103 is formed by families of those slain. The group will be instrumental in fighting for higher standards of airport security and in publicizing investigation information.

**March 14, 1989**
Victims of Pan Am Flight 103 testifies in front of the Senate Transportation Appropriations Sub-Committee, marking the first congressional hearing into the bombing.

**April 3, 1989**
On the 103rd day after the bombing, relatives and friends hold a demonstration in front of the White House. Some members of the Board are invited to meet with President George H.W. Bush to request a congressional investigation into how the U.S. government handled terrorist warnings prior to Pan Am Flight 103.

**August 4, 1989**

President Bush signs an executive order creating the President's Commission on Aviation Security and Terrorism, with a mission to evaluate aviation security.

**May 15, 1990**

The President's Commission on Aviation Security and Terrorism issues its report describing the lapses in security by Pan Am and the FAA and decrying the lack of "national will" to fight terrorism. The report contains over 60 recommendations, which formed the basis for the Aviation Security Improvement Act of 1990.

**October 23, 1990**

The Aviation Security Improvement Act of 1990 is unanimously passed by the U.S. Senate.

**November 14, 1991**

Two Libyan intelligence agents, Abdel Basset Ali al-Megrahi and Lamen Khalifa Fhimah, are indicted by the U.S. and Scotland. The evidence also suggests involvement by high level aides to Libyan leader Moammar Gaddafi.

**January 21, 1992**

A resolution to force Libya to surrender the suspects is approved by the U.N. Security Council.

**April 15, 1992**

The U.N. ceases all air transport links with Libya and bans sales of arms and aircraft to Libya in punishment for its refusal to extradite the two accused agents.

**April 27, 1992**

The civil trial against Pan Am by the relatives of the victims begins.

**July 10, 1992**

Pan Am is found guilty by a Federal District Court jury of "willful misconduct" that made the bombing possible. Pan Am appeals the guilty verdict all the way to the Supreme Court, which, three years later refuses to hear the case, thereby upholding the lower court verdicts. Pan Am Corporation is now forced to settle with the familes.

**April 24, 1996**
President Clinton signs the Anti-Terrorism and Effective Death Penalty Act, containing amendments to the Foreign Sovereign Immunities Act that give any American murdered by state sponsors of terrorism the right to sue that foreign government. This law is unprecedented, and passed only because the Oklahoma bombing in April 19,1995 changed minds in Congress.

**April 24, 1997**
Unprecedented cooperation between the House and Senate Judiciary Committees results in their last-minute (fifteen minutes before Congress' spring recess), unanimous passage of a one-sentence bill giving Americans married to foreign nationals the right to sue under the new law. President Clinton signs it on the afternoon of April 25th.

**August 5, 1996**
President Bill Clinton signs legislation imposing harsh economic sanctions on companies that make future investments in Iranian and Libyan petroleum ventures, and vows to wage an international battle against terrorism.

**August 24, 1998**
At the instigation and under the leadership of U.S. Secretary of State Madeleine Albright, the U.S. and the U.K. propose to convene a Scottish court in the Netherlands in an effort to bring the two Libyan agents to trial.

**August 26, 1998**
Libya accepts the U.S. and British plan.

**April 5, 1999**
The two suspects are handed over to the Scottish authorities in the Netherlands. This action enables the Security Council to suspend the U.N. economic sanctions against Libya.

**May 3, 2000**
Trial begins at Camp Zeist in the Netherlands.

**January 31, 2001**
Abdelbasset Ali Mohmed al-Megrahi is found guilty; Al Amin Khalifa Fhimah, not guilty. Al-Megrahi is given the mandatory sentence of life imprisonment.

**February 8, 2001**

Families meet with U.S. Secretary of State Colin Powell, the Department of Justice and four Senators in Washington D.C. We are reassured that our Justice Department will continue to follow evidence wherever it leads; that our government will pressure Libya to fulfill the remaining requirements of the U.N. Security Council, namely, to accept responsibility for the actions of its officials, to pay appropriate compensation to the families, and to cooperate with the Justice Department in its work to learn all the facts in the conspiracy to bomb Pan Am Flight 103.

**September 11, 2001**

The Chief Executive and Convener of the Dumfries and Galloway Council, Scotland sends a personal letter from Lockerbie to President Bush and Mayor Guiliani, expressing heartfelt sympathy: "The scale of your tragedy is unimaginable, but the individual trauma of the victims and the community is familiar to us and fills us with deep sadness. We received comfort and support from America following the Lockerbie Air Disaster in December 1988. Flags are at half mast here this week." Individual family members respond personally and professionally, many reaching out to the newly created widows and widowers.

**January 23, 2002**

Appeal trial of Al-Megrahi begins at Kamp Van Zeist.

**March 14, 2002**

Decision is reached by the five High Court Appeal judges at Kamp Van Zeist in the Netherlands that "none of the grounds of (Al-Megrahi's) appeal is well founded. The appeal will be accordingly refused. This brings the proceedings to an end." Al Megrahi is flown to a Scottish prison to begin serving a minimum 20-year sentence.

**May 23, 2002**

A Memorandum of Understanding is reached between American and Libyan lawyers in which Libya agrees to pay $10 million per decedent in three installments: the first $4 million linked to the lifting of the U.N. sanctions, the second $4 million to the lifting of the US unilateral sanctions and the final $2 million when Libya is removed from the U.S. State Department List of State Sponsors of Terrorism.

**September 12, 2003**

The United Nations Security Council adopts Resolution 1506, voting 13-0 with two abstentions (U.S. and France) to lift its sanctions against Libya.

**September, 2003**

Libya pays the first $4 million installment to the families.

**November, 2003**

Megrahi's sentence is fixed by the original trial judges to a minimum of 27 years served before parole can be considered. This is an increase from the original minimum of 20 years. Megrahi appeals, asking the Scottish Criminal Cases Review Commission to investigate his case.

**December 18, 2003**

President Bush announces that Colonel Gaddafi has "publicly confirmed his commitment to disclose and dismantle all weapons of mass destruction programs in his country."

**April 23, 2004**

U.S. lifts its economic embargo against Libya.

**December, 2004**

Libya pays second $4 million installment.

**April, 2005**

Libya withdraws the remaining money from the escrow account since it hasnot been removed from the U.S. State Department List of State Sponsors of Terrorism. (Gaddafi was discovered to have instigated a plot to assassinate the crown prince of Saudi Arabia. The Libyan government had also arrested five Bulgarian nurses and a Palestinian doctor who had come to Libya to assist in health care in 1999, charging them with deliberately infecting children with AIDS. The nurses and doctor were tortured, imprisoned for eight years, and sentenced to death by firing squad. They were finally freed in July 2007 and flown to Bulgaria, where they were pardoned — for which the European Union paid 461 million euros into a Benghazi Hospital fund, while Libya also received lucrative anti-tank and civil nuclear technology contracts with France. In April 2009, the nurses and doctor sued the government of Libya for financial compensation for their ordeal.)

**September 16, 2005**

Lobbying day on the Hill. Eleven family members meet with people representing the State Department, Senators Lautenberg, Lugar and Biden, and Congressman Lantos. We demand that Libya be removed from the State Department List only when they fully comply with U.S. specific requirements, which must include full and final compensation to the families as agreed to at the U.N. in September 2003. The State Department tells the family members that it will not act as an agent for us in what is a legal arrangement between the families and the Libyan government, and that the Bush administration is moving ahead with reestablishing full diplomatic ties with Libya.

**May 15, 2006**

The Bush Administration announces that it will reestablish full diplomatic ties with Libya. It removes Libya from the List, though Libya has yet to make the final payment of $2 million per decedent.

**May 24, 2006**

Family members return to the Hill. They are joined by lawmakers from New York, which lost 58 people, and New Jersey, which lost 38, on Pan Am Flight 103. Senators Lautenberg, Menendez, Kennedy, Clinton, Lieberman, Schumer and Biden and Congressmen Ferguson and Andrews submit resolutions blocking U.S. diplomatic ties to Libya until it completes restitution to the families. Over 75 Representatives, Republicans and Democrats, sign the resolution.

**August, 2008**

The U.S./Libya Claims Resolution Act is passed by Congress, reopening the final payment.

**October 31, 2008**

The State Department announces that all of the settlement funds have been transferred from the Humanitarian Fund to the U.S. account for the U.S. plaintiffs.

**November 15, 2008**

Scottish judges reject an appeal for early release due to Megrahi's diagnoses incurable prostate cancer.

**November 25, 2008**
Third and final payment is received from Libya.

**April 29, 2009**
Scottish Criminal Cases Review Commission begins hearing claims that Megrahi's guilty verdict was based on circumstantial evidence.

**May 6, 2009**
Libya officially applies to the Scottish Government to transfer Mr. Megrahi to serve out the rest of his 27-year sentence in Libya. In order to be considered for such a transfer, Megrahi has to drop his appeal to the Scottish Criminal Cases Review Commission and let the guilty verdict stand uncontested.

**August 20, 2009**
Kenny MacAskill, Scottish Minister of Justice, releases Megrahi on grounds of compassion because he is expected to die within three months. Megrahi returns to hero's welcome that night in Libya.

**September 23, 2009**
Libyan dissidents and family members of Pan Am 103 demonstrate outside U.N. protesting Colonel Gaddafi's first address to the General Assembly.

**February, 2011**
Inspired by popular uprisings in Tunisia and Egypt against their dictators, Libyan uprising begins against Gaddafi.

**October 20, 2011**
Gaddafi is killed by Libyan dissidents who finally capture him hiding in his home town of Sirte.

**December 21, 2011**
Libyan Ambassador Adjouli addresses the families at the annual memorial service at the Cairn in Arlington Cemetery, declaring that there is no way that the conspiracy to blow up Pan Am Flight 103 could have taken place without Gaddafi's knowledge and approval, and pledges full cooperation by the National Transitional Government of Libya to release all relevant evidence.

# Bibliography

For anyone who wishes to learn more about the political, legal and personal dimensions of the bombing of Pan Am Flight 103, the Pan Am Flight 103/Lockerbie Air Disaster Archives at Syracuse University is the place to go, actually or virtually at www.archives.syr.edu/panam. Email: pa103archives@syr.edu, or contact Cara Howe, assistant archivist, cahowe@syr.edu.

Below is a very partial list of available materials, arranged by dates of publication.

## Books

*Lockerbie: The Real Story* by David Johnston, 1989, Bloomsbury, London, England.

*The Fall of Pan Am 103, Inside the Lockerbie Investigation* by Steven Emerson and Brian Duffy, 1990, G.P. Putnam's Sons, New York.

*On the Trail of Terror: The Inside Story of the Lockerbie Investigation* by David Leppard, 1991, Jonathan Cape London, England.

*Their Darkest Day, the Tragedy of Pan Am 103 and Its Legacy of Hope* by Matthew Cox and Tom Foster, 1992, Grove Weidenfeld, New York.

*The Media and Disasters, Pan Am 103* by Joan Deppa et al, 1994, New York University Press, New York.

*Miriam's Gift: A Mother's Blessings, Then and Now,* by Rosemary Mild, 1999, Fithian Press (out of print).

*Miriam's World — and Mine,* by Rosemary Mild, 2012, Magic Island Literary Works, Severna Park, MD.

*Pan Am 103, the Bombing, the Betrayals and a Bereaved Family's Search for Justice* by Susan and Daniel Cohen, 2000, New American Library, Penguin/Putnam, New York.

*The Price of Terror: Lessons of Lockerbie for a World on the Brink* by Allan Gerson and Jerry Adler, 2001, Harper Collins, New York.

*Chicken Soup for the Soul: Stories for a Better World*, edited by Canfield et al, 2005, Health Communications, Inc.

*The Boy Who Fell Out of the Sky, a True Story* by Ken Dorenstein, 2006, Random House, New York.

*The Courage to Give,* by Jackie Waldman, 1999, Conari Press.

## Audio Books

*The Longest Night, A Personal History of Pan Am 103,* by Helen Engelhardt, consisting of five CDs, including recordings made of actual events and photographs. Produced in in 2009, nominated for an Audie for "Original Work" in 2010. www.midsummersoundcompany.com.

*Coming Home to Us, A Trilogy of Love, Loss & Healing,* by Helen Engelhardt and Marjorie Van Halteren. The three sections of the Trilogy — "Unquiet Graves," "Mothers and Sons," "Yesterday and Forever"— by Entre Deux Amies productions, were broadcast separately on NPR stations across the U.S. The bonus CD contains "Songs for the Falling Angel" and "The Grieving Parents of Kathe Kollwitz." 2011, produced by Midsummer Sound Company.

## Articles

"Reclaiming the Skies from Terrorism: The Aviation Improvement Security Act of 1990," by Wendy Giebler, *Seton Hall Legislative Journal,* Volume 16 Number 2.

"'Wall of Silence' Angers Kin," by Dennis Duggan, *Newsday,* February 7, 1989.

"Mother Struggles To Fill Void Left By Bombing of Flight 103," by Douglas Martin, *New York Times,* March 18, 1989.

"Indictment for 270 Dead," by Thomas Osterkorn, *Stern* magazine, May 11, 1989.

"Flight 103's Bitter Legacy," by Peter Marks, *Newsday* magazine, November, 1989.

"Brooklyn Man Left a Legacy in Sound," by Peter Marks, *Newsday,* May 14, 1991.

"When Grieving Really Begins," by Helen Engelhardt, *New York Times,* August 10, 1991.

"Using One's Own Anguish to Help Others: Families of Pan Am 103

Victims Reach Out to Those of TWA Flight 800," by Sara Rimer, *New York Times,* August 19, 1991.

"As A Tragedy Is Revisited, A Sisterhood Is Forged; Survivors of Pan Am Flight 103 Victims Wait and View From Afar A Trial On The Bombing," by Laura Mansnerus, *New York Times*, November 20, 2000.

"Kin of Lockerbie Victims: Gadhafi Should Be Next," by Philip Blenkinsop, *USA Today*, February 1, 2002.

"Pan Am Victim's Widow Rages as Khadafy Speaks," by Helen Engelhardt, *New York Post,* September 24, 2009.

"Wounded Families Suffer New Pangs of Justice," by Rick Moriarty and Marc Weiner, Syracuse *Post Standard*, July 20, 2010.

"What Did Fiend Take to Grave?" by Helen Englhardt, *Daily News,* May 20, 2012.

# Acknowledgments

It is my pleasure to thank everyone who made it possible for me to persevere on this project for so many years, among them:

Annette Landau, whose friendship, wisdom and achievements as a writer inspired me.

Barbara Kouts, whose belief in this memoir made it possible for me to write it.

Barbara Glasser, who helped me find the voice to tell this story.

The writer's workshop that met weekly in Merle Molofsky and Les Von Losberg's Brooklyn home from the 1970s to the early '90s, and, from the mid-'90s, the Village Scribblers — Carol Ritter, Marian Calabro, Joan Griffiths and Peggy Troupin — who listened, read, and criticized every chapter as it emerged. I could not ask for more thoughtful and appreciative peers.

Marlene, Michael and Kaethe Fine, whose professional encouragement and friendship have been a continuing foundation.

The Virginia Center for the Creative Arts, which gave me a "room of my own" and a stimulating community of artists.

Barbara Lazear Ascher, nurturing teacher of the non-fiction workshop at Bennington, summer of 1995, who edited the entire manuscript.

Ed Galvin, chief librarian of the 103 Archives at Syracuse University, who not only established the most comprehensive collection of materials, but always welcomed us as extended family.

Judy Dios and Elizabeth St. Hilaire Nelson, who offered their talents and time during the six years I edited *Truth Quest*.

The people of Lockerbie, Scotland, who opened their homes and their hearts to us — especially David Gould, who lost his own stepdaughter to terrorism in the London Underground bombings on July 7th, 1995.

The women at the Scottish Court in the Netherlands: Ann den Bieman, Bernadette Edgar, and Saski t'Hooft, who created a sanctuary for us in the family lounge.

My lawyers, Lee and Jim Kreindler and their secretaries and legal assistants, Pat Robinson and Virginia Parkhouse who treated us all like family and whose kindness I will never forget.

Journalists David Leopard, Margot Adler, Peter Marks, Yolanda Gerritsen, and Brian Lehrer, who offered us personal attention beyond professional expertise.

Lawrence Bush, editor at Blue Thread Communications, who launched this book into print twenty-four years after it was conceived.

Always, my family and friends, both old and new, who nourish my life.